RELIGION AND VIOLENCE

Recent Research in Biblical Studies, 2

Series Editor
Alan J. Hauser

General Editors
Scot McKnight and Jonathan Klawans

RELIGION AND VIOLENCE
THE BIBLICAL HERITAGE

Proceedings of a Conference held at
Wellesley College and Boston University,
February 19-20, 2006

edited by
David A. Bernat
and
Jonathan Klawans

SHEFFIELD PHOENIX PRESS
2015

Copyright © 2007, 2015 Sheffield Phoenix Press

First published in hardback, 2007
First published in paperback, 2015

Published by Sheffield Phoenix Press
Biblical Studies, University of Sheffield
45 Victoria Street
Sheffield S3 7QB

www.sheffieldphoenix.com

All rights reserved.
No part of this publication may be reproduced or transmitted in any form or by any means, electronic or mechanical, including photocopying, recording or any information storage or retrieval system, without the publisher's permission in writing.

A CIP catalogue record for this book
is available from the British Library

Typeset by C.A. Typesetting Ltd
Printed by Lightning Source Inc.

ISBN 978-1-909697-92-8 (paperback)
ISBN 978-1-906055-32-5 (hardback)

Contents

List of Tables	vii
Preface	ix
Acknowledgments	x
List of Abbreviations	xi
List of Contributors	xiii

INTRODUCTION: RELIGION, VIOLENCE AND THE BIBLE
Jonathan Klawans, with contributions by David Bernat ... 1

1. THE SEARCH FOR VIOLENCE IN ISRAELITE CULTURE AND IN THE BIBLE
Ziony Zevit ... 16

2. THE 'PROBLEM' OF VIOLENCE IN PROPHETIC LITERATURE
S. Tamar Kamionkowski ... 38

3. THE PROPHETIC ROOTS OF RELIGIOUS VIOLENCE IN WESTERN RELIGIONS
Stephen A. Geller ... 47

4. HOMICIDE, TALION, VENGEANCE, AND PSYCHO-ECONOMIC SATISFACTION IN THE COVENANT CODE
David P. Wright ... 57

5. THE DEATH OF THE HERO AND THE VIOLENT DEATH OF JESUS
Lawrence M. Wills ... 79

6. ROASTING THE LAMB: SACRIFICE AND SACRED TEXT IN JUSTIN'S *DIALOGUE WITH TRYPHO*
Jennifer Wright Knust ... 100

7. THE LEGACY OF SECTARIAN RAGE: VENGEANCE FANTASIES IN THE NEW TESTAMENT
David Frankfurter ... 114

CONCLUDING REFLECTIONS ON RELIGION AND VIOLENCE: CONFLICT, SUBVERSION, AND SACRIFICE
Stephen Marini ... 129

Bibliography 135
Index of Biblical References 148
Index of Authors 155

LIST OF TABLES

Chapter 5

Table 5.1:	Sequential Similarities between CC and LH in their Casuistic Laws	59
Table 5.2:	String Structure of the Final Apodictic Laws of CC	60
Table 5.3:	Central Chiastic Core of the Final Apodictic Laws	60
Table 5.4:	Correlations between the Apodictic Laws and the Exhortatory Block	61-62
Table 5.5:	Summary Penalties for Injury and Homicide in LH (with LE 13)	77
Table 5.6:	Summary of CC's Penalties for Injury and Homicide	78

Chapter 6

Table 6.1:	Elements of the Cult of Dead Heroes in Ancient Judaism	88

Preface

The presenters invited to speak at Boston University and Wellesley College, in February 2005, were not given a thesis statement. Their precise opinions on the present themes or current theoretical works were largely unknown to us when the invitations were issued. It was rather our belief—our conviction—that assembling a group of scholars known for both exegetical skill and methodological rigor would provide some clarity and, if needed, help set the record straight. Are the Jewish and Christian scriptures inherently violent? What kinds of violence can be found in these documents? What can we and can't we say? What can we and can't we know? The participants are an impressive and diverse group, whose fields of research cover the broad span of biblical studies, from the ancient Near East through patristic and rabbinic literature. The participants include seasoned scholars with established reputations and the wisdom of years, younger scholars just now making their mark, along with scholars at various levels in between. The group includes women and men of a variety of religious backgrounds and commitments, scholars who work at Universities, teaching colleges, as well as Jewish and Christian seminaries. The papers at the conference cohered remarkably: while there was practically no overlap of texts covered, the papers were immediately perceived to be in dialogue, in dramatic and productive ways. There was a genuine excitement as the proceedings progressed, for it became increasingly clear to the participants and the audience that something special was taking place. Upon further reflection—and having now had the opportunity to read fuller and edited versions of the papers—it remains our conviction that the papers presented here constitute an important collection of views on what is perhaps the most pressing issue facing biblical scholarship today.

David Bernat
Jonathan Klawans
June 2007

ACKNOWLEDGMENTS

Before all else, we want to acknowledge and offer thanks to those who hosted, supported and sponsored the conference at which these papers were first presented. Funding came primarily—and quite generously—from The Elizabeth Luce Moore Fund for Christian Studies at Wellesley College. Additional support came from The Luce Program in Scripture and Literary Arts, and the Elie Wiesel Center for Judaic Studies, both at Boston University. We also extend our gratitude for the support and sponsorship of the Departments of Religion at Wellesley College and Boston University. For their hard work in pulling together various aspects of the conference program, we want to thank Dianne Baroz, Administrative Assistant to Wellesley's Religion Department, Katherine MacInnes, Wellesley College Class of 2006, Peter Hawkins, Director of BU's Luce Center, and Cristine Hutchison-Jones, Program Coordinator of BU's Luce Center.

We also wish to thank three further participants in the conference: Benjamin Sommer of Northwestern University, Paula Fredriksen of Boston University and Ithamar Gruenwald of Tel Aviv University. Benjamin Sommers and Paula Fredriksen delivered insightful responses to the panels at the conference devoted to, respectively, the Hebrew Bible and the New Testament. Ithamar Gruenwald delivered a thoughtful and powerful summation of the conference. Our respondents graciously shared their remarks with the respective participants, and the versions of the papers we are printing here are the better for this. It was mutually agreed that the resulting improvements to the original papers pre-empted the value of printing the original responses. But we extend our thanks to these three colleagues for their important contributions to the conference and to the present volume once again.

For assistance in preparing this volume for publication we thank Stephanie White, Wellesley 2009, and Cynthia Harris, Wellesley 2008. For their assistance in shepherding this volume through the editing and production stages, we thank David J.A. Clines, J. Cheryl Exum, Keith W. Whitelam and Ailsa Parkin. We also wish to thank Chris Allen for carefully typesetting the book, and Sarah Armstrong for her diligent work on the indices. For her help with last-minute proofreading, we thank Andrea Ogier, of Boston University's Division of Religious and Theological Studies.

LIST OF ABBREVIATIONS

AB	Anchor Bible
AOAT	Alter Orient und Altes Testament
BASOR	*Bulletin of the American Society for Oriental Research*
BETL	Bibliotheca ephemeridum theologicarum lovaniensium
BibInt	*Biblical Interpretation*
BZAW	Beihefte zur Zeitschrift für die alttestamentliche Wissenschaft
CBQMS	*Catholic Biblical Quarterly* Monograph Series
HTR	Harvard Theological Review
IEJ	*Israel Exploration Journal*
JAOS	*Journal of the American Oriental Society*
JBL	*Journal of Biblical Literature*
JECS	*Journal of Early Christian Studies*
JR	*Journal of Religion*
JRS	*Journal of Roman Studies*
JSJSup	Supplements to the *Journal for the Study of Judaism*
JSOT	*Journal for the Study of the Old Testament*
JSOTSup	*Journal for the Study of the Old Testament* Supplement Series
NTS	*New Testament Studies*
NTSup	Supplements to *Novum Testamentum*
SBLSP	*Society of Biblical Literature Seminar Papers*
VC	*Vigiliae christianae*
VTSup	Supplements to *Vetus Testamentum*
ZAW	Zeitschrift für die alttestamentliche Wissenschaft

List of Contributors

David A. Bernat, Assistant Professor of Religion at Wellesley College, received his doctorate from Brandeis in 2002. Bernat's monograph, *Sign of the Covenant: Circumcision in the Priestly Traditions,* is forthcoming from the SBL. His current research focuses upon the Biblical figure Phinehas and traces attitudes toward religious zealotry in Jewish antiquity.

David Frankfurter, Professor of Religious Studies and History at the University of New Hampshire, received his doctorate from Princeton University in 1990. He has written *Elijah in Upper Egypt* (1993), *Religion in Roman Egypt: Assimilation and Resistance* (1998), and numerous articles. His book *Evil Incarnate: Rumors of Demonic Conspiracy and Satanic Abuse in History* (2006) looks at religious constructions of evil that have motivated violence.

Stephen A. Geller is the Irma Cameron Milstein Professor of Bible at the Jewish Theological Seminary in New York. Much of his publication has been in the areas of biblical language, literature and thought. His most recent book is *Sacred Enigmas: Literary Religion in the Hebrew Bible* (1996). He is currently working on a commentary on the Book of Psalms.

S. Tamar Kamionkowski, Associate Professor of Bible and Academic Dean at the Reconstructionist Rabbinical College, received her M.T.S. from Harvard Divinity School and her Ph.D. from Brandeis University. She is the author of *Gender Reversal and Cosmic Chaos: A Study on the Book of Ezekiel* (2003). Her research interests include Jewish biblical theology, priestly literature, and gender studies.

Jonathan Klawans is Associate Professor of Religion at Boston University. He has published two books: *Impurity and Sin in Ancient Judaism* (2000), and *Purity, Sacrifice and the Temple: Symbolism and Supersessionism in the Study of Ancient Judaism* (2005). He is also an editor of the journal *Currents in Biblical Research.*

Jennifer Wright Knust is Assistant Professor of New Testament and Christian Origins at Boston University. Her publications include *Abandoned to Lust: Sexual Slander and Ancient Christianity* (2005), and a number of other articles and essays. She is currently completing a book-length study of the transmission and reception of the story of Jesus and a woman taken in adultery.

Stephen A. Marini, Elisabeth Luce Moore Professor of Christian Studies at Wellesley College, is author of *Radical Sects of Revolutionary New England* (1982) and *Sacred Song in America: Religion, Music, and Culture* (2003). He is presently writing books on religious change in Revolutionary America and on music and language in American Protestantism.

Lawrence M. Wills, Ethelbert Talbot Professor of Biblical Studies at Episcopal Divinity School, specializes in the social history of ancient Judaism and Christianity. Among his books are *The Jewish Novel in the Ancient World* (1995) and *The Quest of the Historical Gospel: Mark, John and the Origins of the Gospel Genre* (1997).

David P. Wright, Professor of Hebrew Bible and Ancient Near East at Brandeis University, is author of *Disposal of Impurity* (1987) and *Ritual in Narrative* (2001). He is presently working on a book on the Covenant Code and the Laws of Hammurabi for Oxford University Press.

Ziony Zevit, Distinguished Professor of Biblical Literature and Northwest Semitic Languages and Literatures at the American Jewish University published *The Religions of Ancient Israel. A Synthesis of Parallactic Approaches* in 2001. His current research focuses on tracing the evolution of Iron Age religion into the proto-Judaisms of the Early Hellenistic period.

INTRODUCTION:
RELIGION, VIOLENCE, AND THE BIBLE

Jonathan Klawans

(with contributions by David A. Bernat)

1. *Religion, Violence, and the Bible in the Present Day*

The importance of considering the question of religion and violence need hardly be stated. Violence that is motivated by—and justified by—religious ideas, authorities, and texts is too ubiquitous to be ignored or denied. This observation was commonplace even before the events of September 11, 2001,[1] and needless to say, the conversation has only accelerated in the last few years.[2] But much about this relationship remains unclear. Some say that the origins of religion and human violence are intricately and inherently connected, such that the explanation for religious violence is to be found, in part, in 'a strain of violence that may be found at the deepest levels of religious imagination'.[3] Others say that human violence—like primate violence—was there long before religion ever came about, and can be understood as an unfortunate by-product of primate and human evolution.[4] Violence therefore would thrive in the presence or absence of distinctly religious ideas and motivations. Moving closer to the subject of this book, some claim that there is a telling relationship between

---

1. See, for example, David Carrasco, *City of Sacrifice: The Aztec Empire and the Role of Violence in Civilization* (Boston: Beacon Press, 1999), pp. 4-5.

2. For a thorough review of scholarship on the subject, see Hector Avalos, *Fighting Words: The Origins of Religious Violence* (Amherst, NY: Prometheus Books, 2005), pp. 37-90; for modern theories, see esp. pp. 75-90. Avalos also provides a general introduction to religion and violence (pp. 15-35).

3. Mark Juergensmeyer, *Terror in the Mind of God: The Global Rise of Religious Violence* (Berkeley: University of California Press, 3rd edn, 2003), p. 6. See also René Girard, *Violence and the Sacred* (trans. Patrick Gregory; Baltimore: The Johns Hopkins University Press, 1977). Juergensmeyer roots his observation in part on the work of Girard; see further below.

4. For a classic influential treatment, see Konrad Lorenz, *On Aggression* (trans. Marjorie Kerr Wilson; San Diego: Harcourt Brace Jovanovich, 1966). For a more recent treatment, see Richard Wrangham and Dale Peterson, *Demonic Males: Apes and the Origins of Human Violence* (Boston: Houghton Mifflin, 1996). Compare the brief critique in Avalos, *Fighting Words*, pp. 63-64.

religious violence and particular religious ideas such as monotheism or sacred space.[5] Still others claim that even if religion and violence are related in some intimate way, religion—or at least some forms of it—saves itself, as it were, by breaking the cycle of violence or by laying out non-violent visions of world peace.[6]

Reconsidering the biblical heritage as it relates to questions of religion and violence is a narrower—but nonetheless essential—endeavor. As the first paper in this volume states right up front, there is no dearth of violence in the Bible. On top of that, the Bible has also been used as a justification for crusades of various sorts, with painfully violent results.[7] Recognizing this, there has been and continues to be much discussion on this narrower endeavor, asking questions such as: is the Bible uniquely or at least especially violent? Has it played a particularly pernicious role in the history of human conflict? Can studies focused on the Bible prove to be distinctly revelatory with regard to the general problems of human violence and its origin?

Arguably, some general discussions of religion and violence focus too much on the Jewish and Christian scriptures. Surely the Israelites and Christians of biblical times—violent as they were—are not the most vicious societies (even religious ones) on record.[8] But judging from a number of recent books on these subjects, it seems that many scholars do view the Jewish and Christian scriptures as an important locus for discussion. Moreover, they are saying yes to one or more of the questions asked above, and they are doing so in works (and conferences) addressed to the general public. The dangerous and violent nature of the Bible is upheld by various writers, including Hector Avalos (author of *Fighting Words: The Origins of Religious Violence*), R. Joseph Hoffmann (editor of *The Just War and Jihad: Violence in Judaism, Christianity and Islam*), Jack Nelson-Pallmeyer (author of *Is Religion Killing Us? Violence in the Bible and the Quran*), and Regina Schwartz (author of *The Curse of Cain: The Violent Legacy of Monotheism*). Many of the same writers also hold that the study of the scriptures proves revelatory with regard to the nature of religious violence. This point is also exemplified by the recently published four-volume series entitled *The Destructive Power of Religion*, edited by J. Harold Ellens. The title itself anticipates the *Tendenz* of the volumes, which understands the Abrahamic religious communities, along with

---

5. So Regina M. Schwartz, *The Curse of Cain: The Violent Legacy of Monotheism* (Chicago: University of Chicago Press, 1997); Avalos, *Fighting Words*, follows suit.

6. So, for example, Girard, *The Scapegoat* (trans. Yvonne Freccero; Baltimore: The Johns Hopkins University Press, 1986), esp. pp. 100-24, 164-212; Jack Nelson-Pallmeyer, *Is Religion Killing Us? Violence in the Bible and the Quran* (New York: Continuum, 2003), esp. pp. 111-49, and Schwartz, *Curse of Cain*, pp. 143-76.

7. For catalogues of charges against the Jewish and Christian scriptures, see Avalos, *Fighting Words*, pp. 113-58, 175-214, and Nelson-Pallmeyer, *Is Religion Killing Us?*, pp. 27-71.

8. See Carrasco, *City of Sacrifice*, for the sordid details of traditional Aztec religious behavior.

their scriptures, traditions and structures, to be the driving forces behind many incidences of violence in history and contemporary society.[9] All these writers were preceded in this respect by René Girard, whose scholarship looms large over these questions, now for over three decades.

René Girard's *Violence and the Sacred* is not rooted exclusively or even primarily in biblical texts. Yet his subsequent books[10] did focus on the Bible, and these works in turn have inspired something of a cottage industry of 'Girardian' readings of biblical texts.[11] Indeed, René Girard's efforts have been considered—not by all, but by many—to be uniquely insightful. *Violence and the Sacred* has inspired conferences, commentaries, dissertations and many footnotes. Even when Girard's ideas are questioned in part, respectful citations of his works are commonplace in biblical studies scholarship. Girard's theories have also been taken seriously beyond the realm of biblical studies. Girard is viewed as something of an authority by R. Joseph Hoffmann, whose recent collection mentioned above contains essays that build on Girard, and a distinct bibliography section entitled 'René Girard, his Followers and Critics'—the only theorist of violence so honored.[12] Similarly, Girard's theories figure prominently in Ellens's collection, *The Destructive Power of Religion*.[13] Girard's work also serves as one theoretical linchpin for Mark Juergenseyer's popular and well-regarded treatment of terrorism: *Terror in the Mind of God*: in his view, contemporary acts of religious terrorism (planned and committed

---

9. J. Harold Ellens (ed.), *The Destructive Power of Religion: Violence in Judaism, Christianity, and Islam* (4 vols.; Westport, CT: Praeger, 2003). Particularly revealing is the testimonial by Archbishop Desmond Tutu, which appears in each volume of the series. Tutu labels the oppressive policies of South African apartheid as 'religiously driven' (Tutu, 'Ad Testimonium', in Ellens [ed.], *The Destructive Power of Religion*, pp. xv-xvi of each of the four volumes). No one would challenge the characterization of apartheid as evil. But whether the system and those who perpetuated it were motivated chiefly by religious doctrine—as opposed to racial, economic and nationalistic concerns—is certainly open to debate.

10. Girard, *The Scapegoat*; *Things Hidden Since the Foundation of the World* (trans. Stephen Bann and Michael Metteer; Stanford: Stanford University Press, 1987).

11. See, e.g. Robert G. Hamerton-Kelly, *The Gospel and the Sacred: Poetics of Violence in Mark* (Minneapolis: Fortress Press, 1994), James G. Williams, *The Bible, Violence, and the Sacred: Liberation from the Myth of Sanctioned Violence* (San Francisco: HarperSanFrancisco, 1991), and the articles collected in Andrew J. McKenna (ed.), *Semeia 33: Rene Girard and Biblical Studies* (Atlanta: Scholars Press, 1985).

12. R. Joseph Hoffmann (ed.), *The Just War and Jihad: Violence in Judaism, Christianity, and Islam* (Amherst, NY: Prometheus Books, 2006); for praises of Girard, see essays by Hoffman (p. 59) and Charles K. Bellinger (pp. 69-70). For the bibliography compiled by Bellinger (and preceded by further praise), see pp. 291-93.

13. See especially, Ellens, 'Religious Metaphors Can Kill', in Ellens (ed.), *The Destructive Power of Religion*, I, pp. 255-72 (264-67); Mark C. Stirling, 'Violent Religion: René Girard's Theory of Culture', in Ellens (ed.), *The Destructive Power of Religion*, II, pp. 11-50, and Cheryl McGuire, 'Judaism, Christianity, and Girard: The Violent Messiahs', in Ellens (ed.), *The Destructive Power of Religion*, II, pp. 51-84.

by, in his words, 'militant religious activists') can be explained by geo-political factors on the one hand, and the violence in all religions on the other. In defense of the claim that violence is at the heart of religious origins, Juergensmeyer appeals to Girard.[14]

And yet, Girard's scheme has numerous methodological faults, many of which have been pointed out before.[15] His theory is thoroughly reductionist: the essence of all myth and ritual is sacrifice, and sacrificial ritual boils down to criminal violence. Girard's real interests are, moreover, suspiciously selective. After paying lip service to some anthropological work, he focuses on biblical narratives and Greek myths. The traditions of Arabia, India, and China play no role, and presumably contribute nothing to our understanding of how sacrifice and violence began. Moreover, Girard's reading of myth and ritual is in truth an elegant argument *ex silentio*. By claiming to reveal what pre-Christian myth and ritual seek to conceal, Girard can develop his own account that appears to find confirmation precisely in the fact that what he reveals is not actually articulated straightforwardly in these rituals and myths. In other words, his theory is entirely made up. Girard's reading is also distinctively Christian, and notably supersessionist, which can be seen when he turns to Christian narratives and finds *only* in them the revelation of what all earlier myths and rituals conceal. Thus, the Gospels out do and complete all previous mythology, the 'Old Testament' included.[16] And because he believes the Old Testament (like all sacrificial ritual) *conceals* the truth,[17] Girard's Christianity is notably Gnostic. Girard's frequent denunciations of anti-Semitism, while welcome, do not fully counter the fact that his approach to the sources is remarkably anti-Judaic.

But the biggest problems of all concern the very idea of his enterprise. A general theory of religion and violence—one that purports to explain how religion and violence began in the aftermath of murderous primitive behavior—is an odd anachronism at best. Even stranger is the supposition that such a general theory on the origins of all human violence could be based, even in part, on readings of the Jewish and Christian scriptures: Why should the Tanakh and the New Testament be treated by scholars as if they could tell us something about

---

14. Juergensmeyer, *Terror in the Mind of God*, pp. 6, 171-72.

15. For criticisms of Girard, see, e.g. Avalos, *Fighting Words*, pp. 75-78, 205; Ninian Smart, review of *Violence and the Sacred*, by René Girard (Baltimore: The Johns Hopkins University Press, 1977) in *Religious Studies Review* 6.3 (1980), pp. 173-77, and Ivan Strenski, *Religion in Relation: Method, Application, and Moral Location* (Columbia: University of South Carolina Press, 1993), pp. 202-16. See also Klawans, *Purity, Sacrifice and the Temple: Symbolism and Supersessionism in the Study of Ancient Judaism* (New York: Oxford University Press, 2005), pp. 22-26, and further literature cited there.

16. Girard, *The Scapegoat*, pp. 101, 103, 147, 165, 205; *Things Hidden*, p. 158. Compare the critique offered by Daniel Boyarin, *A Radical Jew: Paul and the Politics of Identity* (Berkeley: University of California Press, 1994), pp. 327-28 n. 30.

17. Girard, *Violence and the Sacred*, p. 5.

how religion and/or violence on the whole began? James Frazer, Sigmund Freud, and others who offered unbounded speculations on the hoary origins of religion and violence had their day. Their evolutionist assumptions and methodological shortcomings were lambasted long ago by the likes of E.E. Evans Pritchard and Mary Douglas. It is therefore altogether odd that Girard's resuscitation of the Freudian and Frazerian quest[18] for the origins of religion and violence was and is taken seriously at all.

But even as the Girardian lights begin to dim, another view seems to be taking hold. This approach is less elaborate in that it does not seek to account for the origin of religion or violence. This view simply and easily blames the Bible outright for whatever violence follows from it (and the 'from' is often understood loosely). The recent classic is Regina Schwartz's *The Curse of Cain*, the subtitle of which says it all: *The Violent Legacy of Monotheism*. According to Schwartz, monotheism is inextricably linked with the exclusive, covenantal, land-based, kinship-rooted, national identity created by and remembered in the Hebrew Bible. In a nutshell, the demands of monotheistic exclusivity lead inevitably to ills such as land-possession and attention to kinship. The inescapable result of this is violence against Canaanites long ago, and violence against the enemies of Judaism and Christianity today.[19]

Curiously, Schwartz is, like Girard, a literary critic who turned to the Bible when troubled by questions of violence. And again like Girard, Schwartz finds much in the Bible to condemn, but some to redeem. Schwartz's salvation is to be found not in the Gospels, but in the subversive, pluralistic passages of the Old Testament such as the book of Ruth.[20] She even concludes by calling for the reopening of the canon to revised versions of Exodus, in order to include more inclusive texts.[21] So Schwartz too, like Girard, has been found to be 'propagating a theological agenda'.[22] Schwartz's approach is much less grandiose than Girard's,

---

18. See Girard, *Violence and the Sacred*, p. 91.

19. In a similar vein is Carol Delaney's book, *Abraham on Trial: The Social Legacy of A Biblical Myth* (Princeton, NJ: Princeton, 1998). The work focuses on the *aqedah*, the tale of the binding and near sacrifice of Isaac by his father Abraham (Gen. 22; a narrative mentioned also in the paper in this volume by Ziony Zevit). Delaney treats the implications of the *aqedah* tradition for Bible-reading societies from antiquity until today. She argues that in large measure, assumptions built into the Genesis narrative, and by extension, the Hebrew Bible, New Testament and Quran, account for violent structures in society that give rise to, or enable, child abuse, sexual abuse, poverty, and war. A 'revolution in values' entailed by an abandoning the *akedah* paradigms will give society 'new moral vision [and] a new myth to live by—one that will change the course of history' (p. 251). Delaney's work raises a question fundamental to the purpose of the present volume. Is there any less child or spousal abuse among atheists, or less poverty and subjugation of the vulnerable in the non-Abrahamic religious communities?

20. Schwartz, *Curse of Cain*, pp. 31-32, 90, 142.

21. Schwartz, *Curse of Cain*, pp. 175-76.

22. Brian K. Smith, 'Monotheism and Its Discontents: Religious Violence and the Bible' (review of Schwartz, *Curse of Cain*), *JAAR* 66 (1998), pp. 403-11 (410).

and has, perhaps for that reason, garnered less attention on the whole. But among recent scholarship on religion and violence, there is a turn away from Girard and toward Schwartz. Without referencing Girard once, Nelson-Pallmeyer's *Is Religion Killing Us* refers repeatedly to Schwartz. R. Joseph Hoffmann's selective collection includes an essay by Schwartz. We have noted already that Hector Avalos delivers (yet another) devastating critique of Girard; but he's full of praise for *The Curse of Cain*. Avalos praises her work on the very first page of his introduction, referring to it frequently thereafter, and along the way he concedes that his 'entire thesis is built on the conviction that Schwartz is on the right track'.[23]

So Mark Juergensmeyer's *Terror in the Mind of God* (among other works) rests on Girard. Hector Avalos's *Fighting Words* (among others) rests on Schwartz. If scholars of religious studies are going to go about the important task of speaking about religious violence and even contemporary terrorism by appealing to René Girard or Regina Schwartz, scholars who work primarily with the Bible—on which these theories are (tenuously) based—should be certain to weigh in.

2. *Reconsidering Biblical Violence*

The present collection of papers responds in a number of meaningful ways to the approaches taken by Girard, Schwartz, and the other scholars whose approaches are discussed above. We will not reiterate the specific arguments of our authors here. We wish merely to intimate the ways in which the biblicists whose articles are presented in this volume address, in their own sophisticated fashion, a number of issues dealt with inadequately in other more generalized works on religious violence.

a. *Definitions*

Remarkable latitude is taken in a number of works with regard to the definition and scope of the violence being discussed. Girard, of course, equated violence with sacrifice, whether the victims were human or animal. While Avalos dismisses sacrifice from consideration as a secondary mechanism, he expands the concept of violence in a different direction, including body-marking rituals such as male circumcision.[24] Convinced that violence inevitably results once

---

23. Avalos, *Fighting Words*, esp. pp. 17, 82-86, 93 (82). There are to be sure other voices. John Collins is one ('The Zeal of Phinehas: The Bible and the Legitimation of Violence', *JBL* 122 [2003], pp. 3-21); the papers presented here constitute others.

24. Avalos, *Fighting Words*, p. 77 (sacrifice as a secondary mechanism); pp. 19-20, 149-50 (circumcision as violence). Avalos is not alone in viewing circumcision in this manner. See also Howard Eilberg-Schwartz, *God's Phallus and Other Problems for Men and Monotheism* (Boston: Beacon Press 1994), pp. 137-62 and Hugh S. Pyper, *An Unsuitable Book: The Bible as Scandalous Text* (The Bible in the Modern World, 7; Sheffield: Sheffield Phoenix Press, 2005), pp. 113-34. This view finds a precedent among ancient Romans who did regard the rite, and those

an identity is formed, Schwartz avers that 'acts of identity formation are themselves acts of violence'.[25]

There is no objective definition of violence (readers should note the helpful discussions and references contained in the chapters by Kamionkowski and Zevit below). It must, however, be observed that the broader the definition, the easier it is to indict biblical texts and those who, guilty by association, deem them to be sacred. But the real problem is a lack of precision. If animal sacrifice is to be decried as violent, then so must all human consumption of animals (is the slaughterhouse less violent than the temple?). If body marking is to be decried as violent, then why not include tattooing, ear-piercing, and perhaps even certain forms of hair-cutting?[26] Granted that some view circumcision as barbaric, do we gain or loose by putting such rituals in the same hopper with rape and murder? Curiously, the threatened destruction of religious holy sites like Mecca—a shockingly irresponsible policy urged for consideration by Avalos[27]—is not viewed as inherently violent, because sacred sites can be evacuated prior to their destruction. If circumcision is included but the sudden destruction of forcibly-evacuated sacred property is excluded, have we really hit the nail on the head in defining violence? If identity formation is violent, who doesn't have an identity so as to be able to claim to be non-violent?

The broad definitions recall the rabbinic dictum: *tafasta merubah lo tafasta*, which can loosely be translated to say: 'if you grasp too much, you'll be left with nothing at all' (e.g. *b. Rosh ha-Shanah* 4b). We may do better to follow Ziony Zevit's example and restrict violence to the 'use of extreme, sudden force to injure somebody, usually by surprise'. And we may do well to follow Zevit further by immediately qualifying the definition (he is joined in this effort also by Kamionkowski), and offering sub-categories of violent activities beyond that: it matters whether the violence in question occurs in the context of war or not; it matters whether the violence in question is unnecessarily cruel or not; it matters whether the violence is perceived to be an act of self-defense or an act of aggression. Finally, it matters whether the violence in question is celebrated, legitimated, merely tolerated or even condemned.

b. *History*
A curious motif running through the recent works on biblical violence is a surprising willingness to accept certain violent biblical narratives as historically

---

who practiced it, as barbaric. Conversely, Jews of the same period construed circumcision not as mutilation or wounding, but as a healing practice, akin to removing an infection, or repairing a cleft palate. For a review of ancient Jewish and Roman constructions of circumcision, see David A. Bernat, 'Circumcision', in John J. Collins and Daniel Harlow (eds.), *Dictionary of Early Judaism* (Grand Rapids, MI: Wm B. Eerdmans [forthcoming]).

25. Schwartz, *Curse of Cain*, p. 5.
26. Cf. Avalos, *Fighting Words*, p. 19.
27. Avalos, *Fighting Words*, pp. 375-76.

accurate. Thus writers such as Avalos, Hoffmann, Ellens, and even, at times, Schwartz appear to presume that there was a historical genocide of the Canaanites by land-grabbing Israelites at the time of Joshua.[28] Never mind that the book of Joshua is full of miraculous fantasy: the walls we are told came tumbling down as Israel marched around the city (Josh. 6.1-22). Even leaving the tumbled ramparts aside, archaeological evidence virtually precludes the historical accuracy of even any supposed historical kernel of the book of Joshua. Jericho, for instance, was unsettled at the time, and there is no evidence elsewhere for an organized genocidal conquest of Canaan by Israel.[29] To be sure, some grant that the book of Joshua is late fantasy.[30] Schwartz, moreover, certainly is correct in noting also that various political ideologies (e.g. Marxism) can be seen at work in the scholarly models (such as peasant revolt) that take the place once held by a more literal reading of the Joshua narrative.[31] But there is a remarkable indifference to the well-established a-historicity of the conquest accounts by those who make much of them.[32] Even while she recognizes that Joshua is a fantasy, Schwartz at the same notes, accusingly, 'that the historian's sleight of hand begs a question of ethical accountability'.[33] Nelson-Pallmeyer similarly speaks of the text's sordid afterlife.[34] After a brief discussion of the Deuteronomistic history and the Moabite Stele, Avalos concludes: 'even if the Joshua narratives are meant for in-house consumption, the rhetoric is still premised on principles and policies that were probably carried out against actual people'.[35] In Avalos's case, this all the more surprising since he frequently asserts that his empirico-rationalism allows him to believe only what he can verify.[36] Yet when it comes to doubting the historical validity of biblical texts describing violent genocide, the burden of proof shifts to the doubters—violent texts are historical until proven otherwise.[37]

What is curious—suspicious, in fact—is that these authors are all in the end wedded to the notion that there is a particularly close link, an almost exclusive one, between biblical documents and actual violence. The selective vision required to conjure this picture comes into focus when we consider even just

28. Avalos, *Fighting Words*, pp. 142-44, 162-63; R. Joseph Hoffmann, in Hoffmann (ed.), *The Just War*, p. 7; J. Harold Ellens, in Hoffmann (ed.), *The Just War*, pp. 39, 43; Schwartz, *Curse of Cain*, pp. 57, 153-56.

29. See, e.g. Willam B. Dever, *Who Were the Early Israelites and Where Did They Come From?* (Grand Rapids, MI: Wm B. Eerdmans, 2003).

30. Schwartz, *Curse of Cain*, pp. x, 57; Nelson-Pallmeyer, *Is Religion Killing Us?*, p. 45.

31. Schwartz, *Curse of Cain*, pp. 60-62.

32. Compare Collins, 'The Zeal of Phinehas', pp. 10-12.

33. Schwartz, *Curse of Cain*, p. 61.

34. Nelson-Pallmeyer, *Is Religion Killing Us?*, p. 45.

35. Avalos, *Fighting Words*, p. 163.

36. Avalos, *Fighting Words*, pp. 27-29, 103-104, 216, 227.

37. Avalos, *Fighting Words*, pp. 114-16, 160; cf. p. 180.

for a moment the Joshua narrative in its likely historical context—the late first temple period, during Assyrian hegemony (cf. below both Wright and Zevit). While weakened (monotheistic) Judean authors were imagining the decimation of the Canaanites, Assyrian kings—all good unscriptured polytheists they— were decorating their palaces with graphic depictions of violent conquest and gratuitous torture. Now the siege of Lachish—recorded in 2 Kings and Assyrian annals, depicted on walls of Sennacherib's palace at Nineveh, and supported by archaeological evidence uncovered at the site—can be accepted as an historical fact by any measure.[38] By those same measures, the slaughter of Canaanites at Jericho remains a complete fantasy.[39] The curious history is done not by those who accept this judgment; it's done by those who insist that genocide was in fact carried out against the Canaanites by the Israelites, while at the same time overlooking or downplaying other better-attested incidents of violence from the time-period—such as the Assyrian assaults on Israel and Judah—that are not justified by either monotheistic ideals or scriptural texts.

And what of the accusation—issued by Nelson-Pallmeyer and Schwartz, among others[40]—that a fantasy, once enshrined in scripture, can legitimate violence down the line? This may of course be true at times. But answers to and qualifications of this charge are offered throughout the present volume. Geller will alert us to the difference between a text's potential for violence and its eventual fulfillment. He will also point to the dissonances within the Bible that lead to subsequent confusions and disputes. Frankfurter will also identify another case (the book of Revelation) for which the best evidence suggests that the text's violent potential remained unfulfilled not only in its day, but for sometime thereafter as well. Is it then, he will ask, possible that violent fantasies can in some situations serve to vent the rage that could otherwise be carried out? Kamionkowski will remind us that if we are concerned with afterlives of biblical texts, then other texts (and not just the most violent) should matter as well. Wills reminds us that misunderstandings can sometimes arise very early, such that a text like Matthew 27.25 ('His blood be on us and our children...'—certainly a violent afterlife here) may have had a rather benign intent and meaning at origin. Both Frankfurter and Zevit will remind us that afterlives are afterlives; if we want to reach a full understanding of biblical societies, we can and must determine what these texts meant (and inspired) in their own day. Surprisingly, some evidence suggests that both ancient Israelites and early Christians were less likely to act upon visions of violence than some of their descendants were in the middle ages or are today.

38. David Ussishkin, *The Conquest of Lachish by Sennacherib* (Tel Aviv: Tel Aviv University, The Institute of Archaeology, 1982).
39. Dever, *Who Were the Israelites?*, pp. 37-74.
40. Nelson-Pallmeyer, *Is Religion Killing Us?*, p. 45; Schwartz, *Curse of Cain*, pp. 61-62; cf. Collins, 'The Zeal of Phinehas', pp. 10-11.

There can be no doubt, as one recent author put it mildly, that the narratives of Canaanite genocide in Joshua are 'morally dubious'.[41] But if history matters, then so does the difference between fact and fantasy. Indeed, if historical accuracy matters at all to the academy and the greater public at large, then to gloss over such differences is nothing other than scholarly malpractice. Fortunately, attentive readers of the present volume will note that the authors of the following chapters do not avoid differentiating—when it is academically plausible—literary fantasy from historical reality. They also insist on differentiating between potential implication in biblical texts and actualized implications, as evidenced in the historical record.

c. *Context*

Among the more substantive points raised in recent works on religious and biblical violence is the charge that academicians engage in apologetic activity when biblical and religious violence is explained away as an historical exigency, as having achieved a greater good, or, simply, as an unquestioned aspect of society at that time.[42] Equally apologetic is the effort to isolate and (selectively) elevate certain ostensibly non-violent aspects of the biblical tradition (e.g. Micah 4 or Matthew 5) over other more clearly violent traditions such as Joshua or Revelation. There is a substance to these charges. Indeed, on this very matter scholars from as different perspectives as Hector Avalos and Tamar Kamionkowski reach some similar conclusions: it is not sufficient to point to passages such as Isaiah 2 and Micah 4 and conclude with self-congratulation that the Hebrew Bible at its best provides the basis for world peace.[43] But as Kamionkowski would insist (against Avalos, apparently) it remains important to note that Isaiah 2 does not exhibit the same kind of violence as does, say, the book of Joshua. It also remains to be noted that if we are to be concerned with the negative afterlives of narratives concerning Jericho, should we not also be concerned with the more productive afterlives of texts such as Isaiah 2?

Granting that sometimes the critique of biblical studies can also come from within (see also, for example, Frankfurter's critique of recent works on Revelation), the accusation that biblical studies includes those who engage in apologies for the Hebrew Bible and/or New Testament cannot be safely ignored. Still, the charge of bias cuts in all directions. Surely there are biblical scholars who engage in apology. But we can equally be certain that self-acclaimed secular

---

41. So, e.g. Eryl W. Davies, 'The Morally Dubious Passages of the Hebrew Bible: An Examination of Some Proposed Solutions', *Currents in Biblical Research* 3 (2005), pp. 197-228; compare Collins, 'The Zeal of Phinehas', p. 20.

42. Avalos, *Fighting Words*, pp. 159-74, 215-38, 381-82. See also Avalos in Hoffmann, (ed.), *The Just War*, pp. 60-61; Schwartz, *Curse of Cain*, pp. 60-61. With regard to Josh. 6–11 in particular, see Davies, 'Morally Dubious Passages'.

43. Avalos, *Fighting Words*, pp. 169-70, 220-30; cf. Kamionkowski in this collection.

humanists who wish to 'eliminate religion from human life altogether'[44] engage in selectively literal readings of violent texts in order to indict the religions and books they so despise. Indeed, in too many cases, the accusation of scholarly bias functions rhetorically: having accused biblical scholars of being biased, the writers are then free to proceed as if nothing remains in their way. Since appealing to historical context can be used apologetically, then historical context be damned. Surely it is easier to accuse the Bible of violence once select portions can be taken at their apparent face value, irrespective not only of the difference between fact and fantasy (see above) but also of the historical context in which the texts were composed.

It is the common conviction of the biblical scholars whose works are presented here that context does matter, just as much as history does. If the issues on the table include the role of religion in general and monotheism in particular in the perpetration and justification of violence, then it matters deeply whether the Hebrew Bible and the New Testament are innovating or repeating. If biblical admonitions to annihilate the enemy (see Geller and Zevit), punitive Old Testament laws (see Wright), and New Testament myths (see Wills) all have their analogues and even inspirations in the broader ancient Near Eastern and Hellenistic (polytheistic) contexts, then monotheism in particular—and perhaps religion in general—may have less historical (i.e. real) blame than others might think. Land-grabbing conquest did not begin with Joshua—and may or may not have occurred during Joshua's day, assuming he had one. Thus, the association of monotheism with land-possession can easily be called into question. In the ancient Near East, the great empires of Egypt, Assyria and Babylon, along with the smaller nation states such as Israel, Judah, Moab, Edom, Aram and Phonecia, whether polytheistic or not, all fought over other peoples' lands.[45] Indeed, even the charge that religion (polytheism included) is responsible for this violence begins to look laughable: Would anyone be convinced by the claim that the great (and violent) ancient near eastern empires were driven to conquer primarily by their (polytheistic) religious beliefs alone?

That the Jewish and Christian scriptures are being misconstrued in the name of religion by apologetic biblical scholars is a charge too serious to be dismissed out of hand. To be sure, the appeal to historical context or peaceful texts can be used rhetorically or apologetically by biblical scholars wishing to whitewash the scriptures of Judaism and Christianity. But that the Jewish and Christian scriptures are being attacked by those who wish to salvage only certain parts of them (including Girard, Nelson-Pallmeyer and Schwartz) or by those who wish to destroy religion altogether (including Avalos and Hoffmann) is also a distinct possibility. To those who hold such views, *any* counter-argument will be seen as apologetic. And here we find a curious

---

44. Avalos, *Fighting Words*, p. 371.
45. Compare Collins, 'The Zeal of Phinehas', pp. 3-4.

new form of fundamentalism: a literalist reading of select violent scriptures, divorced from both history and context, with a goal stated with surprising clarity: 'to end religion as we know it'.[46] The charge of apology remains, and it is incumbent upon our readers—scholars and laypeople alike—to look for apology and bias on both sides of the aisle. In the meantime, we might do well to 'neither to condemn nor condone, but to understand and elucidate' (Kamionkowski). Surely without recourse to historical context, elucidation and understanding will continue to elude us.

d. *Scripture and Interpretation*
Any careful consideration of historical context will of course bring us quickly to the irony at the heart of our project: The scriptures cannot be viewed as the cause of the violence they contain, simply because the scriptures were composed and canonized after the events they describe. Let's suppose for a moment there was a historical genocide of the Canaanites; the book of Joshua at most records this event and commends it after the fact. The approval of such behavior is morally problematic in its own right.[47] The problem is only worsened when we consider the potential for actualized violence down the line. But the difference between the various scenarios remains: the contemporary problem driving all the discussion is characterized by the dramatic flourishing of violence done by those who view barbarism as justified by their scriptures. Yes, searching the scriptures will yield many instances of violence, both imagined and real (Zevit). But in the times spoken about in the Bible, the perceived justification for the violence comes, as it must, from elsewhere: from prophets, from kings, from God.

This difference matters, and for more than one reason. For one, *any* significant difference in the reasons for the manifestation of religious violence is of consequence, if for no other reason than the fact that consideration of differences may lead to fuller understanding of this most troubling phenomenon. More to the point, however, is the fact that texts once canonized must be interpreted. And it just may in fact prove to be the case that certain styles of interpretation—particularly literalist ones—may lead to greater propensities for the actualization of the violent potential in scripture (Geller). We should also note again, for the record, that slavishly literal interpretation of violent texts are also, intriguingly, adopted by those who wish to indict the scriptures as inherently violent.

As anyone who has ever read a book knows, arriving at any general agreement on interpretation—literal or not—is by no means a simple process. Disputes over interpretation inevitably arise, and all too often (but not inevitably)

---

46. Avalos in Hoffmann (ed.), *The Just War*, p. 117; cf. Hoffmann in Hoffmann (ed.), *The Just War*, pp. 61-62.
47. Collins, 'The Zeal of Phinehas', pp. 10-11, 20; quoting, in both instances, Barr, *Biblical Faith and Natural Theology* (Oxford: Oxford University Press, 1993).

when the book in question is scripture, interpretive disputes are characterized by violence. A thread running through practically all of the papers presented here is the recognition that the Jewish and Christian scriptures emerged from and speak about varied groups and perspectives, resulting from and in turn yielding disparate interpretations of texts and events. As a result of this, it is incumbent upon modern scholarly interpreters to grasp and then grapple with scriptural diversities. As Frankfurter, Geller, Knust and Zevit point out in their papers, a great deal of the most violent rhetoric in the Jewish and Christian scriptures is aimed not so much at obvious but distant enemies who may strike from the outside, but at those closer to home who disagree over matters of interpretation. One resulting observation is summed up poignantly by Knust, who reminds us that 'the enemy within is always, in the end, the most dangerous enemy of all'.

e. A Deadly Dynamic
If disputes over interpretation are inevitable, and if the danger of violence lurks over such disputes, have we arrived back at an indictment of scriptures as inherently violent? (See Marini's comments below.) We think not. Even here, the all-important difference between potential and actualization emerges. The challenge that remains is to illuminate the deadly dynamic that can transform descriptions of violence past—many of them complete fantasies—into prescriptions for violence now and to come.

In the midst of violent events—or immediately thereafter—the religious person prone to interpret history as the gradual unfolding of God's will is faced with an interpretive dilemma: what is the reason for any particular manifestation of violence? Consider the suffering of the Jews in the late first and early second-century CE. Traditional Jews understood—and continue to understand—the destruction of the temple (70 CE) and the failed revolt led by Bar Kochva (132–135 CE) within the context of the scriptural covenant: the Jews are being punished for sinful behavior. Christians will interpret the events similarly, though the nature of the sins has now changed: in this view, the Romans' violent suppression of the revolts is to be explained as divine punishment for the Jews' rejection of Jesus (see Knust). The difference, though, is in the violent potential of Justin's view, over against the quietist, passive perspective (on this particular matter) adopted by traditional Judaism. To be sure, the Christians in Justin's day didn't act out the violence he describes—there was no need, for the Romans were efficient enough. But as Knust explains, Justin's violent rhetoric will eventually be actualized, disastrously.

What factors contribute to the actualization of the violent potential contained in the scriptures? Power, to be sure, is one important variable; it serves to explain to a large degree how Justin's interpretation of Roman violence can lead to its actualization, once Christians rule Rome. But not all religious violence is enacted by the powerful. Here the contributions by Frankfurter and Geller prove to be strikingly significant (and rather surprisingly commensurate). Geller points to the dangers of apocalyptic literalism, a by-product of biblical prophecy itself. When the scriptures come into the hands of single-minded literalists hell-bent on war, the results are likely to be violent. Frankfurter allows that violent fantasies may have served originally to deflect or channel the rage that could otherwise lead to real violence. But once these fantasies are canonized, they may find their way into the hands of groups who accept without question their own self-righteousness and their enemies' evil nature. When such a group feels threatened on the one hand and empowered directly from God on the other, here too we find a deadly mix.

3. *From Origins to Analysis*

The origins of religious violence will remain elusive. The quests of Girard, Schwartz, and Avalos (among others) are doomed to fail because, simply put, the Jewish and Christian scriptures are neither universal enough nor old enough to shed light on various forms of violence—religious and otherwise—that preceded the composition of these documents, let alone their canonization. In this respect, these theories are not very different from the earlier grandiose (and failed) efforts aimed at explaining the origins of religion itself. Extravagant theorizing on the origins of religious violence will rarely stand up to scrutiny, for scrutiny after all requires evidence, and grandiose theorizing about such origins, by its nature, reaches beyond what the evidence can soundly support. The search for the origins of religious violence in particular may also be terribly misguided in its convenient disregard of the massive evidence that human violence precedes religion. Perhaps Wrangham and Peterson put it best:

> The mysterious history before history, the blank slate of knowledge about ourselves before Jericho, has licensed our collective imagination and authorized the creation of primitive Edens for some, forgotten matriarchies for others. It is good to dream, but a sober, waking rationality suggests that if we start with ancestors like chimpanzees and end up with modern humans building walls and fighting platforms, the 5-million-year-long trail to our modern selves was lined, along its full stretch, by male aggression that structures our ancestors' social lives and technology and minds.[48]

Reading a book like *Demonic Males* is a sobering experience. But one aspect of this book is reassuring in the present context: neither religion nor sacrifice plays significant roles in scientific studies of the origins of human violence.

But there is another mode of analysis, one that should prove to shed light on both the scriptures of old and the problems of today. We should for this purpose put aside the question of origins, and refrain from imagining a vision of early humanity divorced from both religion and violence. We should focus instead

---

48. Wrangham and Peterson, *Demonic Males*, p. 172.

on ways in which religion in general (and for our purposes biblical scriptures and beliefs in particular) serve to accentuate, exaggerate and otherwise bring about acts of human violence *in specific documented historical contexts*. This mode of analysis begins with clear (and meaningful) definitions. It proceeds to work with historical data, and considers context. It then comes to grips with the religious and social dynamics in play, attending to the variables that lead to the manifestation of scripturally-justified biblical violence. Among the recent works known to us that proceed helpfully in this direction with regard to religious violence in general are Mark Juergensmseyer's *Terror in the Mind of God* (once we ignore his occasional Girardian speculations about the origins of religious violence) and Charles Kimball, *When Religion Becomes Evil*.[49] A full treatment along these lines of the Jewish and Christian scriptures remains a desideratum, but we hope that the present volume, on the whole, represents an important step in the right direction.

---

49. Charles. Kimball, *When Religion Becomes Evil: Five Warning Signs* (New York: Harper-Collins, 2002).

THE SEARCH FOR VIOLENCE IN ISRAELITE CULTURE AND IN THE BIBLE

Ziony Zevit

1. *Introduction*

There is violence in the Bible, plenty of it. 1 Kings 11.16 reports that Joab, David's cousin and military commander, and his army occupied Edom for six months and 'cut off every male in Edom'. 2 Kings 15.16 reports that Menahem ben Gadi, a war leader who managed to ascend the throne in the northern kingdom of Israel, smote Tipsah and all who were in it and 'he split open all the pregnant women in the city'. Amaziah, king of Judah, killed ten thousand people in Seir (Edom), during a campaign there, and then he and his Judahite army brought ten thousand captives to Sela 'and cast them down from the top and they all were split open' (2 Chron. 25.11-12). All these actions took place in war. Menahem's cruelty seems to have been intended as a horrific warning to others not to impede his struggle to become king. The acts of Joab and Amaziah, however, seem to reflect a 'take no prisoner' strategy against a hostile, traditional enemy of Judah. They were all acts of war, and war has its own logic. Since he who fights and walks away lives to fight another day, it was thought wise to kill captives if their labor could not be exploited or if they could not be sold as slaves.

Violence against someone recognized and denominated *enemy* is war, and war is a legitimated, comprehensible activity. It is the application of coercive, armed power against an enemy by a legitimate governing authority, be it a king, priest, or tribal leader acting with or through enfranchised followers constituting his army. An unprovoked offensive aggression serving economic or diplomatic ends fall under the war rubric. War may be defensive or retributive, inflicting pain for past wrongs. It may also be waged against real or perceived internal political threats to the legitimate governing authority, as in the case of rebellions, or against those who maintain subversive ideas critically affecting the common worldview of the broader society. Viewed this way, war is a normed behavior supported by social institutions in different ways.

Although all war involves violence, not all violence involves war. *Violence* is the use of extreme, sudden force to injure somebody, usually by surprise. Individual acts of violence may be sanctioned, as in killing somebody in self-defense or legitimate acts of revenge. It may be unsanctioned as in cases of *murder* defined as *illegitimate homicide*. Violence may or may not be *cruel*, intended to inflict pain for no particular reason. In general, Israel seems to have considered cruel violence unnatural and punishable, no matter the perpetrator or the victim: the prophet Amos condemns Israel's neighbors for torture (1.3); handing people over to Edom, a particularly cruel or violent people (1.6, 9, 11); ripping open pregnant women, like the above-mentioned Menahem (Amos 1.13); and desecrating the bones of the dead (Amos 2.1).

All of these types of wars and acts of violence are described in biblical narratives and prophetic texts. In some cases they are rationalized and in others mythologized. This paper inquires as to the extent to which they were incorporated as positive values within the religion and culture of historical Israel on the one hand and within the Bible on the other.

a. *The Hebrew Bible as Cultural Expression*

In *Culture: A Critical Review of Concepts and Definitions* (1952), Alfred Louis Kroeber and his colleague Clyde Kluckhohn defined their subject as follows: 'Culture consists of patterns...of and for behavior acquired and transmitted by symbols, constituting the distinctive achievement of human groups; the essential core of culture consists of traditional (i.e. historically derived and selected) ideas and especially their attached values; culture systems may, on the one hand, be considered as products of actions, on the other as conditioning elements of further action'.[1]

In 2001, I defined Israelite religions as 'the varied, symbolic expressions of, and appropriate responses to the deities and powers that groups or communities deliberately affirmed as being of unrestricted value to them within their worldview'.[2] My definition, like that of Kroeber and Kluckhohn, assumes that religion, like culture, is formed, formulated, and expressed through organized groups of people. Both are expressed semiotically and mediated through external realities such as spoken and written language, arts, and ritual. Though some elements of both culture and religion are private and subjective, most are public and objective. In the ancient Near East, culture was embedded in religion so that there was no intelligible demarcation between the two. The distinction between sacred and secular, between church and state, that evolved in the Christian West was as inconceivable in antiquity as it is in many parts of the Muslim world today.

Pre-exilic biblical texts are expressions of Israelite culture and religion with their attendant values. Written by and for Israelites, earlier tales and texts in the J and E sources of the Torah influenced later productions in D, P, and the

---

1. Alfred Louis Kroeber and Clyde Kluckhohn, *Culture: A Critical Review of Concepts and Definitions* (New York: Vintage Books, 1963 [1952]), p. 357.

2. Ziony Zevit, *The Religions of Ancient Israel: A Synthesis of Parallactic Approaches* (London: Continuum, 2001), pp. 15, 611.

Deuteronomistic history, because authors of the younger works were educated and education involved memorization, internalization and repetition.³ It is through the parsing of pre-exilic biblical texts in order to answer certain questions that the meaning and significance of violence in the culture and worldview of ancient Israel may be ascertained.

b. *Was the Culture of Ancient Israel a Violent Culture?*
There are shame cultures, bellicose cultures, consumer cultures, and there are violent cultures. The adjective selected highlights a dominant trait in the culture. Among the common explanations for violence is that it is instinctual or biochemical, or that it is an expression of anxiety or frustration or that it is social, learned in the family or in some social sub-group that fosters and encourages it through games, stories, or rituals. Allowing that testosterone and atavistic instincts may prime the biological being to act aggressively, in this study I address only psychological, sociological and political explanations, and those indirectly through biblical literature. I am concerned with the people Israel and their literature as known to historical-critical scholarship, not with the pathologies of individuals such as Menahem ben Gadi.

Given the fact that the Hebrew Bible's historiographic literature refers to many wars and describes much violence, that its paranetic literature calls for acts of violence, its liturgical texts are filled with violent metaphors, and its edited prophetic texts call for and describe acts of violence, it is clear that Israelite culture was very familiar with violence. But, was it a culture that reified and valued violence?

c. *Lexemes for Violence in Biblical Hebrew*
The Hebrew verb *hāmās* (חמס) occurs 8 times in the Tanach with the sense to do violence or to violate, to do wrong, to damage physically (Jer. 22.3; Lam. 2.6); twice with the figurative sense of violating divine teachings (Ezek. 22.26; Zeph. 3.4), and once with the sense 'to rob/steal', i.e. violent theft (Prov. 8.35-36).⁴ In one unclear verse it parallels a verb meaning 'to cast off' as when plants shed unripe fruit (Job 15.33). The noun form *hāmās*, best translated by *violence*, occurs 60 times in the Hebrew Bible in a wide range of contexts: theft and misappropriation of property (Isa. 60.18; Ezek. 7.23 ['bloody crimes']; Zeph. 1.9); wrongdoing, injustice and social disorder (Deut. 19.16; Hab. 1.2-3); and it appears 6 times in the context of violence associated with warlike behavior (Gen. 49.5; Judg. 9.24 ['blood']; Jer. 51.35; Obad. 1.10; Hab. 2.17; Ps. 7.17).

---

3. David M. Carr, *Writing on the Tablet of the Heart: Origins of Scripture and Literature* (New York: Oxford University Press, 2005), pp. 110-73, 287-97.

4. In this case, the violence of the thief may be explained psychologically as a response to the frustration of not possessing something owned by another person.

This noun and verb attest that Hebrew of the Iron Age had a word whose semantic range is partially congruent with the way *violence* and *to act violently* are used in contemporary American English. Other words belonging to the same semantic sphere in Biblical Hebrew are *nega* (נגע; Deut. 17.8; 21.5; Ps. 38.12), and *shod* (שד; Isa. 59.6-7; 60.18; Hab. 2.17).

What is significant for the following analysis is that *neither hāmas (the verb) nor hāmās (the noun) occurs* in any of the narratives considered below that exemplify different types of violence in the Bible. Furthermore, it does not appear in texts calling for or predicting violent revenge against those who destroyed the temple.

d. *This Study's Approach*
In this study, I approach the question of whether or not Israel's was a violent culture by considering how Israelites explained or rationalized violent acts, when and why the language of *prescriptive violence* entered the Bible, and how calls for violent behavior were fulfilled. This provides an indirect way of determining how Israelites valued violence. Literary history figures prominently in this analysis both because the gross dating of Pentateuchal and historiographic sources suffice for the enterprise and because it enables producing a nuanced, textured comprehension of changing Israelite attitudes.

2. *Violence in the Bible and in Ancient Israel*

Since many biblical narratives are about violent acts, searching for violence in the Bible is not difficult. Among the narratives are the following: Cain and Abel (Gen. 4.2-16), the Flood story (Gen. 6.9-17), Sodom, Gomorrah and the cities of the Plain (Gen. 19.23-24), Binding of Isaac (Gen. 22.1-14), Simeon and Levi's slaughter of the Shechemites in the matter of Dinah (Gen. 34.1-34), drowning of Israelite males (Exod. 1.22), Moses killing the Egyptian (Exod. 2.11-12), the tenth plague (Exod. 11.1-10; 12.29-32), God's order to blot out the memory of Amalekites and to remember to do so (Exod. 17.14; Deut. 25.17-19), the slaughter of the revelers at the foot of Mt Sinai (Exod. 32.25-29), the strange death of Nadab and Abihu (Lev. 10.1-2), God's destruction of Korah and his followers (Num. 16.31-33), the slaughter of Sihon and Og and their people (Num. 21.23-25, 33-35), the lauded zealotry of Phinehas (Num. 25.6-14), the war against Midianites in which only virgin female infants were spared (Num. 31.1-54), the command to utterly destroy the nations of Canaan (the *herem* [חרם]; Deut. 7.1-2; 20.16-18), the destruction of Jericho and slaughter of its inhabitants (Josh. 6.20-26), the dispatch of Sisera (Judg. 4.17-21; 5.24-27), Abimelech's slaughter of Shechemites and burning of people in Migdal Shechem (Judg. 9.42-49), Jephthah's daughter (Judg. 11.29-40), the ruthlessness of David (1 Sam. 27.8-11; 2 Sam. 8.2), Elijah's slaughter of the Baal prophets on Mt Carmel (1 Kgs 18.40), and Jehu's slaughter of Baal worshippers (2 Kgs 10.18-28).

a. *Explaining and Clarifying Many Violent Acts*

How is all this violence to be explained? Easily, for the most part. Aside from a random, occasional, accidental homicide and the more regular homicides associated with war, people kill people for personal reasons motivated by anger, jealousy, fear, revenge, honor, politics, and personal ambition. Such acts did not fall under censure in Israel unless they were illegal, in which case they were termed *retzach* (רצח, murder).[5] These motivations account for the acts of Cain, Simeon and Levi, Pharaoh, Moses, Abimelech, and David.[6]

War contexts, in which the conventional objective is achieved by utilizing power to either neutralize or destroy an enemy, or by employing a mix of ruthlessness and guile to the same end when power is lacking, clarify the stealthy strategy of Simeon and Levi in overcoming and destroying all male Shechemites, Yael's murder of the sleeping Sisera, and even David's methodical butchering of Moabite males.

The total destruction of Sihon, Og and their followers was due to tactical not strategic considerations. After avoiding Edomite territory by circling into the desert and avoiding Ammon and Moab (Num. 21.4, 11-13, 16) Israel had to make a left turn from the desert toward the northern end of the Dead Sea. This route would take them through Amorite territory, land outside of Canaan but not allocated by Yhwh to any nation. Sihon not only refused the Israelites' request to pass through peacefully, but also approached to attack them in the desert. Israelites killed him, defeated his army, and took over his country (Num. 21.21-25 [J]). In the Deuteronomic retelling of this incident, God hardened Sihon's heart, as he had Pharaoh's, in order to deliver him into Israel's hand (Deut. 2.30-32) and they utterly destroyed his city, leaving nobody alive (v. 33). When Og, also an Amorite according to Deut. 3.8, then attempted to stop the Israelites from crossing his territory without even having asked permission, he and his people met the same fate for the same reasons (Num. 21.33-35 [J]; Deut. 3.1-12).[7]

Louis H. Feldman describes these as 'instances not of mandated genocide but of actual genocide'.[8] Although *not* in Canaan and therefore *not* subject to extirpation, Sihon and Og were the first Amorites, one of the seven Canaanite

---

5. The concept of *retzach* (רצח) illegal homicide, constitutes a qualification of the general principle expressed in Gen. 9.5-6 that God holds to account any shedding of human blood by man or beast because humans were created in the image of God. So too, accidental homicide and homicide in war are exempted from the general rule.

6. Cain's murder was committed before homicide was prohibited in principle and a punishment determined for perpetrators; see Gen. 4.13-15 (an *ad hoc* solution in Israelite mythology) and 9.6 (the general principle for humanity).

7. Only the retellings of the Og and Sihon stories in Deut. 2.34 and 3.6 use forms of the verb חרם (utterly destroy), not the earlier JE narrative traditions in Numbers.

[8] Louis H. Feldman, *'Remember Amalek!' Vengeance, Zealotry and Group Destruction in the Bible according to Philo, Pseudo-Philo, and Josephus* (Monographs of Hebrew Union College, 31; Cincinnati: Hebrew Union College Press, 2004), p. 174.

peoples, to die. Their death, however, was not due to any ideology of *herem*, but to the exigencies of the situation. Given their experience with the Amalekites (on which see below), Israelites were not about to push through hostile territories and leave potential enemies close behind them.

These actions appear extremely harsh only because our popular Western notions about how armed conflict should be conducted derive from concepts of honor, loyalty, gamesmanship, and gallant gestures formed during and after the Middle Ages in Europe. These gave rise to (1) rules that defined combatants and targets, (2) laws of engagement, and (3) conventions for the treatment of prisoners. Underlying many of these rules were theological notions about the individual, natural innocence (particularly that of women, children, and the elderly), the eternity of the soul and the fact that European combatants, until the Reformation, were usually Christians who recognized the validity of each other's faith.

In Israel, where it was known that all the dead reach *sheol*, a successful victory counted more than the noble gesture. (Should David not have beheaded the fallen Goliath because he was down?) Life was infinitively more valuable than the game well played, and was not to be risked.[9] Other acts of violence require additional clarifications.

b. *Death of the Firstborn in Egypt*

God's destruction of Egyptian first-borns should be seen as a final warning to Pharaoh not to trifle with him. (The worst, still to come, occurred by the shores of the sea where Israel saw all of Egypt dead [Exod. 14.30].) It was justified in Israelite thought because it was part of the original warning that Moses had been instructed to deliver: 'Thus Yhwh said, "My son, my firstborn is Israel; and I am saying to you, send out my son so that he may serve me. And, (if) you refuse to send him out, behold, I kill your son, your firstborn"' (Exod. 4.22-23). Although in the following narrative Moses repeats the demand that they be allowed to serve Yhwh many times (Exod. 5.1, 3; 7.16; 8.16; 9.13; 10.3) he did not deliver the death threat. Only when informing Israelites about their imminent departure and the final plague (Exod. 11.1-6) did he announce that the firstborn of all Egyptians and their animals would die (v. 5). In this announcement, however, he did not repeat the demand that Pharaoh allow Israel to leave, not connecting clearly for Pharaoh's benefit the single act by which he might stay the plague.[10] (The speech in Exod. 11.4-8a including the announce-

---

9. My thinking along these lines is stimulated by that of Maurice Samuel, *You Gentiles* (New York: Harcourt, Brace, and Company, 1924), pp. 31-35.

10. What Yhwh took away from the Egyptians in the tenth plague, he also claimed from Israelites in the law of the firstborn of man and beast inserted into the exodus narrative after the laws of the Exodus night vigil and of the Passover offering (Exod. 13.1). The connection between Egyptian and Israelite firstborns is explicit in Exod. 13.15. Israelites must redeem their firstborn males because Yhwh slew every firstborn in Egypt. The implication of this verse is that Yhwh did what was necessary and Israel must remember the price others paid for their redemption from

ment was repeated to Pharaoh. See the pronouns in v. 8a and the description of Moses' angry exit from the court in v. 8b.)

A single idea underlies what contemporary sensibilities might consider unfair about Yhwh's destruction of innocent Egyptians with this plague: the behavior of a monarch vis-à-vis Yhwh's will determines the fate of the people over whom he rules.

This idea underlies the argument of the main Deuteronomistic author of Kings who considered calamities that befell the people of Israel and Judah a direct consequence of their ruler's policies concerning Yhwh's will (1 Kgs 12.26-31; 14.21-24; 2 Kgs 16.2-4; 18.3-7; 22.2). He determined that a most crucial expression of divine will relevant to his composition was expressed in Deuteronomy 12, namely, that sacrificial offerings be brought only to a single place of Yhwh's choosing, and understood that place to be the Jerusalem temple (1 Kgs 8.1-16).[11] Communal punishment is a corollary of the communitarian nature of Israel's pre-exilic social organization.

The eighth-seventh century prophet Isaiah of Jerusalem applied the same principle to the ruler of Assyria. Isaiah pronounced that God had sent Assyria to punish Israel by taking booty and humbling the people (Isa. 10.5-6), but because the prideful king did not plan and think in accord with Yhwh's will but thought in his mind to destroy and cut off many nations, he would be punished: 'And when the Lord carries out all his deeds in Mount Zion and in Jerusalem—"I will act against the arrogant thoughts of the king of Assyria and his overbearing arrogance" ...therefore the lord, Yhwh of hosts will send a against his fatness, a wasting away , and will burn like a fiery flame beneath his glory' (Isa. 10.12,16). So too Nahum in the seventh century: 'Your shepherds are slumbering, king of Assyria, your nobles are tenting, your people wander over the hills and there is no one to gather them... All who hear news clap their hands against you because is there not anyone against whom your evil did not constantly pass? (Nah. 3.18-19)'

c. *Religious Zealotry*
Although religious zealotry is not an admired quality nowadays, it is a comprehensible motive and explains the violence of Phinehas and Elijah. Both are presented as spur-of-the-moment acts under highly charged, public circumstances.

The war against Midian (Num. 31.2-54 [P]) in which all Midianites except virgin infant girls (v. 17) are killed may be described as genocide, but it is pre-

---

Egypt; there is no celebrating the deaths of the Egyptians. Moshe Greenberg draws attention to the role of Yhwh as Israel's avenger. See Moshe Greenberg, *Biblical Prose Prayer as a Window to the Popular Religion of Ancient Israel* (Berkeley: University of California Press, 1983), p. 13.

11. A second Deuteronomistic author (Dtr[2]) writing after the destruction of the Temple, introduced comments to Kings assigning culpability to the people as a collective, e.g. 2 Kgs 21.10-15; 22.16-17.

sented as an act of national revenge on religious grounds against the Midianite men and their secret weapons (Num. 25.16-19; 31.2 [P]). The Midianites sent females to seduce Israelite males into their cult, a plan engineered by Balaam who knew that God would punish Israelites for their cultic unfaithfulness (Num. 31.16 [and see v. 8]). It can also be explained, using a literary argument, as due to religious zealotry because the command to exact revenge is part of the same speech rewarding the zealot Phinehas with an eternal priestly line after he had killed Zimri and his Midianitess paramour Cosbi daughter of Zur.

Jehu's butchery of the Baal worshippers, however, should be evaluated in the context of the other homicides for which he was directly and indirectly responsible in overthrowing the house of Ahab and ascending to the throne (2 Kgs 9.15–10.31). Within this broader context, it is clear that his premeditated act owed less to his professed 'zeal for Yhwh' (2 Kgs 10.16) than to the necessity of eliminating potential opposition from a dedicated, well-organized group. Jehu's violence may be viewed as political skullduggery masking itself as religious zealotry. It is inherent in the nature of revolution that the old guard must be crippled and rendered ineffective if the new regime is to succeed.

d. *Human Sacrifice*

As heinous as some acts performed by religious zealots may be, they are expressions of underlying principles and can be provided with a rationale. Seemingly less explicable, however, in a contemporary rational way is the action of Abraham in the *akedah* story (Gen. 22.1-14). It strikes us as violent, cruel, unnatural and unnecessary. Despite this, human sacrifice, as a form of strong magic, is described once in biblical narrative as having been effective.

In the aftermath of Mesha's ninth century BCE revolt against the kingdom of Israel that controlled Moab (2 Kgs 3.5-27), the Moabites found themselves besieged in Kir-harasheth, modern el-Kerak, by the forces of Israel, Judah, and Edom. Thereupon, the king of Moab sacrificed his 'first-born son who was to succeed him as king, and offered him up on the wall as an *olah* (עלה, completely consumed offering)' and then a great *ketzeph* (קצף, wrath/disgust, or whatever is intended by that word), befell Israel and the attackers withdrew (v. 27). The human sacrifice achieved its objective.

If Jephthah's offering of his daughter—the narrative is unclear whether she was in fact sacrificed or not—is seen in the light of Mesha's, it is the offering that normally would have been made before the battle. Jephthah's conditional promise to provide as an *olah* whatever came out to greet him from his house after his safe return from victory, became an obligation automatically after he defeated the Ammonites (Judg. 11.30-31).[12]

---

12. If so, it is similar to the Israelite oath in the Arad/Hormah narrative preserved in Num. 21.1-3, in which they pledged to utterly destroy the city and its people if Yhwh would deliver the city to their forces. The city was an obstacle interfering with their march north that had to

This understanding is supported by two texts indicating that in Judah there were those who did believe child sacrifice to be a legitimate, though extreme, offering sanctioned by Yhwh. Micah 6.6-7 quotes women in seventh century Judah as saying that sacrificing their own children was the ultimate sacrifice for personal wrongdoing: 'With what shall I approach Yhwh, bow to the god of the uplifted place? Shall I approach him with burnt offerings, with calves a year old? Will Yhwh be pleased with a thousand rams, with a myriad of streams of oil? Shall I give my first-born for my rebellion, the fruit of my body for my own wrongdoing?'

Ezekiel 16.20-21 complains that people in the sixth century sacrificed children in various illegitimate rituals: 'And you took your sons and your daughters that you bore for me, and you sacrificed them for them [i.e. the images mentioned in v. 17] to consume. Are your whorings too few that you slaughtered my children and gave them...to them?'[13]

These attestations make Abraham's decision to offer his son as an *olah* offering moderately rational as a form of religious piety because it was not a singular act bereft of meaning in an Israelite cultural context.[14]

e. *Mandated Genocide in Torah Literature*

The command to exterminate—and I use this term self-consciously—the nations of Canaan recurs in the Torah in Deuteronomy 7, and in Deuteronomy 20. It differs from all the previously discussed cases of violence because it may be classified under the modern term *genocide*.

---

be overcome so that they could advance rapidly and not fear attack from the rear. They gave away plunder that they might have kept had they been able to take the city on their own. The consequences of not giving Yhwh his due is narrated in the story of Achan who pilfered spoil from Jericho (Josh. 7.1, 11-26). The point of these stories is that where Yhwh fought for/with Israel so that the outcome was guaranteed, Israel had no right to gain. Booty was either dedicated to Yhwh or everything was destroyed. Only when there was risk and pain was Israel entitled to gains beyond the success of the battle. See Susan Niditch, *War in the Hebrew Bible: A Study in the Ethics of Violence* (New York: Oxford University Press, 1993), pp. 28-33.

13. See the discussion of these passages in Zevit, *The Religions*, pp. 564-65 (for the Ezekiel passage), and pp. 578-79 (for the Micah passage). Passages referring to burning babies or causing children to pass through fire have nothing to do with child sacrifice. They lack sacrificial terminology and most likely refer to prophylactic rituals involving passing them quickly through flames intended to shield children from harm. See Zevit, *The Religions*, pp. 550-52 and the literature cited there. See also the demurer of Mark S. Smith, review of *The Religions of Ancient Israel: A Synthesis of Parallactic Approaches* (London: Continuum, 2001), by Z. Zevit, in *Maarav* 11 (2004), pp. 145-218 (196).

14. It would not explain, however, why a child strong enough to carry a load of wood up a mountain would support this particular expression of his father's piety unless Isaac is to be compared to Jephthah's daughter. But if so, the narrative does not clarify what Abraham received from God that would have rendered such an offering comprehensible to Israelites from the eighth through the sixth centuries BCE unless it was recompense for the protection provided while Sarah and Abraham were in Gerar.

Deuteronomy 7 instructs that when God brings the Israelites to the land that they are coming to possess, he will dislodge many peoples—the Hittites, Girgashites, Amorites, Canaanites, Perizzites, Hivites, and Jebusites—nations more numerous and powerful than them, and when he delivers them before the children of Israel, 'והכיתם (you will smite them), החרם תחרים אתם (and utterly destroy them). Don't cut a covenant with them and don't pardon them. Don't intermarry with them. Don't give your daughter to his son and don't take his daughter for your son because he will turn your son from me and they will serve other deities and Yhwh's anger will burn against you and he will quickly destroy you' (Deut. 7.1-4). Israelites are then instructed, 'their altars, smash; and their standing stones, break into pieces; and their pillars, hew down; and their images, burn in fire' (7.5). This clear instruction is a redraft of Exod. 34.11-16. After stating God would drive the Canaanite nations from the land (v. 11), the passage warns against making treaties with them because that would lead to intermarriage, and the Canaanite women would then seduce their husbands into worshipping other gods (vv. 12, 15). Therefore, God also demanded the destruction of Canaanite cult objects (v. 13), presumably this was to be done after the Canaanites were gone. Deuteronomy interpreted the expression in Exod. 34.11 (J), 'Here I expel from before you' (הנני גרש מפניך), to mean that God would dislodge them, but Israelites would finish them off.

The Deuteronomist's association of sex/marriage with cult is warranted by the story of Baal Peor, a story to which he alludes in Deut. 4.3 as providing an object lesson for what happens to those who worship foreign gods. The story of Baal Peor, Num. 25.1-9, illustrated how Moabite women—not from the Canaanite people—seduced some Israelite men into illicit worship. Israelite officials at Moses' command killed all these men.

Deuteronomy 12.2-7 repeats the order to destroy Canaanite cult sites and commands that Israelites seek out Yhwh and bring their offerings to him only at the place of his choice.

In Deut. 20.16-18, embedded in a context clarifying who may be killed in war and under what circumstances, the Deuteronomist reminds his audience that the nations of Canaan are excepted from the conventions: 'however, from these nations whom Yhwh your god gives you as inheritance, you may not let a person live. Utterly destroy them...so that they will not teach you to do the disgusting things that they do for their gods, and you will sin to Yhwh your god'.

In no call for the extirpation of Canaanites is the genocide described as a holy act, and the wars of conquest are nowhere deemed holy. Their utter destruction was not dedicated to or executed for the sake of Yhwh, in the manner that Moabites committed genocide for the sake of their deities, as discussed below.[15] It is also clear that the Deuteronomists had no qualms about

---

15. Alexander Rofé, *Deuteronomy: Issues and Interpretation* (London: T. & T. Clark, 2002),

interpreting Yhwh's command as they did, because it was rational and their god was practical.[16]

The Deuteronomic justification for the genocide is twofold: culture contaminates and cult seduces. Canaanites and their religion were held to be so alluring that if left alive, they would inevitably entice seducible Israelites into the worship of their gods. (The seventh century BCE Deuteronomist does not imagine that Canaanites could become Yahwists; only that Israelite Yahwists might worship Canaanite gods. The eighth-seventh century BCE author of Mic. 4.1-5 [= Isa. 2.1-4], however, was capable of imagining that at some time in the future, non-Israelites could acknowledge the significance of Yhwh, come to his house in Jerusalem for instruction, and still maintain their own gods.)[17]

It is not only the Canaanites who pose a threat, but also their cult sites and ritual objects. Deuteronomy assumes that the children of Israel are so attuned to the siren call of the divine that even without instruction they know how to engage in rituals at all places directed to whomever. For the Deuteronomic prohibitionist, elimination of all vestiges of Canaanite religion is intended to save Israelites from themselves. Anticipating the worst, he even legislates in Deut. 13.16-18 that a town filled with Israelite idolaters should be utterly destroyed, like the Canaanites: all the people of the city, their animals, possessions, and the city

pp. 151-52. Jeffrey H. Tigay notes that Deut. 13.17 uses the phrase *kaliyl le Yhwh*, but observes that even if it is a technical sacrificial collocation, neither the town nor the people are killed for Yhwh, only their goods along with the whole town is burnt 'completely for Yhwh'. See Tigay, *The JPS Torah Commentary: Deuteronomy* (Philadelphia: Jewish Publication Society, 1996), p. 539 n. 12.

16. Niditch discusses the qualms of scholars in dealing with the notion that God could issue such a ban (*War*, pp. 40-43). Commenting on the Peasants' Revolt in mid-May 1525, Martin Luther wrote: '...let everyone who can, smite, slay, and stab, secretly or openly, remembering that nothing can be more poisonous, hurtful, or devilish than a rebel' (*Against the Robbing and Murdering Hordes of Peasants*). This and similar statements—many commending washing hands in the blood of enemies—are collected, color-coded by degree of violence, and posted on-line at: http://socrates58.blogspot.com/2004/05/martin-luthers-violent-inflammatory.html (viewed 4/25/07).

17. Yair Hoffman argues that the initial calls for *herem* are late accretions, first in Deuteronomy 20 and then in Deuteronomy 7 (where it interrupts the narrative continuity between 6.9 and 7.6). He argues further that the insertion was formulated sometime after the return of Zerubbabel in the sixth-fifth centuries, expressing opposition to the foreigners whose practices are described in Ezra 9.1-2 as like the abominations of the Canaanites. That is, Hoffman sees the texts in Deuteronomy as modeled after those in Ezra. See, 'The Deuteronomistic Concept of the Herem', *ZAW* 111 (1999), pp. 196-210 (201-202, 205-207). Actually, since most specific references to law in Ezra clearly reflect Deuteronomy, and since Ezra's list adds Moabites and Egyptians and Ezra is against all intermarriages, whereas Deuteronomy allows it under certain circumstances, it is safer to assume that Deuteronomy has influenced Ezra and not *vice versa*. Finally, the term 'peoples of the land' in biblical idiom refers to ethnic groups beyond the tribal borders. Hoffman's observation about the prohibition in Deuteronomy 7 is unaffected by this critique and is part of the editing history of the pre-exilic book.

itself, even if their activities do not follow the Canaanite model. He had both legal and historical precedents on his side. Exod. 22.19 (J) legislates 'he who sacrifices to a god other than Yhwh alone will be utterly destroyed'. This was applied to the Israelite men in the case of Baal Peor. Another precedent is found in Exod. 32.26-9, an unclear story about how Moses punished those who apparently bore major responsibility for the Golden Calf. After the Levites gather to him because they are 'For Yhwh', he instructs them to kill 'each man his brother and each man his friend and each man his relative'. After about 3000 people are killed—it is unclear if they are only from the tribe of Levi—Moses says, 'Dedicate yourselves (literally, 'fill your hand') for Yhwh today, because a man was against his son and against his brethren, and for putting a blessing on you today'.

A different justification for killing off the nations of Canaan is provided in Leviticus 18 (P), a chapter listing what the author considered perverse sexual liaisons between family members, bestiality, and some form of male homosexuality, all of which are described as the 'practice (מעשה) of the land of Egypt where you dwelt and the practice of the land of Canaan to which I am taking you' (Lev. 18.3). The fleshy practices of the Canaanites polluted them, i.e. rendered them impure, and the land in which they lived as well, 'and the land became polluted', with the consequence that God 'punished it for its iniquity, and the land vomited out its inhabitants' (Lev. 18.25).[18] Thereupon, Israel and aliens who live in the land are warned not to act as did the Canaanites, because should they engage in such immoral practices, the land would vomit them out also (Lev. 18.27-30).[19] Moral iniquity, according to Leviticus, explains the physical departure of Canaanites.[20] Deuteronomy provided a practical clarification of how the land would disgorge the iniquitous Canaanites and purge itself. It mandated genocide.

The Mesha inscription from the mid-ninth century BCE indicates that Israel's neighbor not only knew the concept of *herem*, the utter destruction of an enemy, but that they practiced it as well. In lines 14-16, Mesha describes his campaign against Nebo:

---

18. The past tense of the Hebrew verb is problematic and defies philological explanation. Julius Wellhausen provided an historical answer. It betrays the time of the writer. This is cited by Jacob Milgrom in *Leviticus 17–22* (AB, 3A; New York: Doubleday, 2000), p. 1580.

19. Gen. 15.16, which employs the same idea and metaphor, suggests that it required about four generations of such perverse behavior until the amount of iniquity reached the point at which the land retched: 'and the fourth generation will return here because the iniquity of the Amorites is not complete until then'.

20. On moral impurity, a type that cannot be ritually expurgated through Yahwistic rituals, see Jonathan Klawans, *Impurity and Sin in Ancient Judaism* (New York: Oxford University Press, 2000), pp. 26-31; 'Pure Violence: Sacrifice and Defilement in Ancient Israel', *HTR* 94.2 (2001), pp. 154-55; and Christine E. Hayes, *Gentile Impurity and Jewish Identities: Intermarriage and Conversion from the Bible to the Talmud* (New York: Oxford University Press, 2002), pp. 22-24.

> (14) And Kemosh said to me, 'Go seize Nebo from Israel' and I (15) went at night and fought against her from the rising of the morning star until noon and I (16) seized her and I killed all of her, seven thousand men and young men and women and young wo(17)men and virgins, because for Ashtar-Kemosh I utterly destroyed her.

The word used by Mesha for 'utterly destroy' is the same *herem* used in Hebrew.

In his detailed study of this inscription as a religious text, Philip D. Stern concluded that the *herem* 'must be understood as an intensely moral-religious act, reasserting the rule of the god(s) and reflecting the victory of Kemosh and Mesha over the 'monsters of chaos', i.e. Yhwh and Israel. Moab was able to slaughter the Israelites without a qualm with the aid of this mythopoeic conception'.[21] Stern's point is that theology salved the Moabite conscience and that the hypothesized myth was well known in Moab before the slaughter.

A pragmatic explanation for Mesha's utter destruction of Israelites is the same as the one submitted above for Israel's utter destruction of the Transjordanian Amorites. Having conquered Israelite clans settled by Omri in the heart of traditionally Moabite territory, he could not allow potential enemies with allies across the border to reside in Moab or to become, resentful, landless farmers a few miles away.

Other examples of genocide in times of war are mentioned in both historical and literary sources from the ancient Near East, as well as in Hellenic, Hellenistic, and Roman sources. These suggest that the phenomenon, while rare, was known from Syria to Europe from the second millennium BCE through the third century CE. In many cases genocide was accompanied by cultic activities or explained in mythological terms.[22]

Lines 11-12 of Mesha's inscription describe a similar slaughter but the vocabulary is subtly different. He describes his campaign against the Israelite town of Ataroth:

> (11) I fought against the town and I captured it and I killed all the pe[ople from]
> (12) the town rayat (רית) for Kemosh and for Moab

Although the reading is certain, the meaning of the word, pronounced perhaps *rayat*, remains problematic 150 years after the discovery and initial decipherment of the inscription.[23] Its meaning could be adverbial, describing how the killing was done, or it could be a noun describing what the killing was: a gift, an offering, a gesture.

---

21. Philip D. Stern, *The Biblical Herem: A Window on Israel's Religious Experience*, (Brown Judaic Studies, 211; Atlanta: Scholars Press, 1990), p. 50.

22. Stern, *The Biblical Herem*, pp. 57-87; Feldman, *Remember Amalek*, pp. 2-7 with bibliography.

23. For the reading, see Aaron Schade, 'New Photographs Supporting the Reading *ryt* in Line 12 of the Mesha Inscription', *IEJ* 55 (2005), pp. 206-207.

The significant difference between the Mesha's narratives of *herem* (lines 14-17) and *rayat* (lines 11-2) is the following. The god Kemosh instructed Mesha to attack Nebo, but in the attack on Ataroth, Mesha acted privately on his own. In both cases, however, the Israelites were slaughtered for deities: Ashtar-Kemosh in the case of Nebo, and two deities, Kemosh and Moab in the case of Ataroth.

The institution of *rayat* has its parallel in Lev. 27.28-29, laws for the private *herem*: 'Every חרם that a person declares will be חרם for Yhwh, from all that he has, from a person, from a beast, from the field of his holding, cannot be sold and not redeemed; every חרם is most holy for Yhwh. Any חרם declared חרם from people cannot be ransomed; he will be put to death'.[24] In Israel, it was only the private *herem* that was dedicated as holy for Yhwh, because individuals proscribing their own property did it as a type of senseless freewill offering.

f. *Mandated Genocide in the Historiographic Tradition*
Israel's historiographic tradition indicates that Canaanites were not utterly destroyed. The elaborate but fictional stories in the early chapters of Joshua about the conquest and destruction of Jericho and Ai set a misleading tone to the book.[25] Although Joshua reports many successful campaigns against the Cisjordanian kings and the inhabitants of their cities, Joshua refers also to many sections of the land where the original population remained intact: Jebusites in Jerusalem (Josh. 15.63), Canaanites in Gezer and in the midst of Ephraim (Josh. 16.10), many Canaanites throughout the territory of Manasseh (Josh. 17.12-13), and Canaanites in Dan's original allotment (Josh. 19.47). Joshua himself was duped into making a treaty with the Hivites who lived in Gibeon and their kinsmen (Josh. 9.1-26) in territory allotted primarily to Benjamin and Judah. On the day that he discovered what had happened, he made them 'hewers of wood and drawers of waters for the Israelites for the community for the altar of Yhwh unto this day...' (v. 27).

Likewise, the book of Judges contains a list of Canaanite urban centers and their surrounding villages unaffected by the Israelite invasion (Judg. 1.27-36). In fact, aside from the story of Deborah and Barak's conflict with the forces of Jabin from Hazor, none of Israel's enemies in the battles described in this book are Canaanites: Arameans, Moabites, Philistines, Midianites, Amalekites, Kedemites and Ammonites. According to the Deuteronomistic editors of the

---

24. This law appears in a context discussing the value of items donated or dedicated to the sanctuary as a matter of freewill. Lev. 27.26-29 deals with items that cannot be donated since they are, according to Priestly legislation, Yhwh's property anyway. This includes livestock promised, i.e. not firstlings, along with real estate, or slaves (27.28). Lev. 27.29 suggests that human donations must be utterly destroyed, killed.

25. Zevit, 'Archaeological and Literary Stratigraphy in Joshua 7–8', *BASOR* 251 (1983), pp. 23-35 (33-35).

historiographic literature, the worst fears of the Deuteronomic writer were realized: Israelites settled among Canaanite people, intermarried, and worshipped their gods (Judg. 3.5).

One historiographic tradition suggests that by the time of the United Monarchy, most of the Canaanite peoples had assimilated into the Israelite tribes or integrated themselves into the tribal structures. Some, however, did not. 1 Kings 9.20-21 records that 'of these Solomon made a labor force unto this day'. This is the last reference to Canaanite people in a historiographic context in the Tanakh.

Whether or not all this information is accurate is less important than the fact that it indicates that the Deuteronomistic historian was aware that though there had been and still were Canaanite people in the land—note the expression 'unto this day' in Josh. 9.27 and 1 Kgs 9.21—there had been successful wars of conquest and many deaths, but no genocide.

This awareness led the Deuteronomistic historian to qualify the call for immediate genocide. In Judg. 3.1-4, he explained that it was God's plan to leave the nations in the land so that Israelites could gain experience in warfare on the one hand and to test Israelite faithfulness to his commands on the other. (This may have been his explication of Exod. 23.29-30 [J]: 'I will not drive them out before you in a single year ... little by little...') The fact that they failed this test of faithfulness (v. 5) is what, according to the Deuteronomistic historian, set off the cycle of wars (involving non-Canaanite peoples) intended to punish Israel. This in turn led to a similar qualification being inserted at Deut. 7.17-24 to indicate that the future conquest would be gradual.

g. *Mandated Genocide in Light of the History of Biblical Literature*

The idea of Israel's methodical, genocidal *herem* may have been inspired by Assyria during the eighth century. Assyria, aggressively pushing into the Levant, was perceived as almost unstoppable, capable of destroying whomever it wished, whenever it wished (Isa. 5.26-28; 10.6, 13; 8.7-8; 37.24) and capable of destroying complete populations as object lessons. Peter Machinist has demonstrated that after the mid-eighth century BCE Judahites not only had knowledge about what Assyrian forces did, but also were familiar with Assyrian propaganda claims in written and other representations.[26] In 701 BCE, Judahites witnessed and experienced directly Assyrian military power, strategy, and organization and this knowledge may even have left a trace in the Deuteronomistic conquest narrative in Joshua.

Joshua's conquest is described as taking place in three regional campaigns: the first into the central highlands, the second towards Jerusalem and cities to its south and west, and the third into the Galilee. This may have been modeled loosely on Sennacherib's tactics with two major armies during his 701 campaign

---

26. Peter Machinist, 'Assyria and its Image in the First Isaiah', *JAOS* 103 (1983), pp. 719-37 (722-26, 737).

in the same regions. The list of cities in Isa. 10.28-32 describes the march of one Assyrian army from the north, south to Jerusalem along the central mountain road. The list in Mic. 1.10-16 describes the march of a second army that came down the coast, took care of matters in Philistia and then turned to Lachish and the areas south-west of Jerusalem. From there, the army would have moved northeast toward Jerusalem.

Deuteronomy, the book mandating genocide, achieved its extant shape during the seventh and sixth centuries BCE, after whatever Canaanites there were in Cisjordan had ceased to exist as recognizable, identifiable peoples. The Deuteronomistic recasting of early conquest stories as fulfillment of the *herem* come from the same chronological and a similar ideological horizon.[27] The form of the stories in Joshua cannot predate Deuteronomy's interpretation of the J narratives in which God said 'I will send my terror (אימתי) before you...and I will make all your enemies flee' (Exod. 23.27; see also 34.11), and 'I will send the hornet (הצרעה) before you and it will chase the Hivvites and Canaanites...before you' (Exod. 23.28) as mandates for genocide. The Deuteronomistic historian's sense of how the conquest might have taken place in accord with the *herem*, was influenced by J's narrative about the Amorite genocide in Transjordan.

But to what end? What circumstances in the seventh-sixth centuries BCE lent plausibility and relevance to these themes?

h. *Mandated Genocide in the Light of Israelite History*

From the vantage point of seventh century Judah—the northern kingdom of Israel having been destroyed and dismantled by Assyria in 722 BCE—there were no Canaanites in the land. Foreign peoples from the east were settled in Samaria and other territories of the northern tribes. Assyria loomed as a powerful threat over Judah. Therefore, zealous, Yahweh-alone thinking explained that the destruction of Israel must have come about on account of disloyalty to Yhwh. The passion of Jehu in ridding the north of Ahab's descendants—Ahab who had married Jezebel, daughter of Ethbaal king of Sidon and who served Baal (1 Kgs 16.30)—and of dedicated Baalists had not saved the kingdom.[28] The Judahite equivalent of Ahab and Baalism in Deuteronomistic perception was Manasseh and southern polytheism. Accordingly, the call to eradicate people could not have been directed against non-existent Canaanites whom, as even

---

27. Moshe Weinfeld proposes that the original conquest stories first developed in local, tribal traditions were then shaped into a national tradition during the early monarchy, more than a century before the Deuteronomistic historians began to mold some evolved form of them into his theologically didactic narrative. See *Deuteronomy 1–11* (AB 5; New York: Doubleday, 1991), pp. 377-84.

28. Sidon occurs in some of the non-stereotyped lists as one of the Canaanite nations: Gen. 10.15-18; Judg. 3.3; 2 Sam. 24.6-7. See the table in Stern, *The Biblical Herem*, p. 95.

the Deuteronomists knew, could no longer be found in the land, but against unfaithful Judahites, be they prophets giving authenticating signs, family members, or even complete towns (Deut. 13.1-19). The internal enemy was to be extirpated—leftover business from the time of the conquest was to be concluded—in a preemptive war designed to ward off Yhwh's anticipated reaction to the tribal kingdom that tolerated unfaithfulness.

Josiah, who understood and acted on the cultic implications of the paranesis in Deuteronomy 12, turned a blind eye to the demand in Deuteronomy 13 that he execute his own tribesmen. In the course of his reform, described in 2 Kings 22–23, he dramatically executed only priests of shrines far from Judah, slaughtering them on their altars, in the area of Samaria (2 Kgs 23.20). Although he may have been as zealous as Jehu, Josiah was a reformer of practical bent who could not cast his own tribesmen as internal enemies. His zealotry did not lack political sophistication. He ignored Deuteronomy's call for blood. Even as he rid the temple of idolatrous worship, he left untouched even the Jerusalem priests who had maintained these cults.[29]

John J. Collins observes that whether or not the biblical narratives about these violent destructions are historical is not relevant. They are 'programmatic ideological statements' that 'project a model of the ways in which Israel should relate to its neighbors'.[30] Alastair G. Hunter described these texts as 'the potential for violence built into the Bible'.[31] Both these scholars are correct, *but not with regard to pre-exilic Israel*.

Josiah, with prescriptions for and descriptions of genocide available to him and Deuteronomic paranesis in his ears, did not emulate the concocted past and did not execute Deuteronomy's injunctions.[32]

i. The Special Case of the Amalekites
The case of the Amalekites is unlike and not connected at all to that of the nations of Canaan.[33] The command to remember what the Amalekites did to Israel at the beginning of the Exodus, and to wait until some indefinite time in

---

29. Josiah's reform is considered as one of many cultic policies enacted in Judah during the seventh-sixth centuries, each with its own inherent logic in Zevit, *The Religions*, pp. 470-76.

30. John J. Collins, 'The Zeal of Phinehas: The Bible and the Legitimation of Violence', *JBL* 122 (2003), pp. 3-21 (11).

31. Alastair G. Hunter, '(De) Nominating Amalek: Racist Stereotyping in the Bible and the Justification of Discrimination', in Jonneke Bekkenkamp and Yvonne Sherwood (eds.), *Sanctified Aggression: Legacies of Biblical and Post-Biblical Vocabularies of Violence* (JSOTSup, 400; London: T. & T. Clark, 2003), p. 107.

32. The *Nachleben* of the narratives and laws considered in this article during Late Antiquity is described and analyzed by Feldman, *Remember Amalek*. Acts of violence perpetrated by Jews such as the Hasmoneans in post-biblical periods were not justified in terms of these laws or narratives.

33. *Pace* Feldman, *Remember Amalek*, p. 145.

the future when Israel had no more enemies, and not to forget to blot out their mention/memory from beneath the heavens is unique (Deut. 25.17-19 and see Exod. 17.14-16 [J]) in that it is unconnected to the *herem* tradition. (Samuel, however, ordered Saul to utterly destroy them and kill men, women, infants, and animals, 1 Sam. 15.1-3, 8-9.[34])

The Hebrew Bible does not record what original heinous act Amalekites committed against Israelites, but the calls for retribution suggest that it was grievous. The figurative language in Deut. 25.18, ויזנב בך כל הנחשלים אחריך, which translates literally as 'and he "un-tailed" in you all stumblers behind you' is interpreted as indicating that Amalekites attacked stragglers behind the main group from the rear.

The Amalekites were not one of the Canaanite peoples. In fact, they seem to have been a western branch of some Edomite group (Gen. 36.12; Ps. 83.7-8).[35] At one time, perhaps in the thirteenth century BCE, some of them lived as far north as what became the territory of Ephraim where a region known as Amalekite Mountain existed (Judg. 12.15 and see 5.14). Biblical narratives locate them somewhere in the Negev region, ranging across Sinai toward Egypt (Gen. 14.7; 1 Sam. 27.8) where they attacked Israelites (Exod. 17.8), were attacked by Saul and David (1 Sam. 15.4-7; 27.8), and had at least one urban settlement (1 Sam. 15.5) along with many encampments. They are mentioned as allies of the Ammonites, Moabites, and Midianites—Transjordanian groups that attacked and harassed Israel during the period of Judges (Judg. 3.13; 6.3, 33; and 7.12). In the biblical presentation of events, Amalekites were Israel's consistent adversaries from the time that they left Egypt through the establishment of the monarchy.

Israel's hostility is reflected in the calls for revenge in Exodus and their interpretation in Deuteronomy, in Samuel's exaggerated instructions to Saul, in David's practice of leaving nobody alive after looting Amalekite groups

---

34. The decision to take spoil and save Agag, the Amalekite king, contrary to Samuel's instructions, indicates, perhaps, that Saul thought that what he did was permitted—'Blessed are you for Yhwh, I have fulfilled the word of Yhwh' (1 Sam. 15.13)— and that Samuel had exaggerated a traditional understanding of Yhwh's command on how to handle the Amalekites by turning it into a *herem* mandate. David's activities, approved by the Deuteronomistic historians, suggest that Saul and his army were correct.

35. The reference in Psalms also associates them with groups settled mainly east of the Jordan. For the Hagrites in Gilead, see 1 Chron. 5.10, 18-22. According to the Genesis genealogy, Jacob's brother Esau fathered Eliphaz who fathered Amalek. If those who attacked Israel are considered fourth-generation descendants of Esau, they are at the same remove from their founding ancestor as the Israelites undergoing the Exodus. Speculating midrashically, perhaps they were taking care of what they considered unfinished family business. Amos expressed anti-Edomite hostility in terms of the relationship between Jacob and Esau in the middle of the eighth century BCE (Amos 1.11-12). Extant biblical stories about Jacob and Esau contain no story that could function as an analogy to whatever (almost) current event Amos referred. If, however, Amos was alluding to the Amalek story, he may have had a complete analogy.

(1 Sam. 27.9,11), and in the inner dialogue imagined in Ps. 83.5: 'They said, "let us go and cut them off from being a people, and let the name of Israel not be mentioned again"'. The tone suggests that some authentic festering memory underlies these traditions.[36] The literary sources conveying the story date to the ninth-eighth century (Exodus), and the seventh (Deuteronomy, 1 Samuel) while the narratives concern events that occurred, according to the historiographic tradition, in the twelfth, eleventh, and tenth centuries BCE.

Their final comeuppance occurred after a large force of Amalekite raiders successfully captured David's unmanned stronghold at Ziklag, when David and his men were away, burning the city, taking booty, and capturing all women and children (1 Sam. 30.1-2). A few days later, David pursued them, recovered all the captives, and killed all but four hundred young men who fled on camels (1 Sam. 30.17). What happened to those who escaped may be intimated from a single pericope in the book of Chronicles, a post-exilic composition of the fourth century BCE.

Amalekites are last mentioned in a genealogical note about the tribe of Simeon. According to this note, five hundred Simeonites migrated to Mount Seir in Edomite territory during the reign of Hezekiah, perhaps after the Assyrian invasion of 701 BCE, where they found Amalekites 'and they smote the remnant of the Amalekite fugitives, and settled there until this day' (1 Chron. 4.41-43).[37] The Chronicler did not connect their final demise to any demand for their extirpation. What surprises, though, is that the Deuteronomistic historians made no mention of the end of Amalek.

The Amalekites are the only indigenous people killed out by Israelites whose story can be traced from traditional but historically unreliable sources in J, through more reliable-appearing sources used by the Deuteronomistic historians in Judges and Samuel, until their final elimination some time in the seventh century. They were highlighted in seventh century Deuteronomy because at the time of its composition, they were still known to exist.

j. *Violence after 586 BCE*
Iron Age war conventions apparently allowed for the taking of booty that included women, children, animals and goods (Deut. 20:.10-14; Jud 5.30) and Israelites apparently adhered to these conventions (Deut. 21.10-11).[38] With the exile of

---

36. The wording of Ps. 83.5 suggests that it was concocted on the basis of wording known to us in the Pentateuchal traditions. Mention of the Assyrians and Tyrians in verse 9 supports a late eighth century BCE date for the psalm, before the Assyrians and their Levantine allies destroyed Samaria in 722 BCE.

37. The expression could have been in the original source used by the Chronicler since it is generally restricted to parallel texts, e.g. 2 Chron.5.9//1 Kgs 8.8. See Sara Japhet, *I & II Chronicles* (OTL; Louisville, KY: Westminster/John Knox Press, 1993), pp. 125-27.

38. Lev. 19.18 forbids Israelites from exacting revenge only from fellows (1 Sam. 22.17-18; 24.12; Jer. 15.15) and so Yhwh was expected to do it, e.g. Ps. 94.1, 'God of vengeance, Yhwh,

586 BCE, something changed. William Morrow proposes that the destruction of Jerusalem gave rise to changes that are aptly, not figuratively, characterized as reflecting post-traumatic stress disorder. One symptom of PTSD is reflected in the violation of various cognitive systems that inject confusion into a coherent worldview. Such shifts in meaning systems include loss of faith, a sense of hopelessness and despair, and a desire to escape violence. This shift is discernible in biblical texts bearing on violence and national revenge.[39]

In Ezekiel's apocalyptic vision of Gog and Magog, those who threatened Israel are to be destroyed, not by Israel, but by their own swords. Then, birds and beasts invited by Yhwh will mutilate the dead, as if enjoying a sacrifice that he prepared for them. Israelites, however, will make fires and burn the weapons of their enemies and bury the dead (Ezek. 38.21-23 + 39.17-28 + 39.9-16).[40] Ezekiel is unable to imagine Israel engaged in violent revenge even against men, only in the pious act of cleaning up the carnage. A similar retreat from violence is seen in Isa. 34 (generally believed to be post-exilic), and in Jer. 50.34-39; 51.34-40.

In the second part of post-exilic Psalm 137, 'By the waters of Babylon', the psalmist's sadness and despair erupt in anger. When expressing his desire for revenge against the unprecedented acts perpetrated against his people during the destruction of Jerusalem he exclaims: 'blessed be he who repays you the payment that you paid us; blessed be he who seizes and smashes your babies on the rock' (v. 8).[41] The psalmist did not pray for the privilege of doing unto others, because, beaten, defeated, and returned from an exile, in his conception, that was not what Israelites did any more.

God of vengeance, appear!' They were, however, allowed to exact it from foreigners (1 Sam. 14.24; 18.25).

39. William S. Morrow, 'Post-Traumatic Stress Disorder and Vicarious Atonement in the Second Isaiah', in J. Harold Ellens and Wayne G. Rollins (eds.), *Psychology and the Bible: A New Way to Read the Scriptures* (Westport, CT: Praeger, 2004), pp. 168-71, and 'Comfort for Jerusalem: The Second Isaiah and Counselor to Refugees', *Biblical Theology Bulletin* 34 (2004), pp. 80-86 (80-81).

40. Ezekiel's imagery of bodies spread across a plain in ch. 39 (or in a valley in ch. 37) may have been influenced by Mesopotamian imagery. Shalmaneser III wrote on the Kurkh Monolith c. 853–852: 'I decisively defeated them. I felled with the sword their fighting men. Like Adad, I rained down upon them a devastating flood. I piled them in ditches (and) filled the extensive plain with the corpses of their warriors. Like wool, I dyed the mountain with their blood'. Ninurta-Kudurru-Usar-Suha, a warlord in the late eighth century wrote: 'I caused their blood to flow like waters of a river. The road with their corpses was visible to the eagles and vultures. I filled the mountains and wadis with their skulls like mountain stones. Birds made nests in their skulls'. See William W. Hallo (ed.), *The Context of Scripture*. II. *Monumental Inscriptions from the Biblical World* (Leiden: E.J. Brill, 2000), pp. 262, 280.

41. Obad. 12–14 lists what he considers Edomite sins during the destruction: gloating, jeering, pillaging, killing fugitives, and handing refugees over to the Babylonian authorities.

3. Conclusions

Historical Israel did not develop a vocabulary for violence. Historical Israel did not evolve a symbol system for violence.

Historical Israel did engage in wars that involved ruthless violence but did not evolve an ideology of violence that esteemed war itself or the killing of enemies. Israel most likely extirpated Amorites in Transjordan and maintained a vendetta against Amalekites that ended without fanfare in the seventh century BCE. No guilt was associated with such acts, but no particular glory was connected to them either. Israel was hardly pacifistic. It did celebrate Yhwh as a 'man of war' on specific occasions and acknowledged singular acts of prowess and bravery, whether against man or beast (2 Sam. 21.15-22; 23.8-23).

Historical Israel valued neither war nor warriors. It celebrated victory (Exod. 15.1-21; Judg. 5.1-31; 11.34; 1 Sam. 18.6-7) and elected successful warriors as leaders and kings (Judg. 8.22-23 [the offer of kingship was refused]; 11.4-11; 1 Sam. 11.5-15; 2 Sam. 5.1-3). The closest biblical poetry approaches celebrating warriors is a single verse in David's dirge over Saul and Jonathan emphasizing their unwavering bravery in battle (2 Sam. 1.22).[42] The closest it comes to recognizing a code of warrior behavior and privilege is an expression placed in the mouths of Zebah and Zalmunah, Midianite kings, who ask that Gideon himself kill them: 'Rise and smite us because like the man [i.e. who kills another] is his heroism' (Judg. 8.21).[43] The Deuteronomistic historian, for all his literary bloodthirst, apparently considered it improper for a person who was essentially a warrior—David, conqueror of Jerusalem and founder of the legitimate dynasty of Israel's kings—to build Yhwh a temple (2 Sam. 7.1-16 ; see in particular verse 9, and 1 Kgs 5.17 and compare 1 Chr. 22.7-8).

Historical Israel, in the seventh–sixth centuries BCE, recreated a past in which her ancestors had engaged in genocide, but did not pursue any mimetic activities to reenact that past against current enemies. Prophets did not cast Arameans or Ammonites or Philistines or Assyrians or any enemy, as Canaanites or Amorites or Girgashites in the same way that later Jewish tradition created an identity between Edom, Amalek, and Rome.[44]

In sum, although there was much that was violent in the life of ancient Israel that is reflected or surmised from the biblical texts considered above, there is no evidence suggesting a cultural pattern of overt or suppressed violence. A violent pattern might have included violent crimes including murder, which seems not to have been much of a concern in ancient Israel, regular social dissention, internal wars (deemed unacceptable in Judg. 21.15-18; 1 Sam. 11.12-13; 1 Kgs 12.21-24), combat sports, and malevolent magic.[45]

---

42. Samuel, *You Gentiles*, pp. 52-57.
43. See Niditch, *War*, pp. 99-100.
44. See Feldman, *Remember Amalek*, pp. 62-83.
45. Carol R. Ember and Melvin Ember, 'Issues in Cross-Cultural Studies of Interpersonal

After 586 BCE, the desire for vengeance was directed into language. Expressions of might came to be imaged in metaphor and not imagined in battle. Psychically seared, militarily powerless, Israelite aggression was sublimated into *Schadenfreude* and fantastic dreams. Only with the rise of the Hasmonean dynasty three centuries later, a dynasty that rose bloodily in the war-culture of the Hellenistic Near East, did the above-mentioned pattern of cultural violence become prominent and common in the political life of local Jews and in both their historical and mythopoeic literature.

Violence', in R. Barry Ruback and Neil A. Weiner (eds.), *Interpersonal Violent Behaviors, Social and Cultural Aspects* (New York: Springer Publishing, 1995), pp. 25-42 (34). I thank Dr Sue Kapitanoff for this reference.

The 'Problem' of Violence in Prophetic Literature: Definitions as the Real Problem

S. Tamar Kamionkowski

1. *Introduction*

The problem of violence in prophetic literature has been addressed by a number of Biblicists, primarily those concerned with the theological implications of divine violence and divine wrath. It is my intention to reframe the notion of 'problem' and the definition of 'violence' in a manner that I believe enables us to more honestly understand the prophetic materials in their original contexts and that is also more socially responsible.

I talk about social responsibility in this paper because the necessity for this collection of essays does not exist in a vacuum. Since 9/11, popular awareness of the intersections between religion and acts of violence has taken a center stage in public discourse. Those of us who engage in historical and literary inquiry cannot disengage ourselves from this public discourse. We must act with integrity which means being both honest with respect to the ancient texts and recognizing that our interpretations become a part of our public discourse as much, if not more than the ancient texts themselves.

Some of the recent attempts at dealing with divine violence in prophetic literature unwittingly contribute further to a culture of violence even as the writers are troubled by that very violence. Let me begin by offering an example of a recent work by Terence Fretheim that results quite unintentionally in a dangerous conclusion. Fretheim surveys the enormous volume of human and divine violence found throughout the Hebrew Bible. As a liberal Protestant, he is troubled by the degree of divine violence in the texts. To address the problem, Fretheim stresses the overwhelming number of cases of human violence, from Genesis to Proverbs to which God must respond. He asserts that 'Such a resolute divine opposition to human violence is important to remember in reflecting upon divine violence. In sum: if there were no human violence, there would be no divine violence'.[1] In other words, God uses violence as a means of judgment

---

1. Terence Fretheim, 'God and Violence in the Old Testament', *Word and World* 24 (2004), pp. 18-28 (21). See also his article, '"I Was Only a Little Angry": Divine Violence in the Prophets', *Interpretation* 58 (2004), pp. 365-75.

and salvation. It is never gratuitous violence. 'God chooses to become involved in violence so that evil will not have the last word. In everything, including violence, God seeks to accomplish loving purposes'.[2]

Fretheim is significantly influenced by Abraham Joshua Heschel. Heschel speaks specifically of divine anger, not violence (although divine anger is not just a divine state of mind but includes action). He asks us not to view divine violence as allegorical, but as 'a stark reality', one that must be understood within his definition of divine pathos.[3] In other words, he argues that God does not act out of spite or recklessness. God's wrath and accompanying actions teach us that indifference and complacency are the greatest evils. 'He is always concerned, He is personally affected by what man does to man. He is a God of pathos'. He continues, 'Man's sense of injustice is a poor analogy to God's sense of injustice. The exploitation of the poor is to us a misdemeanor; to God, it is a disaster'.[4]

Heschel frames the discussion within the context of divine pathos; Fretheim frames the discussion within the context of justice. Fretheim justifies God's use of violence by arguing that it is in the service of justice and not gratuitous violence.[5] Heschel and Fretheim go further, arguing that divine acts of violence can ultimately be understood as signs of divine love because God's violence functions to make humanity more just. Although I assume that Fretheim, Heschel and others do not intend this, I hear the same argument used today by the present U.S. administration in justifying the curtailment of civil rights and in its policies on the 'war against terror'. I also hear the same rhetoric used by 'freedom fighters' who believe that their violence is serving a greater purpose in ousting the godless West from its lands.

Any attempt to condone divine violence in the Hebrew Bible cannot help but become part of the system of violence. So I propose that as scholars we seek neither to condone nor to condemn, but to understand and elucidate. We begin doing this by acknowledging, as we do in other areas of critical inquiry, that the problem is not one of divine violence, but human projections or intuitions about divine violence. My methodological assumption is that the prophetic texts are ideological texts that reveal more about the producers of the text and the world in which they lived than any transcendent truths.[6] The problem is therefore not

2. Fretheim, 'God and Violence', p. 27.
3. Abraham Joshua Heschel, *The Prophets* (Philadelphia: Jewish Publication Society, 1962), p. 280.
4. Heschel, *The Prophets*, pp. 284-85.
5. For other attempts at justifying divine violence, see Harry M. Orlinsky, 'The Situational Ethics of Violence in the Biblical Period', in Salo W. Baron and George S. Wise (eds.), *Violence and Defense in the Jewish Experience* (Philadelphia: Jewish Publication Society, 1977), pp. 37-62 and Edwin C. Hostetter, 'Prophetic Attitudes toward Violence in Ancient Israel', *Criswell Theological Review* 7 (1994), pp. 83-89.
6. For a clear explication of ideology as presented by a Biblicist, see Gale A. Yee, *Poor Banished Children of Eve: Woman as Evil in the Hebrew Bible* (Minneapolis: Fortress Press,

one of divine violence, but of a culture's imposition of violence upon the divine to understand and legitimate the world they know.

2. *Definition of Violence*

In order to understand prophetic writings about violence, we need a more sophisticated understanding of violence. Fretheim offers a common definition of violence: 'any action, verbal or nonverbal, oral or written, physical or psychical, active or passive, public or private, individual or institutional/societal, human or divine, in whatever degree of intensity, that abuses, violates, injures, or kills'.[7] The limitation of this kind of definition become apparent when we consider the definition of Hauerwas and Berkman:

> ...a criminal and a public officer may commit the same act, and yet their differing status leads us to call the former 'violence' and the latter 'enforcement of the law'. Their actions may be equally coercive, and yet assigned radically different moral status. Thus we see that our very descriptions of some rather than other acts as 'violent' or 'coercive' presumes prior commitments to certain kinds of act which we wish to justify.[8]

According to this definition, violence is embedded in a more complex matrix of coercion and the justification of certain power dynamics.

I would like to use Johan Galtung's understanding of violence as a useful framework to approaching the biblical texts. Galtung, an accomplished Scandinavian scholar of peace and conflict management, has argued that we must distinguish between direct, structural and cultural violence. Direct violence would correspond to the common definition of violence; Fretheim's definition quoted above is a good example. Structural violence refers to forms of violence that correspond to the systematic ways in which a given social structure prevents individuals from achieving their full potential. Racism, classism and sexism are examples of structural violence. Policies like intentional marginalization, oppression and disempowerment of segments of society are examples of structural violence. Cultural violence is represented by 'those aspects of culture, the symbolic sphere of our existence—exemplified by religion and ideology, language and art, empirical science and formal science... —that can be used to justify or legitimize direct or structural violence'.[9] Cultural violence blurs reality or influences our moral codes so that we do not always see the violent

---

2003), esp. pp.9-28. Yee is profoundly influenced by Terry Eagleton's *Ideology: An Introduction* (London: Verso, 1991).

7. Terence E. Fretheim, 'God and Violence in the Old Testament', p. 19.

8. Stanley Hauerwas and John Berkman, 'Violence', in Paul Barry Clark and Andrew Linzey (eds.), *Dictionary of Ethics, Theology and Society* (London: Routledge, 1996), pp. 866-70) (866).

9. Johan Galtung, 'Cultural Violence', *Journal of Peace Research* 27 (1990), pp. 291-305 (291). Galtung first introduced the concept of structural violence in his article, 'Violence, Peace and Peace Research', *Journal of Peace Research* 6 (1969), pp. 167-91.

act. Galtung urges us to notice the ways in which certain types of violence may be diminished at the expense or maintenance of other kinds of violence. (This tension should be apparent to all Americans who have followed the debates regarding the Patriot Act and related governmental policies.) Finally, Galtung argues that direct violence is an event, structural violence is a process and cultural violence is an invariant that remains essentially the same for long periods of time.[10] There is no question that Galtung's definition of violence is a maximalist one; that is, some of us might use terms such as power or inequality. He subsumes all of these dynamics under the rubric of violence.

A cursory reading of prophetic literature reveals that direct violence permeates these writings. Acts of human and divine violence dominate the discourse. So, I believe the more interesting question is not how to understand such examples of direct violence, but to examine those texts in which violence appears to be absent. In other words, to what extent are the prophets able to step outside of the dominant structures of violence embedded in their societies to imagine a world of peace. If they are indeed envisioning peace, is it the absence of war and conflict, thus negative peace[11] that they are advocating; or is the prophetic voice calling for a completely new utopian society in which peace is marked by as yet unknown modalities of cooperation, loving-kindness and goodness.

3. *Isaiah 2.2-4*

Within the context of Galtung's analysis of violence, I will examine Isaiah 2.2-4 (to examine its parallel in Micah goes beyond the scope of this paper),[12] a classic prophetic text of peace. The words: 'They shall beat their swords into plowshares, and their spears into pruning hooks: nation shall not lift up sword against nation, neither shall they learn war any more' (Isa. 2.4) appear in large letters on the wall opposite the United Nations Headquarters in New York City.[13] Isaiah's vision has captured the attention of peace-workers and commentators drawn to an idyllic vision of a future without borders or strife, and connected by a shared vision of peace and justice. What was is the nature of the peace that Isaiah imagined as he invoked these words?

---

10. Galtung, 'Cultural Violence', p. 294.

11. I intend the term 'negative peace' as defined by Galtung whereby the absence of violence does not necessarily indicate a positively defined condition of peace (Galtung, 'Violence, Peace and Peace Research', p. 183).

12. Most studies attempt to establish an original or primary text from which the other prophet borrowed. For a more complex approach, see Marvin A. Sweeney, 'Micah's Debate with Isaiah', *JSOT* 93 (2001), pp. 111-24. Sweeney's argument is based on the assumption that both texts came into their final form during the Persian period.

13. This was brought to my attention by James Limburg, 'Swords to Ploughshare: Text and Contexts', in Craig C. Broyles and Craig A. Evans (eds.), *Writing and Reading the Scroll of Isaiah: Studies of an Interpretive Tradition*, I (VTSup, 70/1; Leiden: E.J. Brill, 1997), pp. 279-93.

My assumption in reading this text is that it is an eighth-century prophetic oracle likely delivered by Isaiah ben Amoz, and that the oracle ends at v. 4, not v. 5. I am interested in the meaning that the oracle may have had at its earliest stages and not in its reinterpretation as the book was redacted.

Verse 2 offers a mythic, cosmological introduction to the heart of the prophecy that comes in vv. 3-4. Verse 2 offers a broad description in hyperbolic and illogical language while vv. 3-4 telescope in to the details of the vision.[14] The verse reads, 'In the days to come, the mountain of the house of Yhwh shall stand firm above the mountains and tower above the hills, and all the nations shall stream up to it'.

The prophecy begins with a cosmological tone, invoking Zion imagery in which Yhwh's mountain stands at the center of the world, the tallest mountain both literally and figuratively. The nations of the world stream upward to the source of the earth's fount of water.[15] I believe that Isaiah deliberately uses the verb נהר 'to flow' in this surprising reversal of expectation; that is, he suggests a stream of people upwards, defying gravity. By using this language, he invokes Zion imagery and he catches the reader by surprise—the unimaginable is about to happen—pay attention to what follows.

The next verse brings the spotlight onto the people: 'Many people shall go and say: 'Come let us go up to the mountain of Yhwh, to the House of the God of Jacob that he may instruct us in his ways and that we might subject ourselves to his system of justice'. For instruction shall emerge from Zion and the rulings of Yhwh from Jerusalem'.

The identification of תורה 'torah, instruction' in this verse has understandably received the greatest attention among commentators. The debate centers on whether this is Mosaic Torah, generalized prophetic teachings with a wisdom bent, or both—that is, the original meaning did not refer to Mosaic law but came to be associated with it in the final stages of the book's redaction.[16] The same ambiguity exists around the phrase 'word or utterance of Yhwh' and scholars have debated the nature and function of this utterance as it relates to the nations of the world.

---

14. Baruch J. Schwartz rejects the root נהר as 'streaming' in part because of the reverse order of people streaming up and then saying in the following verse, 'Come let us ascend'. See Schwartz, 'Torah from Zion: Isaiah's Temple Vision (Isaiah 2:1-4)', in Alberdina Houtman, Marcel Poorthuis and Joshua Schwartz (eds.), *Sanctity of Time and Space in Tradition and Modernity* (Jewish and Christian Perspectives Series, 1; Leiden: E.J. Brill, 1998), pp. 11-26. According to my reading of these verses, this argument becomes moot.

15. Cf. Ps 46.5.

16. See Joseph Jensen, *The Use of tora by Isaiah: His Debate with the Wisdom Tradition* (CBQMS, 3; Washington, DC: Catholic Biblical Association, 1973) and more recently, Marvin A. Sweeney, 'The Book of Isaiah as Prophetic Torah', in Roy F. Melugin and Marvin A. Sweeney (eds.), *New Visions of Isaiah* (JSOTSup, 214; Sheffield: Sheffield Academic Press, 1996), pp. 50-67.

When some words are ambiguous, it is best to ground an interpretation on the more certain terms, so leaving v. 3 open for the moment we proceed to v. 4. Verse 4 reads: 'He will judge between the nations and arbitrate for many peoples. They shall beat their swords into plowshares and their spears into pruning hooks: Nation shall not take up sword against nation neither shall they train again for war'.

The unambiguous terms שפט 'judge' and הוכיח 'reprove' explain the setting for this vision. The nations are coming to Zion for arbitration and judgment and it is in the juridical context that I believe the entire passage should be understood. Thus 'torah' and the word of Yhwh refer to rulings and edicts. An interesting parallel exists in Deut. 17.10 which commands that in the case of a dispute, the litigants should ascend to the place of God where the case will be adjudicated. The words and verbal roots that we have discussed thus far all appear in both texts. Baruch Schwartz has concluded that Isaiah imagines a High Court of Arbitration with a reputation of being such a fair and respectable court that nations would choose to bring their grievances to Zion.[17] While I agree that this setting is more juridical than educational or ritual, I would not describe it as a High Court of Arbitration. The prophet, imbued with Zion theology, imagines Zion as the center of the world, the capital city of all lands, with the mountain towering above all the others. Peoples will be united in their *shared submission to the dominion of the God of Israel and his human representative from the Davidic line*.[18]

The word of Yhwh and the edicts come out from Zion; they do not simply reside in Zion. I am reminded of the proclamation of royal edicts such as those found in Est. 2.8 (דבר המלך ודתו) or Qoh. 8.4 (דבר המלך), where the word of the king is absolute and his proclamation extends out throughout the kingdom. I am also reminded of the Mesopotamian prologues for the law codes in which the king establishes his ultimate power and sovereignty, and sets it within the context of social justice, equity and peace. Hammurabi boasts of establishing *shulmu* for his people and urges anyone with the need for arbitration to read his stele. In other words, the rhetoric of the kings of Mesopotamia includes a claim of absolute power and demand for complete obedience, but it is set within a framework of teachings or instruction: *shulmu* is subject to submission to the king and his laws. We get another glimpse of this model in the Enuma Elish, as we observe Marduk's absolute sovereignty exercised in the ability to use the power of his word to create new realities to which all are subject. Tablet IV, lines 1-10 read:

---

17. Baruch J. Schwartz, 'Torah from Zion'. Hans Wildberger also connects Isa. 2.1-4 to Deut. 17 and concludes that the 'torah' is primarily juridical; see *Isaiah 1–12: A Commentary* (trans. Thomas H. Trapp; Minneapolis: Fortress Press), pp. 91-92.

18. See John T. Willis, 'Isaiah 2:2-5 and the Psalms of Zion', in Craig C. Broyles and Craig A. Evans (eds.), *Writing and Reading the Scroll of Isaiah: Studies of an Interpretive Tradition*, I (VTSup, 70/1; Leiden: E.J. Brill, 1997), pp. 295-316, for a systematic study of the connection of this passage to Zion traditions.

> They erected for him a princely throne.
> Facing his fathers, he sat down, presiding.
> 'You are the most honored of the great gods,
> Your decree is unrivaled, your command is Anu.
> You, Marduk, are the most honored of the great gods,
> Your decree is unrivaled, your word is Anu.
> From this day your pronouncement shall be unchangeable.
> To raise or bring low—these shall be in your hand.
> Your utterance shall be true, your command shall be unimpeachable.
> No one among the gods shall transgress your bounds...

For Isaiah, the vision is one of the transference of power from Nineveh to Zion. The word and law from Yhwh and presumably his human representative on earth will be incontestable. Francis Landy asks if the voice of Isaiah 1 and the voice of the first part of Isaiah 2 are reconcilable.[19] While he answers this question through a complex literary reading of the book, I would simply answer that the worldviews of the two sections are the same at their ideological and moral foundations.

Heschel writes of Isa. 2.2-4: '...in the vision of Isaiah the nations will no more turn their eyes to Nineveh, the seat of human power, but to Jerusalem, the seat of divine learning, eager to learn God's ways, eager to learn how to walk in His paths'.[20] 'What to us seems inconceivable, to Isaiah was a certainty: War will be abolished. They shall not learn war any more because they shall seek knowledge of the word of God. Passion for war will be subdued by a greater passion: the passion to discover God's ways'.[21] Given this study, I do not see here a model of substitution, as Heschel has argued, but rather a model of transference. Just as fledging Israel transferred its servitude from Pharaoh to Yhwh, so now the nations will transfer their servitude from Nineveh to Zion.

Returning to Galtung's analysis of violence, we might argue that Isaiah envisions an eradication of one type of direct violence—war; but this is achieved by the establishment of one incontestable center of authority to which all will submit. He replaced the direct violence of war with a new structure of violence—full submission to one power at Zion. As Johan Galtung has written:

> 'war' is only one particular form of orchestrated violence, usually with at least one actor, a government. How narrow it is to see peace as the opposite of war, and limit peace studies to war avoidance studies... Important interconnections among types of violence are left out, particularly the way in which one type of violence may be reduced or controlled at the expense of increase or maintenance of another.[22]

---

19. Francis Landy, 'Torah and Anti-Torah: Isaiah 2:2-4 and 1:10-26', *Biblical Interpretation* 11 (2003), pp. 317-34.
20. Heschel, *The Prophets*, p. 183.
21. Heschel, *The Prophets*, p. 184.
22. Galtung, 'Cultural Violence', p. 293.

Isaiah 2.2-4 does indeed envision the eradication of war, but not the eradication of violence.

4. Conclusions

I believe that we must evaluate the value of Isa. 2.2-4 in its 'original context' and as a source text for peace activism today. In the world in which Isaiah lived, his vision for peace as a condition of absence of war and shared submission to a single divine will was truly visionary. I think it unreasonable to have expected Isaiah to question the moral implications of hegemonic systems and the ways in which individuals in power use the language of submission to the divine as a means to power.

Even in today's world, with more sophisticated theories regarding peace and justice studies, there is room for Isaiah's vision to be held in a positive light. I still want my daughter to experience the joy of singing 'nation shall not lift up sword against nation' in Jewish day school. I do not want to deny the beauty of this vision to those of us who use it to support our peace work. However, there must be those among us who can also speak honestly about this text and its limitations.

Since I have started looking at Isa. 2.2-4 through this lens, I have become more sensitive to the ways in which our own culture is so deeply steeped in cultural violence. Looking at Isa. 2.2-4 through this lens can serve as a mirror for our own modes of structural violence and the more invisible cultural violence that lies behind it.

The prophets stood out as individuals who were deeply troubled by injustices. They hoped for a world of more stability and order framed by various visions of justice. But they were not peace activists. They believed that order and stability would come about through acts of divinely orchestrated violence. In the end—whether Isaiah's vision of Zion or Jeremiah's new covenant (Jer. 31) or Ezekiel's description of the gathering of the people to the land of Israel (Ezek. 36)—the classical prophets believed that this was rooted in total submission to the divine will and by extension, to a particular leadership group (most often the Davidic royal line).

Divine violence in prophetic literature is not simply a justified, proportional response to human violence. Human imaginations of divine violence cannot be studied as an isolated phenomenon; it is part of the same system that both condones and condemns the monarchy, that demands absolute loyalty to a single deity, that assigns distinct roles to individuals based on gender, circumstances of birth, and so on. All of these marginalize some while centering power with others; all of these involve levels of coercion, all of these are based on an 'us versus them' model. The prophets were products of their age; cultural violence was so embedded in their world, as it is in our today, that they were unable to step outside of themselves.

The next steps I would take with such a study would be to engage in a more nuanced and in-depth analysis of the structures of violence with which various prophets found themselves. While cultural violence is deeply rooted and long-standing, the structures of violence can change from time to time. A more comprehensive study of this type might look at the socio-economic and political conditions of each prophet's world from the perspective of structural violence, noting how the prophet's response and use of violence matched the particular conditions of his time. Such a study might find interesting subtle variations.

If we are to be honest with ourselves, we must acknowledge that the problem of divine violence in prophetic literature is a problem of deeply embedded cultural violence. Power, submission, war, and acts of direct violence were deeply imbued into the societies that produced the Hebrew Bible. However, for us to think that the roots of the current violence can be found and traced to the Bible, then we shall surely fail to achieve any new understandings. The prophetic texts express and represent the same complex interweaving of politics, economics and religion that we experience today. We use violence to 'establish order and justice' just as our ancestors did. We can use the biblical texts to help us more clearly reflect on our own challenges. Returning again to Galtung, 'Cultural violence makes direct and structural violence look, even feel, right—or at least not wrong'.[23] The challenge for us is to step outside the framework long enough to have it feel not right. An honest look at this fact may help us to take the blindfolds off of our own eyes, to notice how deeply cultural violence and power are embedded in our world today, to notice what we have not yet noticed.

---

23. Galtung, 'Cultural Violence', p. 291.

THE PROPHETIC ROOTS OF RELIGIOUS VIOLENCE IN WESTERN RELIGIONS

Stephen A. Geller

1. *Introduction*

The acts of religiously motivated violence perpetrated on 9/11 have frequently, and reasonably, been characterized as apocalyptic. Once again, it seemed to many, religion was being perverted and the language of sacred text, in this case, the Quran, was being used to justify intolerance, hatred and, finally, murder. Many people, including students of religion, pointed their fingers, as so often, at what they saw as the ultimate culprit, the bloodthirsty 'Old Testament', the parent of Judaism, Christianity and, more distantly, Islam. In truth, one does not have to read very far in the Hebrew Bible before one comes across fulminations to destroy God's foes in holy war, put them to the *herem*, the total ban of physical extermination, i.e. murder. Midianites and Amalekites are to be extirpated and erased. Above all the Canaanites, the aboriginal inhabitants of the Promised Land, are to be slaughtered down to the last man, woman and child. The earliest descriptions and names of God are military: 'Yahweh of Armies', 'The Lord is a man of war' (Exod. 15.3); '(he) makes his arrows drunk with the blood (of the foe)'; Deut. 32.42; etc.). The Nazis were fond of citing such passages to show how bloodthirsty Jews were.

Now, on the historical level this accusation against the Hebrew Bible is quite unjustified. Scholarship long ago proved that the biblical tradition of holy war is the exact opposite of the Christian crusade or the Muslim jihad. In the latter the community of believers fights for its God, to destroy unbelief and spread the faith. In the Bible the reverse is true: God is believed to intervene and fight for His people. Evidence of immanent divinity in the form of miracles and angelic armies are *sine qua non* in biblical descriptions of holy war. The armies of Israel merely mop up an already shattered foe. It is clear to scholars that the tradition of *herem*, though old, has become an historical-religious typology, in the Hebrew Bible.[1] Historical scholarship seems to be coming to a consensus that there never was a national war against Canaanites, let alone a mass slaughter of them. Instead, a very ancient military-religious tradition, general

---

1. On holy war as a theology in the Hebrew Bible, see Milford C. Lind, *Yahweh as a Warrior: The Theology of Warfare in Ancient Israel* (Scottdale, PA: Herald Press, 1980).

in the ancient world, was taken up by developing biblical religion and used as a militant metaphor for faith. Indeed, the genesis of the concept of faith was in war, when the people were exhorted not to fear but to put their trust in God. So by 'Canaanites' is meant Israelite opponents of the dogmas of biblical religion; and by 'kill' is meant reject. The battleground is not so much outer as inner, one's own fears and doubts. The metaphors are unfortunate, but the real danger is taking them literally. Instead the vicious holy war themes of combat and killing are a perhaps clumsy attempt to express the inner ideal of struggle for faith. Indeed, many Muslims claim that the true sense of jihad, holy war, is also primarily inner discipline and spiritual battle against sin and one's own unbelief.

Yet is the ideology of holy war any less repugnant, and dangerous, as the outer garment of an ideal, a theology? In the Hebrew Bible the war-like motifs are taken up by prophecy and become ever more elaborate and wild: 'The Lord has a sword, it is stated with blood. The Lord is angry at all the nations; he has doomed them, given them to slaughter, their slain will be cast out, the stench of their corpses will mount, the hills will be melted by their blood...' (Isa. 34.2-3). The especially grisly scenario of Ezekiel's War of Gog and, later, the apocalyptic theme of the final battle of Armageddon between cosmic good and evil are well known examples of biblical and post-biblical religious militarism. War seems an essential, inalienable heritage of biblical religion. The Old Testament God seems a God who loves war. The New Testament God of universal love and peace also soon succumbed to his role as the God of battles at the head on the Church Militant. Islam grew by war and divides the world into the realm of submission, Islam, and the realm of war, to be subjugated.

The explanation of 9/11 in religious terms might simply be that the warlike language of the Bible, even if it is metaphorical, creates the danger of arousing in minds ignorant of the true poetic and literary nature of the motifs actual emotions of intolerance, and literal deeds of violence. It is the furnace of concepts and imagery where the politically and socially frustrated and furious can stoke their rage. But this seems to me to be too simple an explanation to explain the depths of the phenomenon of religious violence in Western religions. The struggle today seems to be not just between religious traditions, and political social and cultural differences, but rather, more deeply, between differing views of reality itself. This discussion will suggest that one root of the religious violence and intolerance that mark all western religions to some degree is not mere misunderstanding of metaphor but a dissonance that goes back to the origin of biblical religion in prophecy, a conflict between the private religious visionary experience of the prophet and his outer mission to bring a divine message to society. This dissonance expressed itself in military terms, and gave to western religions a potential for religious violence that they have all too often fulfilled.

We shall trace very briefly the fateful interpenetration of prophecy and war through three major stages: first, 'holy war' (*herem*), as an actual institution in ancient Israel; second, the stage of developing biblical religion; and third, the exilic and postexilic rise of book religion. Then the thesis of this discussion will be presented.

2. *Israelite Religion*

Holy war is attested outside of the Bible (Mesha and elsewhere) and is, indeed practically a universal. In *herem* the enemy was 'devoted' to God, i.e. killed. Prophets were undoubtedly involved in the preparation for war by providing kings with oracles sanctioning the campaign and predicting victory. 1 Kings 22 is a classic text reflecting the ancient association of war prophets and sacred war. *Herem* as an actual practice did not survive the extinction of the kingdoms of Israel and Judah; yet the ideas associated with *herem* did not die, because by then they had been developed by some prophets into an ideology of biblical religion. Of all the stages, that in which holy war was actually practiced is the least relevant to later religious developments.

3. *Biblical Religion*

Biblical religion grew out of the activity of some prophets of Yahweh and their followers. Its initial impetus, many scholars hold, was in the struggle between Baal and Yahweh, and their respective prophets, in ninth century northern Israel. The prophets Elijah and Elisha viewed themselves as actually at war with the foreign queen Jezebel, devotee of Baal, and her weak husband Ahab. The ancient prophetic function of sanctioning holy war by providing rulers with oracles was immensely expanded by the religious warfare of the ninth century. Elijah, like his God, was full of 'zeal' (*qin'a*), militant passion. Elisha actually instigated a war of extermination against the Baalists. Prophecy and violence entered a permanent symbiosis. War on at least four levels became a dominant feature of prophecy in biblical religion as it continued to develop.

a. External religious-national conflict against 'foreign' gods, represented at first by the threat of Phoenician Baal of the Heavens, and later by the forms of worship introduced by Ahaz and Manasseh as the result of their vassalhood to Assyria, as well as by such cults as that of the 'Queen of Heaven'.

b. Societal conflict between the prophets representing nascent biblical religion and the wider societies of Israel and Judah, the leaders of which—kings, officials, priests, and other prophets—are regularly portrayed by the Bible as idolatrous and corrupt, with very few exceptions. But the societal conflict is even more basic, because it really reflects a general tension between prophets, seers, shamans and ecstatics of all types and the society to which they belong.

As Robert Wilson has shown, there is a practically universal struggle of prophets in world cultures be viewed as central to their society rather than peripheral.[2]

c. Inner-prophetic conflict between groups of prophets of Yahweh themselves, whom the Bible divides into 'true' and 'false', without ever offering a useful practical guide to distinguish between them. Both claim to have messages from Israel's God, and even 'false' prophets may not be lying because there is a disturbing possibility that the deity may intentionally deceive his own prophets by sending a 'lying spirit' (1 Kgs 22). This internal weakness of the institution of prophecy was undoubtedly a major cause of its being replaced by book religion.

d. Most significant for later developments was the fourth level of warfare: internal psychic conflict in the prophet himself. This took two forms, which mutually reinforced each other. The first is inner doubt about the validity of one's own prophetic calling, a doubt most dramatically revealed in the 'confessions' of Jeremiah, in which that prophet seems to suspect that he has been deceived by God and is actually a false prophet. As Wilson showed, visionaries are expected to struggle against their missions; it is a sign of their authenticity that they do so. But biblical prophets carry demurral to new heights. They need constant reassurance by God, and even the greatest, such as Moses, were torn by doubt and despair. (Isaiah seems to be an exception).

The second form of inner warfare was to prove most fateful in perpetuating the tradition of religious violence in later religions. This was the conflict between the very nature of the prophetic experience of the divine, the private and personal act of revelation, and the prophet's public mission to deliver the message received in that revelation to a stubborn people. But what reason did ordinary people, lacking the original and confirming revelation, have to heed any prophet? (One must remember that the great literary prophets did not have the ability to perform the miracles that would have authenticated their mission to the public). All the major canonical prophets failed in their missions. The inner dissonance of experience and mission engendered a bitter frustration in the prophets, which expressed itself in the only language at hand, that of holy war.[3]

With warfare on all the levels just described, with foreign cults, society as a whole, other prophets of Yahweh and, most bitterly, with the prophetic self and its mission, biblical prophecy was an inherently and immensely conflicted phenomenon. It is not surprising that religions based on it, beginning with biblical religion itself, absorbed and expanded the use of warlike language to express the underlying, and unconscious, religious dissonance described above

---

2. See Robert Wilson, *Prophecy and Society in Ancient Israel* (Philadelphia: Fortress Press, 1980).

3. On the religious dynamic, see Stephen A. Geller, *Sacred Enigmas: Literary Religion in the Hebrew Bible* (London and New York: Routledge, 1996).

between experience and mission; all the more so after the states of Israel and Judah were faced by the threat of extinction in war by the empires of Assyria and Babylonia. It was a warlike age.

But it is important to understand that for the prophets the language of holy war had mutated from its root in actual military practice into metaphor, as a source of imagery to express their profound frustration on all levels. The battle was not, as in original *herem*, Yahweh's campaign against foreign foes on the 'Day of the Lord'. Rather, as reinterpreted by the prophets, the 'Day of the Lord' was God's fight against his own sinful people, using foreign empires as his tools. The metaphorization of holy war was extended by the later dominant Deuteronomic tradition to a fantasy of a supposed 'conquest' of Canaan by Israel's ancestors, projected into the distant past. Above all, the prophets developed an eschatology, in which ancient royal themes of battle became images of hopes for the future, in which God would vindicate Israel and His own Name in the eyes of the nations. The problem with metaphors is that they are liable to be taken literally.

4. *The Exilic and Postexilic Period*

With the composition of the first biblical books in the Exile, prophetic biblical religion began to become the world's first religion of the book. By the mid-fifth century BCE, when Ezra promulgated the Pentateuch, the shift to textual religion was almost complete. Prophecy gave way to the covenantal formulation of religion, which by now had taken the form of canonical, immutable text. There were many reasons for this momentous shift, political, social and cultural. But relevant to the thesis of this discussion is that book religion resulted partially from dissatisfaction with the inner turmoil of prophecy and, specifically, the inability of people to tell true from false prophets. Part of the strategy of developing text religion was to outlaw prophecy as a living phenomenon. It did this through a clever tactic, much used today in the world of business, politics and academe. It promoted it upstairs, sent it to the House of Lords, made it emeritus. Prophecy was given an honorable retirement, as text. Old prophets were canonized and made into safe books, but dangerous contemporary prophets were excoriated and future prophets excluded, even as a possibility. Text religion wanted no new revelations to compete with its formulation of the old one.

But, ironically, book religion inherited the old inner tensions and conflicts of prophecy, transmuted into a new form, but still unsolvable. The struggle between true and false prophets became the struggle for interpretation, between true and false understandings of the text. *Qin'at sopherim*, the zealous conflict of scribes, replaced prophetic *qin'a*. Above all, the eternal prophetic dissonance between the inner, secret and private prophetic experience of revelation and the outer, public mission to the world of humanity also survived in fateful form in book religion. The sacred canon was the outer, public expression, at hand to anyone who could read or listen, and seemingly accessible to all. But the inner, the primal religious experience of revelation, the contact with God that the book recorded. was in the past, sealed off forever from today. When biblical religion became book religion it created a central dilemma, which all western religions share to some degree: believers have access only to a secondary manifestation of revelation, the original experience they can never have. The later Rabbis called this *hastarat panim*, the hiding of God's face. Theologians call it transcendence, God's increasing remoteness from the world.

This was an insoluble religious problem for the religion of the book. In the types of religion that are essentially nature worship the gods are permanently accessible as the natural forces they represent. Eastern religions promise that believers can attain buddhahood or even godhood through self-discipline and asceticism, through a series of ascending rebirths. But Jews, Christians and Muslims can never become legitimate prophets. They cannot hope to experience God directly as the prophets did, except, perhaps, in mystical visions—but such things were always rare and suspect in main-stream religion in the West. Nor is the ritualization of personal religious experience in such practices as the eucharist a substitute for the plenitude of direct divine revelation to all believers. The blossoming of charismatic sects in some religious traditions is evidence of the longing for direct experience of the divine.

The struggle against the implications of this self-exile from the divine marks book religion from the beginning. Already Deuteronomy worries about how the original Mosaic revelation can be actualized to later generations. Christianity claimed it arose through a new upswelling of the prophetic spirit, but as soon as it became a book religion, church fathers sealed it off again. The same was true of Islam. Muhammad is not just the last prophet relatively, but absolutely, there can be no other. In sum, the tension in prophecy between divine inner and public outer, two extremes that belong to different levels of reality and are therefore irreconcilable, became an equally great tension in book religion between original, but inaccessible, revelatory experience and its secondary public manifestation in text. And this new tension was to prove itself as warlike as the inner prophetic struggles.

Book religion gradually developed two great competing modes, reflecting different views of the very nature of religious reality. One is the interpretational mode, the other the literal mode.[4] Both modes can be held by different groups or individuals at different times, or even simultaneously; but it must be stressed that they are still, I believe, fundamentally different and distinct. The interpretational mode holds that the sacred text can and must be interpreted, but with the guidance of an equally sanctified tradition. In terms of the prophetic dichotomy discussed before, it grows out of the outer, the public mission of the prophets to communicate a message to the world of humanity. Rabbinic Judaism is a

---

4. I am grateful to Ben Sommer for helping me to clarify this distinction.

leading example of this mode. It maintains that a body of oral tradition was also given at the primary revelation at Sinai, by means of which the written text can and must be understood. The aim of this seemingly absurd dogma is to legitimize the process of interpretation by tradition, since the oral law was forgotten and has to be recovered by rabbinic debate and midrash of all types. Ordinary people, the *am haarets*, cannot do it. Interpretational religion has a horror of direct interpretation of the Bible, of unmediated dialogue between the sacred text and the mind of the believer. It is viewed as a challenge to tradition and dangerous to understanding. The Catholic Church similarly upheld the principle of sanctified interpretation and until the Protestant reformation forced it to change, discouraged non-clergy from reading the Bible. In fact, if they did so, it burned them. Rabbinic Judaism preferred to insist that ordinary Jews become educated enough to read the text surrounded by a hedge, or maze, of traditional commentaries. Islam, in its classic era, also allowed the interpretational mode.

The interpretational mode may declare belief in an afterlife (which biblical religion never did), but its reality is that of this world. The sacred text is a guide to living for the living. This world is the reality that projects its needs and concerns back to the sacred texts, which one searches, with tradition as a teacher, for relevant meaning. One must not be deceived by rabbinic protestations about the unchangeability of canon, its eternity, its preexistence. These are typical rabbinical preemptory declarations. The real meaning of such statements is that interpretation must proceed by dialectical tension between a fixed canon and a mutable tradition, responsive, but not servile to the needs of change in the human world. Change will come, even if unacknowledged, through progressive interpretations of the authoritative text, bending it if necessary, sometimes with audible creaking, to the requirements of interpretation by an equally authoritative tradition. The Rabbis disliked *peshat*, the plain contextual meaning of the biblical text, and as a Bible scholar, I used to dislike them for that. Their readings of verses often seem wildly arbitrary compared with the steady, sober, plodding progress of modern historical scholarship. None of the rabbis even had a PhD! Now, I have come to understand that the very wildness of some midrash is itself the message: this book dare not be taken literally. They knew that literal interpretation was no interpretation at all, and that their enemies were literalists like the Sadducees and, later, the Karaites.

The interpretational mode is relatively tolerant. Competing interpretations are encouraged in *aggadah*. In *halakhah* they are tolerated, if no decision can be reached, which is often the case. Of course, there were hatreds and rivalries, *qin'at sopherim* could be bitter. But the dialectical form of the Talmud, its exaltation of the dialogue of competing interpretations, is the norm, or at least the ideal.

The opposite of all this is the other, the literal mode. It abjures all interpretation. Nothing must come between the contemporary reader and the ancient text. All complications of context, such as language, culture and history, are of no account or concern. Mediating tradition is evil and must be swept away if it is perceived of as conflicting with the clear sense that emerges from the text to those pure in heart and simple in faith. If interpretation be needed for some seemingly obscure passage, there is in principle only one correct one. A leader chosen and inspired by God will tell you what that correct interpretation is. But, of course, one interpretation means in effect no interpretation, which always proceeds at least in pairs if not in multitudes.

What is reality for the literal mode? It certainly does not grow out of blind cultural conservatism or love of text for its own sake. Rather, the main impetus that drives literalism is actually a passionate longing for the experiential aspect of prophecy, the direct contact with the divine the prophets claimed to have had and that book religion sealed off. One might therefore suppose that literalists would reject the book as a secondary, mediated and pallid religious phenomenon, in favor of charismatic, spontaneous and immediate interaction with God directly. Yet, such sects, where they exist, practically never free themselves from the sacred book. They are usually fanatical literalists. Not direct prophetic experience is for them the ground of reality, but rather the sacred text itself, not as words, but as experience. The text is not a guide to life; it is life itself, to which this existence must be bent. For literalists, text is ultimate, eternal and unchanging myth.

Moreover, the literal mode is intolerant and, by inclination, warlike, whether in defense of its view of reality, or in offence against its perceived foes. The superficial reason is that literalists must adhere to the text of scripture itself, which is replete with the language and imagery of sacred war. But the deeper reason is that they share the prophetic zeal for actual experience of God, beyond the possibilities of text religion. Yet, at the same time, they must also view everything through the prism of the book, which is the only basis of reality. The answer to this conundrum was the tradition of apocalyptic literature, the final expression of biblical militarism and also a classic obsession of most adherents of the literal mode. Apocalyptic grew out of prophecy, but specifically from a narrow and literal understanding of prophecy as prediction. True to the literalist orientation toward reality, apocalyptic views history as the working out of patterns established mythically at creation, and therefore predestined by God. Even He cannot change what He has decreed must happen. Contemporary events are shadows cast by the text. And apocalyptic literature is typically war-like. It is usually written by people who view themselves as standing at the moment of final cosmic battle predicted by the biblical prophets, as literalists understand them. After the battle, and the day of judgment, an Edenic paradise will be projected by the text onto this world. No deviation from the pattern is tolerated. Every word in the text will come true, exactly as stated. The text is a blueprint to reality. If interpretation is needed (as it certainly is in some of the wilder apocalyptic visions) a seer instructed by an angel, not tradition, will inform believers of the true meaning of the text. It is ironic that for apocalyptic literalists adherence to the word of the sacred book is not an end in itself, but rather a means to enter the post-Armageddon messianic realm, in which the faithful will bask directly in the light of the divine presence. As saints, they will actually be divine themselves (cf. Dan. 12.3), outdoing the prophets, who always remained human. There could be no clearer indication of the fact that the true passion of literalists is not text but experience.

The apocalyptic tradition of Judaism was marginalized by the Rabbis, though it popped up from time to time when Jews were in deepest despair. It seems to be reviving today, in some circles. Christianity has a well-developed apocalyptic stream, and so, today, does Islam. Apocalyptic literalism is the resort of the desperate, as interpretational tolerance is of the contented.

4. Conclusion

This kind of seething pottage of perfervid literalism and visionary violence is what we saw on 9/11. Not all literalists are religiously violent and intolerant. One thinks of quietist literalists like the Amish. But I believe it is the case that most religiously violent people are also literalists. They rarely view their militant passion as arising from a loose metaphorical or allegorical understanding of scripture. Rather, in acts of martyrdom, they hope to bring this world closer to the reality of the book, and in doing so, transcend the book itself to experience the divine.

Which mode does the Bible itself support? The Bible I know, for all its warlike language in places, is a tolerant book, especially in the Ketuvim, the latest section. Its very literary form bespeaks this tolerance. It would rather be inclusive than clear, a joy to tradition but a curse to scholars. Practically everything is recounted twice, in forms that often conflict. The Bible seems unconcerned about how the laws of Deuteronomy differ from the same or similar laws in Exodus, or about how Chronicles distorts its sources in Samuel and Kings. The Bible presents the opposition to its own pieties, Job next to Proverbs, Qoheleth next to Canticles. It never fails to undermine the greatest heroes: Moses and David are presented with their faults. There is no sickly sentimentality or whitewashing. The prophetic dilemma discussed before is not papered over. It seems to me that the medium is the message, and in the Hebrew Bible the message is *dorsheni*, 'interpret me'! In the Christian scriptures, the competition of four accounts of the career of Jesus gives a similar message. The Bible itself opts for the interpretational mode (indeed, there are many inner-biblical interpretations, as Michael Fishbane and Ben Sommer have shown). Literalism is therefore no homage to the Bible but a betrayal of the text itself. The first and greatest illusion of literalism is that it is being faithful to the text.

The crimes of 9/11 were, in terms of religion, caused by a pernicious form of apocalyptic literalism. One must abhor it, but one must also recognize that the impression that two competing views of reality had come into conflict was true. For us, the terrible events were like a window into a horrible anti-reality of chaos. For the terrorists, they were the portal into the true reality of paradise projected by their sacred text, not liable to interpretation. The events have a pedigree that goes back far beyond the text the terrorists were claiming to fulfill, to the inner conflicts of prophecy passed on to book religion.

HOMICIDE, TALION, VENGEANCE, AND PSYCHO-ECONOMIC SATISFACTION IN THE COVENANT CODE

David P. Wright

1. Introduction

The Covenant Code (CC;[1] Exodus 20.23–23.19) is the earliest substantial law collection in the Hebrew Bible.[2] It also has the most similarities of any single law collection in the Bible to Mesopotamian legal collections, especially the Laws of Hammurabi (LH). These facts have led scholars to read CC against its Near Eastern background in an attempt to uncover some of the Bible's and Israel's fundamental and unique legal and social ideals. The laws of CC, it is claimed, demonstrate that biblical Israel had a more ethical attitude toward human life than did Mesopotamia. The unique requirement to stone a goring ox, for example, shows that even animals are responsible for taking the life of a human being who is uniquely created in the image of God. The strict requirement of capital punishment for homicide is also though to reveal a sacral attitude toward human life.[3]

A new evaluation of the underlying perspectives of CC is required in view of new evidence that indicates that LH was a direct literary source for the entirety of CC. This paper will first review the basic evidence for this dependence and

---

1. Abbreviations in this paper include: CC = Covenant Code; HittL = Hittite Laws; LE = Laws of Eshnunna; LH = Laws of Hammurabi; LLI = Laws of Lipit-Ishtar; MAL = Middle Assyrian Laws. For recent translations of LH see Martha Roth, *Law Collections from Mesopotamia and Asia Minor* (Atlanta: Scholars Press, 2nd edn, 1997); M.E.J. Richardson, *Hammurabi's Laws* (London: T. & T. Clark, 2000). Roth's volume contains translations of other legal collections.

2. See the review of its relationship to Deuteronomy in Bernard Levinson, *Deuteronomy and the Hermeneutics of Legal Innovation* (New York: Oxford University Press, 1998), pp. 6-11; 'Is the Covenant Code an Exilic Composition: A Response to John Van Seters', in John Day (ed.), *In Search of Pre-Exilic Israel* (JSOTSup, 406; London: T. & T. Clark, 2004), pp. 272-325.

3. See primarily Moshe Greenberg, 'Some Postulates of Biblical Criminal Law', in M. Haran (ed.), *Yehezkel Kaufman Jubilee Volume* (Jerusalem: Magnes Press, 1960), pp. 20-27. See also Greenberg, 'More Reflections on Biblical Criminal Law', *Scripta hierosolymitana* 31 (1986), pp. 2, 9-17; Shalom Paul, *Studies in the Book of the Covenant in Light of Cuneiform and Biblical Law* (VTSup, 18; Leiden: E.J. Brill, 1970), pp. 79, 81, 82; J.J. Finkelstein, *The Ox That Gored* (Transactions of the American Philosophical Society, 70/2; Philadelphia: American Philosophical Society, 1981), pp. 26-28, 70; Nahum Sarna, *Understanding Exodus* (New York: Schocken, 1986), pp. 179-80; Joe M. Sprinkle, *'The Book of the Covenant': A Literary Approach* (JSOTSup, 174; Sheffield: JSOT Press, 1994), pp. 123-28.

then provide a reassessment of the system of punishments found in the various homicide and injury laws of CC over against their cuneiform source. It will raise the possibility that the goal of CC may not be so much to legislate but to respond ideologically to Assyrian political and cultural hegemony. It transforms a genre and text with international cultural prestige into a new work with a counter-imperial voice.

2. *Literary Dependency*

The Laws of Hammurabi come from the reign of that Old Babylonian king, from about 1750 BCE. Ever since they were rediscovered in 1901 and published in 1902, scholars have recognized their similarity to the laws of Covenant Code (CC).[4] But the correspondences with LH are much broader than what scholarship has observed over the last century.[5] CC's middle body of laws mainly in casuistic or case form (formulated 'if...then...', 21.2–22.19) display the same or nearly the same order as laws in the last half or so of the casuistic laws of LH.[6] They correspond in fourteen points or topics, summarized in Table 5.1. The few divergences are explainable in terms of the creativity that CC used in revising its source, as the second half of this paper will show. As CC used the sequence of LH as a guide, it folded in laws from other places in LH outside of the sequence.[7] CC also included a few laws based on other cuneiform collections, examples of which we will discuss, below.[8]

---

4. Some have believed that even on the basis of limited similarities the two collections must be connected. See Meir Malul, *The Comparative Method in Ancient Near Eastern and Biblical Legal Studies* (AOAT, 227; Kevelaer: Butzon & Bercker; Neukirchen–Vluyn: Neukirchener Verlag, 1990).

5. For the details of the evidence presented here, other views, and bibliography, see David P. Wright, 'The Laws of Hammurabi as a Source for the Covenant Collection (Exodus 20:23- 23:19)', *Maarav* 10 (2003), pp. 11-87; 'The Compositional Logic of the Goring Ox and Negligence Laws in the Covenant Collection (Ex 21:28-36)', *Zeitschrift für altorientalische und biblische Rechtsgeschichte* 10 (2004), pp. 93-142. I am in the final stages of preparing a full-length monograph for Oxford University Press.

6. The reason for CC's beginning with debt-slavery which appears in the *middle* of Hammurabi's casuistic laws is because of priority of the theme of poverty, which also has primary position in the two strings of the final apodictic laws (see below). For more detail on the dependence of CC on LH, see David P. Wright, 'The Laws of Hammurabi and the Covenant Code: A Response to Bruce Wells', *Maarav* 13.2 (2006), pp. 209-58. In addition to poverty, the cult is a topic of emphasis, especially in the apodictic laws.

7. Non-sequential correspondences between CC and LH include: boring/cutting off the ear of a slave (Exod. 21.6 // LH 282; see below); kidnapping (Exod. 21.16 // LH 14); negligence (Exod. 21.33-34 // LH 125); burglary (Exod. 22.1-2a // LH 21); grazing (Exod. 22.4 // LH 57–58); safekeeping (Exod. 22.6 // LH 120, 124–25); animal rental (Exod. 22.13-14 // LH 244, 249).

8. Correspondences between CC and other law collections include: talion in miscarriage (Exod. 21.22-25 // MAL A 50, 52); an ox goring an ox (Exod. 21.35 // LE 53); burglary (Exod. 21.1-2a // LE 13); burning a field (Exod. 22.5 // HittL 105–106); seducing a virgin (Exod. 22.15-

	Casuistic Laws of CC	Casuistic Laws of LH
	(21.2-11 family law) —	— (117-119, 127-191 family law)
1.	21.2-6 debt-slavery of males —	— 117 debt-servitude of males +175 (children of slave), 182 (master relations)
2.	21.7-11 debt-slavery of daughter —	— 117 debt servitude of daughter + 148-149 (taking second wife), 178 (three means of support)
3.	21.12-14 death from striking, intent ⌐	
4.	21.15, 17 child rebellion —	— 192-193, 195 child rebellion
		⌐ 196-201 talion laws, injury to slave
5.	21.18-19 men fighting, injury, cure	206 men fighting, injury, cure
		⌐ (206) 207 death from striking, intent
6.	21.20-21 killing one of lower class —	— 208 killing one of lower class (cf. 116) (cf. 196-205, 209-223)
7.	21.22-23 causing a miscarriage —	— 209-214 causing a miscarriage
8.	21.23-27 talion laws, injury to slave ⌐	
		⌐ 229-230 negligence (cf. 125)
9.	21.28-32 goring ox —	— 250-252 goring ox
10.	21.33-34 negligence —	
	21.35-36 goring ox —	(similar to Laws of Eshnunna 53)
11.	21.37; 22.2b-3 animal theft —	— 253-265 animal theft
12.	22.6-8 safekeeping —	— 264-266 'safekeeping' of animals (cf. 120, 124-125)
13.	22.9-12 injury and death of animals —	— 266-267 injury and death of animals
14.	22.13-14 animal rental —	— 268-271 animal rental (cf. 244-249)

Table 5.1: Sequential similarities between CC and LH in their casuistic laws

In addition, the apodictic laws, which appear as bookends before and after the casuistic laws of CC (20.23-26 and 22.20–23.19), show an equally tight set of correspondences with LH.[9] The key to understanding these is to recognize that the final apodictic laws exhibit a two-string structure with four corresponding themes or elements (see Table 5.2). These strings are set around and augment a chiastic core of laws dealing with judicial propriety in 23.1-8 (see Table 5.3).[10]

16 // MAL A 55–56). It cannot be assumed that CC used any of these other known other collections in particular (though a Neo-Assyrian fragment of MAL A has been found; cf. Roth, *Collections*, 152-154). One assumes the existence of other, perhaps limited collections, which had laws like those that CC and the known non-LH cuneiform sources manifest in common (see Wright, 'Compositional Logic', pp. 122-23).

9. This description of the relationship of the apodictic laws of CC to LH supersedes what I said about the matter in my initial publications listed in n. 5.

10. I have strenuously critiqued of the notion of chiasmus in general and of structures proposed for CC in particular in 'The Fallacies of Chiasmus: A Critique of Structures Proposed for the Covenant Collection', *Zeitschrift für altorientalische und biblische Rechtsgeschichte* 10 (2004), pp., 143-68. In that study I concluded that the only true chiastic structure, i.e. intended by the author, of all those proposed was that in Exod. 23.1-8 (see pp. 156-57). I made this conclusion before I recognized any of the evidence about a string structure in the final apodictic laws and how they coordinate with LH.

The whole of the final apodictic laws is thus a carefully calculated structure. The chief comparative point to note is that the final apodictic laws and also the apodictic laws at the beginning of CC replicate *in exact sequence* the themes of what I call the exhortatory block of the epilogue of LH (columns 47.59-49.17), as summarized in Table 5.4.

	Topic	String I (Exod. 22.20-30)	String II (Exod. 23.9-19)
1.	general law about the poor	22.20-23: three classes—resident alien, widow, orphan—not to be oppressed; Egypt rationale	23.9: resident alien not to be oppressed; Egypt rationale
2.	two specific laws benefiting the poor	22.24: interest not to be taken from poor; 22.25-26: garment pledge not to be retained	23.10-11: poor may eat from produce of seventh-year field; 23.12: poor to rest on seventh-day
3.	two short laws about speaking about sovereigns	22.27: God not to be cursed; 'chieftain' (= king) not to be cursed	23.13b: names of other gods not to be memorialized; name of these gods not to be heard on lips
4.	cultic laws	22.28-30: miscellaneous cultic rules: *first produce* (wine/oil) to be offered, first born humans to be dedicated, *first born* animals to be offered after remaining with *mother* a week, carrion not to be eaten because people are holy	22.17-19: three annual festivals to be observed where people appear before the deity; miscellaneous cultic rules: leaven with sacrificial blood not to be offered, festival offering not to remain till morning, *first fruits* to be offered, kid not to be boiled in *mother's* milk

Table 5.2: String structure of the final apodictic laws of CC

(a) ¹Do not promote a *false report*. Do not conspire with an *evil person* to be a witness that causes *violence*.
    (b) ²Do not follow the majority to do evil. Do not testify in a dispute to *perversely follow* the majority to pervert (justice). ³*Do not show deference to the poor in his dispute*.
        (c) ⁴*When you encounter the ox or ass of your adversary wandering, return it to him*.
        (c') ⁵*When you see the ass of your foe suffering under its burden and you would hesitate raising it, you must raise it*.
    (b') ⁶Do not *pervert* the case of your *impoverished in his dispute*.
(a') ⁷Keep yourself away from a *lying word*. Do not *kill* the *innocent and blameless*, for I will not exonerate an *evil person*.
(x) ⁸Do not take a bribe, because a bribe blinds the clear-sighted and distorts the words of the innocent.[11]

Table 5.3: Central chiastic core of the final apodictic laws

---

11. The x-member may be considered secondary, or may be an augment of the structure for the purpose of providing closure.

Initial Apodictic Laws (Exod. 20.23-26)	Exhortatory Block of the Epilogue of LH (columns 47.59–49.17)	String I of Final Apodictic Laws + Judicial Core (Exod. 22.20–23.8)	String II of Final Apodictic Laws (Exod. 23.9-19)
	Three individuals (the 'weak', orphan girl, widow) not to be oppressed, to be treated justly (47.59-73)	*Three* individuals (resident alien, widow, orphan) not to be oppressed (22.20-23)	Resident alien not to be oppressed (23.9)
		(String I adds two topically related laws benefiting the poor; 22.24-26; Table 5.2)	(String II adds two topically related laws benefiting poor; 23.10-12; Table 5.2)
Statues of (other) gods not to be made. Instead, an altar, a symbol of the divine sovereign, is to be made (20.23)	Hammurabi's statue set up in the Esagil temple. His law stele is set up before this (47.75-78)		
Yahweh memorializes (*zkr*) his name ('my name'; Semitic *šmy*) in cult place (20.24a)	Hammurabi's name ('my name' Semitic *šmy*) is to be memorialized (*zkr*) in the Esagil temple. No other king like Hammurabi (47.93–48.2)	God and the people's chieftain (= king) are not to be cursed (22.27)	Names (*šm*) of other gods not to be mentioned (*zkr*) (23.13)
	Wronged man to visit the temple for judicial clarification. He appears before Hammurabi's statue and stele and prays in praise of Hammurabi, to the gods Marduk and Zarpanitu. King and gods are called 'lords' (48.3-58).	Sacrificial and cultic prescriptions (most of these have a connection with the sanctuary and altar) (22.28-30) [Primarily a counterpart to the corresponding element in string II]	Every male to appear before (or 'see') Yahweh at the sanctuary for pilgrimage festivals. Yahweh called 'Lord'. Offerings to the deity (23.14-19). [End of CC]
Yahweh comes to the cult place and blesses the people. (20.24b) Laws added on the materials used for the altar and stairs in 25-26, but connected to materials mentioned in 20.23-24a.	Hammurabi provides well-being (= blessing) for the people. (48.34-36). Reflection on the visit to the temple refers to the gods that 'enter (=come to) the Esagil temple'. Request for good reputation (or omens) (48.48-58).		

	Admonition to the future king to ensure justice. Laws not to be altered. Eradicate wicked. Partial reversing structure (48.59-49.17).	Laws ensuring justice. Justice not tobe perverted. The wicked and innocent. Full-blown reversing structure (23.1-8).	

Table 5.4: Correlations between the apodictic laws and the exhortatory block

The correspondences between the apodictic laws and the exhortatory block are especially visible once it is realized that CC has replaced Hammurabi and Mesopotamian gods with Yahweh. He is now law author and revealer. His cult symbol, the altar, replaces Hammurabi's temple statue. While the exhortatory block would have Hammurabi's name memorialized at a cult site ('May my name [*šumī*] be remembered [*lizzakir*] in the Esagil temple favorably forever'), CC has Yahweh's name memorialized at a cult site ('In every place where I cause my name [*šĕmî*] to be recalled [*ʾazkîr*]') and prohibits memorializing other gods ('you shall not mention' [*lōʾ tazkîrū*] their name [*šēm*]'). CC extends and transforms the motif of name memorialization in a prohibition not to curse the deity and the native 'chieftain' (i.e. the king). The coming of a wronged man before Hammurabi's statue and stele at the Esagil temple is replaced with the annual visit of male pilgrims for the festivals (e.g. 'three times a year may every male among you appear before [emended: 'see'] the Lord, Yahweh' *šālōš pĕʿāmîm baššānâ yērāʾeh* [*yirʾeh*] *kol-zĕkûrĕkā ʾel* [*ʾet*]-*pĕnê hāʾādōn Yhwh*). The deity of CC provides blessing to the people just as Hammurabi provided well-being to his people. Yahweh even comes to the cult site like the gods who 'enter' (*erēbum*) the Esagil temple, though he appears in theophany not in ritual procession.[12]

Other correlations are visible. The chiastic core in 23.1-8 is similar to a partial reversing structure visible in the future king passage of the exhortatory block ('[a] may he not alter...[b] may he not remove... [c] let him give heed to my words that I have written on my stele... [c'] If that man gives heed to my words that I wrote on my stele [b'] and he does not remove... [a'] he does not alter'). The transitional introduction to the casuistic laws in 21.1 ('These are the laws that you shall set before them') correlates with the transitional introduction at the end of the prologue, just before the casuistic laws ('I placed truth and justice in the mouth of the land'). CC's transitional introduction also correlates

---

12. The only element of the final apodictic laws that is unaccounted for in terms of the string structure and sequential correspondence with the exhortatory block is the very short general command in 23.13a: 'Be observant with regard to all that I have said to you'. This still corresponds with a general command to the future king in the exhortatory block: 'Let him be obedient to the words that I inscribed on my stele' (*ana awatim ša ina nariya ašṭuru liqūlma*).

with the transition out of the casuistic laws into the epilogue ('[These are] the just laws that Hammurabi, the capable king, established'). Lastly the placement of the apodictic sections around the casuistic laws matches the overall A-B-A structure of LH with its prologue-casuistic laws-epilogue.

The correspondences between CC and LH cannot be attributed to coincidence, shared generative legal logic, oral tradition, or mediating Northwest Semitic texts.[13] It is more reasonable to believe that the biblical writer used LH directly. The opportunity for this would have been during the Neo-Assyrian period, specifically in the century of 740–640 BCE. This was a period of intensive cultural contacts between the Assyrian imperial power and the subjugated states of Israel and Judah, and numerous copies of LH were available in Mesopotamia at this time.[14]

This estimate of the text of CC carries with it a number of implications. One is that for the most part CC has a single author or perhaps a committee of authors working in collaboration. Moreover, the text is product of academic reflection, not a collection of native customs. Furthermore the goal of CC

---

13. Most scholars explain the limited similarities they have heretofore observed between CC and LH as due to oral tradition. See Eckart Otto, 'Town and Rural Countryside in Ancient Israelite Law: Reception and Redaction in Cuneiform and Israelite Law', *JSOT* 57 (1993), pp. 3-22; 'Aspects of Legal Reforms and Reformulation in Ancient Cuneiform and Israelite Law', pp. 160-96 in Bernard M. Levinson (ed.), *Theory and Method in Biblical and Cuneiform Law* (JSOTSup, 181; Sheffield: Sheffield Academic Press, 1994); *Wandel der Rechtsbegründungen in der Gesellschaftsgeschichte des antiken Israel* (Studia biblica, 3; Leiden: E.J. Brill, 1988); Ludger Schwienhorst-Schönberger, *Das Bundesbuch (Ex 20,22–23,33)* (BZAW, 188; Berlin: W. de Gruyter, 1990); Ralf Rothenbusch, *Die kasuistische Rechtssammlung im 'Bundesbuch' (Ex 21,2-11.18–22,1)* (AOATS, 259; Münster: Ugarit-Verlag, 2000). The most recent work that charts a compositional history based on oral tradition (largely influenced by Otto) is Bernard Jackson, *Wisdom-Laws: A Study of the Mishpatim of Exodus 21:1–22:16* (New York: Oxford University Press, 2006), chapter 14 (I thank Professor Jackson for sharing a copy of his book proofs in advance of publication). Oral tradition is problematic because it cannot explain the similar order of laws or the detailed correspondences in wording. It either has to resort to a claim of coincidence or claim that cuneiform models (perhaps retained in scribal memory; cf. Otto) influenced the organization at a late stage. This last option, however, is not parsimonious since it bifurcates the phenomenological connection with Mesopotamian law, saying that similar content arose from oral tradition but similar order arose from literary modeling. It is easier to claim that all similarities arose from literary modeling.

14. For the textual attestation of LH during the Neo-Assyrian period and contacts between Assyria and Israel/Judah, see Wright, 'Laws of Hammurabi as a Source', pp. 47-54, 58-71. See also Levinson, 'Is the Covenant Code an Exilic Composition?', pp. 288-97. CC must predate Deuteronomy's laws, which I date, as many scholars do, to around the end of the seventh century BCE (see n. 2). This means that John Van Seters's contention of an exilic date for CC and its (reverse) dependence on Deuteronomy must be rejected (see his *A Law Book for the Diaspora: Revision in the Study of the Covenant Code* [New York: Oxford University Press, 2003]). See Levinson, 'Is the Covenant Code an Exilic Composition?', for a response to Van Seters's book, and my review in *JAOS* 124 (2004), pp. 129-31.

may be something other than to encode and prescribe law. Given its changes in the political landscape of LH, on exhibition particularly in the prologue and epilogue of LH, I would argue that CC is a symbolic response to Assyrian hegemony. It adopted the culturally prestigious genre of the Mesopotamian law code yet modified this to reflect native nationalistic interests. It eliminated the Mesopotamian king—and even downplayed the position of the native king (cf. 22.27)—and replaced him with the native deity. It also replaced the 'weak' person at the beginning of the exhortatory block with the resident alien, accompanied by the national memory of being aliens in Egypt. This nationalistic perspective in regard to the disadvantaged was underscored by treating 'Hebrew' slaves, an ethnic designation, at the beginning of the casuistic laws. The systematic revisions that CC made in the casuistic laws may not have been mere ethereal academic formulations, but calculated to create a 'better' system of laws compared to LH. I am not making the questionable claim that CC's laws are in fact *theological and ethically* superior than those of LH. Rather, I am suggesting as a *historical* observation that from its own compositional perspective, CC revised LH and other cuneiform law with a goal of producing a corpus that was more coherent legislatively than its sources by its solving problems and questions in those sources, similar to how Deuteronomy and the Holiness Legislation later sought to improve on their sources.

3. *Homicide, Talion, Vengeance, Satisfaction*

CC's laws about homicide and injury take on a new significance in this context of textual dependence. Knowing the major source of CC's legislation, one is able to reconstruct the compositional logic and what Bernard Levinson calls the 'hermeneutics of innovation' that CC employed to achieve its particular legal expression. Indeed, what Deuteronomy and the Holiness School do by way of interpretation and legal revision to CC is what CC is already doing to its cuneiform sources. In many respects the differences in CC's laws about homicide and injury laws can be explained as reactions to inconsistency found in or questions raised by the Mesopotamian source or sources. One of CC's major concerns was to provide a victim or his family with appropriate psychological and/or economic satisfaction. In what follows we will examine the homicide and injury laws in four topical sections: the goring ox, talion and injury, homicide and injury of a slave, and homicide of a burglar.

a. *The goring ox*[15]
CC's laws about an ox fatally goring a human being (21.28-32) closely follow the model provided by LH 250–252:

---

15. For a detailed analysis with bibliography, see Wright, 'Compositional Logic'.

Exodus 21.28-32	Laws of Hammurabi 250–252
²⁸If an ox gores a man or woman and he dies, the ox shall be stoned, its flesh shall not be eaten; the owner of the ox is not liable.	²⁵⁰If an ox gores a man (*awīlum*) while passing through the street and kills (him), that case has no claim.
²⁹If an ox is a habitual gorer, from previous experience, and its owner has been warned, but he did not restrain it, and it kills a man or woman, the ox shall be stoned and its owner shall also be put to death. ³⁰If ransom is laid upon him, he shall pay the redemption price for his life, according to whatever is laid upon him. ³¹Or (if) it gores a son or daughter, it shall be done for him according to this law.	²⁵¹If a man's ox is a habitual gorer, and his district has informed him that it is a habitual gorer, but he did not file its horns and did not control his ox, and that ox gores a person (literally: son of a man) and kills (him), he shall pay one-half mina (= thirty) shekels of silver.
³²If the ox gores a male slave or a female slave, he shall pay thirty shekels of silver to his (the slave's) master and the ox shall be stoned.	²⁵²If it is the slave of a free person, he shall pay one-third mina (= twenty) shekels of silver.

CC has the same basic three cases as LH: (a) ad hoc goring, (b) goring by an ox whose owner has been warned about the habit of his animal, and (c) goring a slave.

CC has an extra verse about a child as a victim (v. 31). CC is reacting explicitly here to other laws in LH that speak of the homicide of a child (a debt-servant child LH 116; a pregnant 'daughter of a man' LH 210; and a child killed by a collapsing house LH 230). These other laws prescribe that the offender's child be killed. The motivation for CC's inclusion of the law about a child victim, specifically in the ox laws, is the ambiguous idiom of LH 251 which refers to the victim as a 'son of a man' (*mār awīlim*), though here the idiom probably refers to the victim's class, not age. The rejection of vicarious punishment is a foundation of CC's revision and will be apparent in its revisions of LH 116 (vv. 20-21) and LH 210 (v. 23), to be discussed later. This rejection not only protects the innocent from unwarranted punishment, it also provides proper satisfaction to the aggrieved party by punishing the actual offender.

The most salient difference in CC's ox laws and in its penalties is the requirement to stone the animal (vv. 28, 29, 32). Other notable differences are the possible execution of an owner who has been warned about his animal and raising the fine for killing a slave to thirty shekels. These elevated penalties, I submit, grow out of solving a contradiction between LH 250 and another source that CC used for its law about an ox goring another ox in 21.35. This verse is almost verbatim what we find in Law of Eshnunna (LE) 53:

Exod. 21.35	LE 53
If the ox of a man knocks the ox of his neighbor and it dies, they shall sell the live ox and divide the resulting silver, and also divide the dead (ox).	If an ox gores an(other) ox and kills (it), both ox owners shall divide the price of the live ox and the carcass of the dead ox.

As note 8, above, indicated, we cannot claim that it knew LE *per se*. But we can surmise, given CC's clear dependence on LH and the near identity in formulation to LE 53, that CC used another lesser collection that had a law similar to LE 53.

Both LE 53 and LH 250 deal with a case of ad hoc goring, but are inconsistent in their prescriptions of compensation. The owner of a gored ox in LE receives half the carcass of the dead animal and half the price of the live ox, but the family of the human victim in LH receives nothing—'that case has no claim'. It is reasonable to suppose that CC added the requirement that the ox be stoned to resolve this contradiction. This is clearly a punishment, indicated by the adverb 'also' (*gam*) in the next case (v. 29) which shows that the stoning has the same legal force as the execution of the owner. Since stoning the ox is a punishment and because it employs a technique of killing that is not appropriate to food preparation, the animal may not be eaten (cf. 22.30). CC replicated almost exactly the wording of its source that was similar to LE 53 because this provided a baseline for its system. CC's substantial modifications are in the laws taken from LH 250-252.[16]

The addition of the requirement of stoning to the basic law of ad hoc goring of a human (v. 28) led to an increase of other penalties in vv. 29 and 32. Even though CC first prescribes capital punishment for an owner who did not control his animal after being warned (v. 29), it allows the option of monetary compensation—called a 'ransom'—if the family (presumably, cf. v. 22) so desired (v. 30). This monetary penalty essentially correlates with LH 251. The reason why CC does not prescribe a specific amount in this law is because CC has taken the thirty shekels of LH 251 as the amount to be paid for a slave in v. 32, replacing the twenty shekels of LH 252.[17]

The increase in CC's penalties and the requirement to stone the ox in particular do not seem to arise from theo-anthropological considerations (see note 3). Priestly or Holiness School perspectives that prohibit homicide because human beings are created in the divine image and judge an animal guilty when it kills a human being (Gen. 9.4-5; cf. 1.26-27; Lev. 17.4) are later than CC and may actually derive in part from an interpretation of CC's law about stoning an ox. CC does not otherwise contain decisive evidence that it has a higher estimate of human life over against LH. CC, in fact, replicates the basic penalties about homicide explicit or implicit in LH. It agrees with LH in requiring capital punishment for intentional homicide (the implication of laws such as LH 116, 207, 210, 229). And it does not require capital punishment when there are mitigating factors (inadvertence, a victim's lesser social status, etc.).

---

16. CC's striving for systematic correlation between the laws where animals and humans are victims of a goring ox is found further in its invention of v. 36, modeled on v. 29.

17. This increase may also be partly due to the conflation of debt and chattel-slaves (see below).

b. *Talion and compensation for inadvertent homicide and injury*
CC's miscarriage ('eye for and eye...' and talion) laws exhibit another set of modifications to penalties found in LH. As with the goring ox laws, CC replicates the basic cases found in the miscarriage laws of LH:

Exodus 21.22-25	LH 209-210
²²When men struggle and they knock a pregnant woman and her children come out, but there is no injury (to the woman), he shall be fined as the husband of the woman exacts from him, and he shall pay *biplīlîm*.[18]	²⁰⁹If an *awīlum* strikes an *awīlum*-woman (literally: daughter of an *awīlum*) and he causes her to miscarry her fetus, he shall weight out ten shekels of silver for her fetus.
²³If there is injury (to the woman), you shall give (= pay) life for life, ²⁴eye for eye, tooth for tooth, arm for arm, leg for leg, ²⁵burn for burn, injury for injury, wound for wound.	²¹⁰If that woman dies, they shall kill his daughter.

The first law deals with the loss of the child; the second law deals with the death (and as CC adds, the injury) of the woman.[19] The most visible modification in CC is the replacement of the punishment of LH 210 with a digest of the talion laws that appear slightly earlier in LH:

Exodus 22.23b-25	LH 196-201
²³...you shall give (=pay) life for life, ²⁴eye for eye, tooth for tooth, arm for arm, leg for leg, ²⁵burn for burn, injury for injury, wound for wound.	¹⁹⁶If an *awīlum* blinds the eye of a member of the *awīlum* class, they shall blind his eye. ¹⁹⁷If he breaks the bone of an *awīlum*, they shall break his bone ¹⁹⁸If he blinds the eye of a commoner or breaks the bone of a commoner, he shall weigh out one mina (sixty shekels) of silver. ¹⁹⁹If he blinds the eye of an *awīlum*'s slave or breaks the bone of an *awīlu*'s slave, he shall weigh out half of his value. ²⁰⁰If an *awīlum* knocks out the tooth of an *awīlu* of the same rank, they shall knock out his tooth. ²⁰¹If he knocks out the tooth of a commoner, he shall weigh out one third mina (twenty shekels) of silver.

18. The meaning of this term is not clear. Possibilities include: 'for the abortions' (emended: *binpālîm*); 'by arbitration/mediation'; 'by assessment' (E. Speiser, 'The Stem PLL in Hebrew', *JBL* 82 [1963], pp. 301-306); 'according to the stage of gestation' (HittL 17).

19. The term *'āsôn* refers to injury or death that the woman suffers. For other interpretations, which cannot be accepted, see Wright, 'Laws of Hammurabi', p. 22 n. 16. Other cuneiform miscarriage laws also break down cases on the basis of loss of the child and death of the woman (LLI d-e; MAL A50, 53).

CC's eye and tooth are found expressly in Hammurabi's laws (LH 196, 198, 199, 200-201). CC's arm and leg come from laws referring to the breaking a bone (LH 197, 199). The various wounds at the end of the list are probably influenced by the mention of a 'wound' (*simmum*) found in the nearby laws of LH 215–220 and especially LH 206. As the discussion below will lay out in more detail, LH 206 generated vv. 18-19. These verses require payment for the person's idleness caused by the injury. This is a disability payment essentially equivalent to talion. The reason for CC's reducing the talion laws to a list in vv. 23-25 is so they can be plugged into the apodosis of LH 210. And one reason for replacing this apodosis with the talion laws is because CC rejects vicarious punishment, as noted above.

CC makes other changes in the miscarriage and talion laws that reveal other systematizing interests. While Hammurabi's miscarriage law involves intentional injury, marked by direct striking and capital punishment, CC presents its case as one of inadvertence, where two men fight[20] and one of them happens to knock (*nāgap*) the woman. Judged by the criteria of the main homicide law in vv. 12-14, this is inadvertent.

The talion penalty provides additional evidence that this is a case of inadvertence, and this shows another contrast with LH. As opposed to Hammurabi's talion laws whose main cases prescribe bodily mutilation, CC's talion laws do not. The verb 'you shall give' (*wĕnātattâ*) in v. 23b which governs the talion dyads means 'you shall pay'. This is the meaning of the verb *nātan* in other laws in CC (21.19, 22, 30, 32) and it is consistent with the use of *nadānum* 'to give' in LH which is used idiomatically in other laws of making a payment.[21] Hence, when the text says 'you shall give life for life, eye for eye...', it means making equivalent payment.

CC also wrote its talion law as a general law. That this is its force is indicated by the use of the second person verb 'you shall give (pay)' instead of the normal third person verb. The occasional use of the second person within the casuistic laws is a way of connecting the content of the laws with the second person communal addressee of the initial apodictic laws (20.23-26), which are to be considered part of CC's original composition. The first law in the casuistic laws begins with a second person verb to tie the collection to the apodictic introduction (21.2 'If you acquire...', *tiqneh*). The appearance of a second person form in the homicide asylum laws ('you shall take him' *tiqqaḥennû*; v. 14) ties the context to the earlier altar laws in 20.24-26. The second person at the beginning of the talion list addresses the community and thereby generalizes the law beyond its specific application to a context of miscarriage.[22]

---

20. Fighting is introduced from vv. 18-19 which themselves derive the condition from LH 206; see below.

21. LH 101, 106–107, 112–13, 120–21, 124, 126, 138–40, 217, 221–25, 228, 234, 238, 239, 242/243, 247, 248, 251–52 [// Exod. 21.29, 32], 258–61, 264, 267, 271, 273–74, 276–78.

22. It does not seem to mean, however, that the community pays the penalty (so Raymond Westbrook, 'Lex Talionis and Exodus 21, 22-25', *Revue biblique* 93 [1986], pp. 52-69).

Another sign that CC's talion law is a general law is that its list of injuries goes beyond what is expected for miscarriage. The only element in CC's list that has a specific contextual relationship with the corresponding miscarriage in LH is 'life' since LH 210 is a case of homicide. Hammurabi's miscarriage law does not include a case of injury. Moreover, an injury such as a 'burn' does not fit the case of men fighting and knocking a woman. Put another way, the talion list is overkill if it is to apply specifically to miscarriage. It makes perfect sense, however, as a general law.

As such, the talion law applies to all cases of homicide and injury described in vv. 12-21. It means that all cases of *inadvertent* injury and homicide require indemnification, paid to the victim or the victim's family. This fills a prominent gap left in the initial and primary homicide legislation in vv. 12-14.[23] These first verses say that an intentional killer is to be put to death and that an inadvertent killer is not. But they say nothing about any further obligation that an unintentional killer might have. It seems as if the inadvertent killer gets off scot-free. One would not expect this, however, from the Akkadian law that lies behind vv. 12-14. These verses correspond with LH 207 which is part of a larger series of laws on inadvertent injury and homicide in LH and which are the basis for other laws in CC:

Exod. 21.18-21	LH 206–208
[18]When men fight and one strikes his fellow with a stone or (even) with (just) a fist, and he (the latter) does not die but takes to his bed—[19]if he gets up and walks about outside on his staff, then the striker is absolved, but he must recompense him for his period of inactivity and provide for his cure.	[206]If an *awīlum* strikes another *awīlum* in a fight and injures him, that *awīlum* shall swear (saying), 'I did not strike him with intent', and he shall pay the physician.
[12]He who strikes a man so that he dies shall be put to death. [13]If he did not plan it, but God caused it to occur, I will appoint a place for you to which he may flee. [14]If a person plots against his fellow to kill him by deceit, you shall take him from my altar to be put to death.	[207]If he dies from his being struck, he shall also swear (as in previous paragraph). If (the victim) is an *awīlum*, he shall weigh out one-half mina (= thirty shekels) of silver.
[20]If a man strikes his male slave or female slave with a rod and he (or she) dies under his hand (i.e. immediately), he is to be avenged. [21]But if he lingers for a day or two, he shall not be avenged, since he is his (the master's) property.	[208]If (the victim who dies when struck) is a common person, he (the assailant *awīlum*) shall weight out one-third mina (= twenty shekels) of silver.

23. For homicide see Pamela Barmash, *Homicide in the Biblical World* (Cambridge: Cambridge University Press, 2005). For a corrective to Barmash's analysis of the relation of D and CC, see Jeffrey Stackert, 'Why Does Deuteronomy Legislate Cities of Refuge? Asylum in the Covenant Collection (Exodus 21:12-14) and Deuteronomy (19:1-13)', *JBL* 125 (2006), pp. 23-49.

Verses 18-19 contain all the main points of LH 206: fighting, striking, injury, and paying medical expenses. Verses 12-14 echo LH 207 in dealing with homicide and specifically being concerned about lack of intention. The oath required by LH 207 (also 206) would have been done *maḥar ilim* 'before the god' according to other laws in LH (9, 23, 106, 120, 126, 240, 266, 281), which may be understood as taking place at a temple/sanctuary.[24] Hammurabi's and CC's homicide laws thus correlate further in having ties to a cult place. Verses 20-21 deal with striking and killing one of a lower class. Though LH 208 treats a commoner rather than a slave, a number of laws in the neighborhood of LH 206-208 reflect social graduations that include slaves (LH 196–201, 202–205, 206–208, 209–14, 215–17, 218–20, 221–23). CC has replaced the commoner with a slave, more consistent with its sociological perspective.

The main difference between these series is CC's divergent order. CC has simply moved the topic of homicide from the middle of the series in LH and placed it at the beginning of its assault and capital punishment laws. Verses 18-21 still reflect the original context of LH, however, inasmuch as vv. 18-19 deal only with injury, the topic of LH 206, whereas vv. 20-21 deal with homicide, the topic of LH 208. The transitional law equivalent to LH 207 has been removed from the sequence. The relocation of the homicide law allowed CC to reformulate the homicide law in participial form, perhaps under the added influence of a native source.[25] CC makes up the omitted requirement of indemnification in the case of inadvertent homicide in the first dyad of the talion law of v. 23a. This clarifies that the killer is to pay the equivalent the life lost.[26]

CC exceeds the requirements of LH in requiring indemnification in the case of inadvertent injury according to its talion law. According to LH 206, one only pays for the physician in such a case; no additional payment is required. CC apparently thought that it was inconsistent to require this in the case of homicide but not in the case of injury. This, coupled with the rejection of vicarious punishment, may be seen as the primary factors in modifying the miscarriage and talion laws from LH.

The requirement of indemnification for inadvertent injury is also found in vv. 18-19. These verse display one significant difference over against LH 206 (see the texts above). In addition to paying for the injured individual's recuperation, one who injures another is also to pay for the period of idleness caused by the

---

24. The term (*hā*)*ʾĕlōhîm* '(the) God', which refers to the place of judicial procedures (i.e. the sanctuary) in 21.6; 22.7, 8 (cf. 10), is a reflex of the generic *ilum* in such passages in LH. Likewise the *hāʾĕlōhîm*, which refers to an 'act of God' in 21.13, echoes the descriptions of a generic *ilum* causing accidental death in LH 244, 266.

25. On the use of a native source for the participial laws in CC, see Wright, 'Compositional Logic', pp. 111-12 n. 42.

26. The miscarriage laws of MAL A 50, 52 have the motif of talion appearing in connection with miscarriage. Laws like these may have been partly influential in leading CC to including talion in its miscarriage law.

injury. This payment is required in cases of both inadvertent and intentional injury. These two modalities are encoded in the two instruments of assault described in v. 18, the *stone* and the *fist*. The use of a fist may be inadvertent, since this is the instrument of concern in the main homicide law of vv. 12-14 (note 'striking' in v. 12 and the use of a 'hand' in v. 13). As there striking by the hand may be inadvertent, so here in v. 18. The inclusion of a stone, however, points to greater aggression and hence possibility of intention. By including both hand and fist, v. 18 is saying that it does not matter whether the injury is intended or not, the penalties outlined in v. 19 apply.

The significance of vv. 18-19 is that payment for the injured person's idleness is not appreciably different from paying the worth an injured body part. Both are compensations for *disability*. CC has apparently described the same payment in two different ways in vv. 18-19 and in vv. 23b-25.

That indemnification is required in the case of inadvertent homicide answers a question in the asylum law of vv. 12-14: How long does the killer stay at the sanctuary or altar? CC implicitly sees this as a temporary refuge, lasting only as long as it takes to adjudicate and settle the case. If it is determined that the killing was intentional, the killer is taken from the altar to be put to death. If it is determined that the killing was unintentional, it can be assumed that the killer would leave the sanctuary as soon as he paid or made arrangements to pay the victim's family. The later interpretations of Deuteronomy (19.4) and the Holiness School (Num. 35.25-28) that the inadvertent killer resides in the city of asylum are based on a misunderstanding of CC, probably due to CC's separation of the talion law in vv. 23b-25 from the main homicide law. Deuteronomy and the Holiness School read vv. 12-14 as a self contained unit and took it to mean that inadvertent homicide does not require any indemnification. This misreading is confirmed by how these later legal understood CC's talion laws. They misinterpreted these also as referring literal bodily mutilation (cf. Deut. 19.21; Lev. 24.19-20).

The philosophy of punishment in the homicide and injury laws of vv. 12-25 is consistent with what we have seen in the goring ox laws. Both sets of laws are interested in providing satisfaction to the victim or victim's family. In the case of intentional homicide, this is achieved through exacting vengeance by executing the killer. In the case of inadvertent homicide or injury, it is achieved through receiving indemnification. When execution serves as the means of requital, indemnification is not also required, as indicated by the goring ox legislation (cf. 21.29-30). The two methods of satisfaction thus are complementary.

c. *Killing and injuring a slave*

The foregoing section noted above that vv. 20-21 correlate with LH 208. Besides dealing with a slave instead of a commoner, CC's law also differs from LH 208 in distinguishing between cases in which a slave owner is liable for killing his slave. The decisive criterion is the immediacy of the death. If the slave dies the day that the owner beat him or her, the owner 'suffers vengeance' (*nāqōm yinnāqēm*). If the slave lives for a day or two and then dies, the owner 'does not suffer vengeance' (*lōʾ yuqqam*). The vengeance here must refer to capital punishment, to tell from other instances of the verb and root *nqm* in the Bible.

How this vengeance is prosecuted depends on understanding another systematic change that CC wrought upon Hammurabi's laws. It blended together the categories of chattel (property) slaves and debt-servants in its various laws where the specific category of slave is not defined (21.20-21, 26-27, 32).[27] These two categories are phenomenologically separate in LH. The Akkadian collection uses distinct terminology: a chattel-slave is a *wardum* 'male slave' or *amtum* 'female slave' while a debt-servant is a *nipûtum*. In LH, chattel-slaves are the permanent property of an owner, whereas debt-servants are temporarily enslaved, for three years, to pay off a debt. In fact, Hammurabi's law about temporary debt-servitude is the basis for CC's famous law about a slave serving for six years and being released in the seventh (21.2):

Exodus 21.2	*LH 117*
If you acquire a Hebrew slave, he shall work for six years. In the seventh he shall go free, without further obligation.	If an obligation has come due for a man, and he sells his wife, son, or daughter, or is himself surrendered for debt servitude, they shall work in the house of their buyer or creditor for three years. In the fourth year their freedom shall be effected.

CC has changed the period of servitude to echo the seven year agricultural cycle (23.10-11).

The conflation of slave types, most visible in vv. 20-21, explains the tension in how the death of a slave is judged. The owner's liability for killing in v. 20 is based on the laws about debt-servitude in LH. LH 116, the law just before the law that inspired CC's basic debt-slave law, sets down a creditor's liability for killing a debt-servant through a severe beating:

> If the debt-servant dies from beating or from mistreatment in the house of his/her creditor, the owner of the debt-servant (= the debtor) shall bring proof against his merchant. If (the debt-servant was) the man's son, they shall kill his son. If (the one in bondage was) the man's slave, he shall weigh out one-third mina (= twenty shekels) of silver. He shall forfeit as much as he gave as a loan.

---

27. For biblical slavery, see the recent extensive works by Gregory C. Chirichigno, *Debt-Slavery in Israel and the Ancient Near East* (JSOTSup, 141; Sheffield: JSOT Press, 1993) and Innocenzo Cardellini, *Die biblischen 'Sklaven'-Gesetze im Lichte des keilschriftlichen Sklavenrechts. Ein Beitrag zur Tradition, Überlieferung und Redaktion der alttestamentlichen Rechtstexte* (Bonner biblische Beiträge, 55, Königstein: Peter Hanstein, 1981).

Verse 20 follows the essence of this law. CC does not describe the victim as a debtor's son partly because it wants to generalize the law and partly because it rejects vicarious punishment. Still, LH 116 indicates that death of a debt-servant by mistreatment is a capital offense, and CC follows this.

The contrasting lenient rule in v. 21 is based on the institution of chattel-slavery in LH. LH only includes laws about others injuring or killing a slave (e.g. LH 213–14, 219, 231, 252), not about an owner himself doing so. The reason for this is because the law would be meaningless legally. By killing a chattel-slave, an owner would be destroying his own property. This may be foolish, but it is not prosecutable. CC follows this logic in v. 21 and allows the slave owner to beat a slave to death as long as the death happens a day later. CC justifies this with the principle operative in LH: 'because he is his silver (i.e. property)' (*kî kaspô hû'*).

The prosecution of the penalty for the death of a debt-slave would be different from that for a chattel-slave. Since a debt-slave would be a member of the native ethnic group, technically a 'Hebrew slave' (*'ebed 'ibrî*) as in 21.2, his family would prosecute the penalty against the creditor. A chattel-slave, however, may not have family members present or in a position to prosecute the case. It may be that CC imagined the state taking over the prosecution, perhaps hinted at in the second person verb in the phrase '*you* shall take him from my altar to be put to death' in v. 14. Alternatively, the owner may have been able to avoid prosecution. This ambiguity may be responsible for the text's using the verb 'suffer vengeance' with the root *nqm* rather than the more direct prescription 'be put to death' (*môt yûmat*; cf. 21.12, 29).

The laws about the permanent injury of slaves in Exod. 21.26-27 also reflect the conflation of slave types. These verses, which follow CC's main talion law, are based on the talion laws of LH and reflect the social gradations presented there:

Exodus 22.26-27	*LH 198–99, 201*
[26]If a man strikes the eye of his male slave or eye of his female slave and destroy it, he shall send him free for his eye.	[198]If he blinds the eye of a commoner or breaks the bone of a commoner, he shall weigh out one mina (sixty shekels) of silver.
[27]If he knocks out the tooth of his male slave or the tooth of his female slave, he shall send him free for his tooth.	[199]If he blinds the eye of an *awīlum*'s slave or breaks the bone of an *awīlum*'s slave, he shall weigh out half of his value.
	[201]If he knocks out the tooth of a commoner, he shall weigh out one third mina (twenty shekels) of silver.

Since these laws are independent from the miscarriage law, CC retains a full casuistic formulation. CC nonetheless makes two significant changes that show that debt-slaves are included in it legislation as opposed to its source. It portrays the striker as the owner/master of the slave. Secondly, it prescribes that the injured slave is to go free, the lot of a debt-slave after six years of service (21.2, 7). One assumes that the injury cancels any debt claim that the owner/creditor may have against the slave or his family.

The conflation of slave types has had the effect of worsening the lot of debt-slaves vis-à-vis Hammurabi's laws. Debt-slaves in CC have to work twice as long as debt-servants in LH and they may be beaten to death as long as they do not die the day of their beating. But the conflation has brought an improvement to the lot of chattel-slaves in CC over against LH. While they are permanent possessions, they nonetheless are protected to some degree against the harshness of their owners. Deuteronomy later builds on CC's debt-slave laws in 21.2-11 and ameliorates their treatment, especially that of female debt-slaves (Deut. 15.12-18). The Holiness School restores the distinction between debt-servants and chattel-slaves similar to what is found in LH and allows harsh treatment of the latter though it also on average lengthens the period of servitude for native debt-servants (Lev. 25.39-46).

d. *Killing a Burglar*

The primary homicide and injury laws are found in 21.12-32. Another homicide law (22.1-2a) appears later, in the middle of the animal theft law (21.37 + 22.2b-3). It is not entirely clear why this law appears exactly where it does. It is clear, however, that it was conceived in connection with the safekeeping laws of 22.6-8. Conceptually it fits well just after or near v. 6 (connecting motifs are italicized):

> ⁶If a man gives to his fellow silver or objects to safeguard and it is stolen from the man's *house*,
> if *the thief is found*, he shall pay twofold.
> > ¹If *the thief is found* in the act of tunneling [into the *house*] and is struck and dies, there is no bloodguilt for him.
> > ²If the sun has risen on him, there is bloodguilt for him.
>
> ⁷If *the thief is not found*, the owner of the house shall approach the God (saying that) he did not misappropriate the property of his fellow.
>
> ⁸For every criminal matter—whether an ox, ass, flock animal, article of clothing, or anything lost about which one might claim 'this is it—the case of the two of them shall come to the God; he whom God convicts shall pay twofold to his fellow.

Verses 6-8 were created by cross-referencing to various laws in LH. The animal theft laws of LH 264–65 in the topical sequence of LH that CC follows for the order of its casuistic laws (see Table 5.1, above) contain the idiom 'to give for shepherding' (*ana reʾîm nadānum*). This is similar to the idiom for 'to give for safekeeping' (*ana maṣṣarūtim nadānum*) found in the safekeeping laws of LH 122–25. The idiom in the shepherding law gave CC grounds to bring in the earlier safekeeping laws at this point in its composition. In turn, one of the safekeeping laws (LH 125) speaks about the property held by a custodian as being stolen 'by digging through' (*ina pilšim*). This allowed CC to bring in the still earlier laws on burglary (*palāšum* 'to dig through') and robbery from LH 21–23 (LH 21 is cited below). The robbery laws (LH 22–23) provided the datum about a thief's being apprehended or not apprehended in vv. 6 and 7 and in the burglary law in v. 1.

Use of the burglary law in LH 21 allowed CC to utilize another burglary law from another source, similar to, but probably not the same as LE 13 (LH 21 is included here for fuller comparison):

Exod. 22.1-2a	LH 21 and LE 13
¹If the thief is found in the act of digging, and he is struck and dies, there is no blood guilt for him. ²ªIf the sun has risen over him, there is blood guilt for him.	ᴸᴴ ²¹If a man bores into a house, they shall kill him in front of that breach and hang him up. ᴸᴱ ¹³A man who is seized in the house of a commoner in the house at midday shall weigh out ten shekels of silver. He who is seized at night in the house shall die; he shall not live.

LE 13 correlates better with CC's law than does LH 21 in distinguishing between burglary during the day and night, conditions not raised by LH 21. The main difference between the biblical and Akkadian laws is that CC is concerned about the guilt of the killer (probably imagined to be the householder) whereas the Akkadian laws are concerned about the guilt of the burglar. CC may have creatively transformed Akkadian sources like LH 21 and LE 13 to formulate its burglar homicide law. But we have to admit that it is possible that CC was influenced by an unknown law interested in the killer's culpability. Such a law obtained in the Roman Twelve Tables that are dated to c. 450 BCE. The laws of this collection are known by their scattered citation by various later Latin writers, which makes their original context and exact formulation difficult to ascertain. Nonetheless, two burglary laws as they have been extracted and collocated by modern scholarship read:

> VIII.12: If a thief commits a theft by night, if the owner kills the thief, the thief shall be killed lawfully.
> VIII.13: By daylight...if a thief defends himself with a weapon...and the owner shall shout.[28]

Certainly one cannot argue for a genetic connection between the Roman laws and Near Eastern law given the present state of evidence.[29] There are too many

---

28. For this translation, see Allan Chester Johnson, Paul Robinson Coleman-Norton and Frank Card Bourne, *Ancient Roman Statutes* (Austin: University of Texas Press, 1961), p. 11. For an edition of the Latin text, see Salvator Riccobono, *Fontes iuris romani antejustiniani. Pars prima: Leges* (Florence: S.A.G. Barbèra, 1941), pp. 57-58.

29. Nor can one argue for the influence of biblical law on the Roman laws.

differences otherwise to make such a conclusion and the cultural and geographical gaps are too great. But the Roman laws point to the theoretical possibility that there may have existed an Akkadian law that was more similar to Exod. 22.1-2a than LE 13 and which served as a source for CC's law. If so, CC has been less creative in formulating its burglary law than if it had only laws like LH 21 and LE 13 as sources.

CC's burglary law presents a case of homicide with the least liability. Not only is the killer not capitally liable, he or she apparently does not need to pay indemnification if the burglar is killed at night. The burglar has altered the starting balances on the ledger sheet, as it were. He has theoretically created an obligation for himself by intending to commit a theft. This cancels any requirement of indemnification that the killer may have, and the burglar's indeterminable violent intentions against the inhabitants of the house allows his being killed. If the burglar is killed during the day, however, the householder incurs liability for intentional homicide since, presumably, the burglar can be determined to not be intent on injuring the household members.

4. Conclusion

The penalties for intentional and inadvertent injury and homicide in LH and CC are summarized in Tables 5.5 and 5.6. The primary modifications that CC makes in the material derived from its Akkadian sources is the rejection of vicarious capital punishment, making penalties for inadvertent homicide and injury systematically consistent, solving inconsistency in the laws about the ad hoc goring of an ox, and blending the categories chattel and debt-slaves together. The rationale that lies behind these modifications as a whole is an interest in providing appropriate psychological and economic satisfaction to victims or their families. This comes by taking vengeance on intentional killers, including oxen, or receiving compensation.

CC's modifications do not primarily seem to have a theological rationale. This may only be argued indirectly by saying that they reflect a concern for justice, and that a concern for justice is ultimately theological. But even here CC must be seen as under the influence of LH. The prologue and epilogue of LH explain Hammurabi's laws as arising from a divine injunction for the king to promulgate justice. CC transforms this by making the deity the lawgiver, evident particularly in its apodictic laws. This appears to have an ideological purpose, to counter the royal and imperial power-structure portrayed in the Akkadian source and which reinforced and reflected Assyrian political and cultural dominance. CC's systematic 'improvements' to Akkadian casuistic laws served its larger ideological goal of the text by proffering what it believed was a more coherent and consistent body of legislation.

source	modality	homicide		injury	
		free person	slave	free person	slave
LH	intentional direct	[capital punishment], including vicarious option (cf. LH 116, 210, 230)	[if own slave, no penalty; if slave of another, payment of value of slave]	talion mutilation (LH 196-197, 200) [payment for recuperation (implied from LH 206)]	payment of 1/2 value of slave (LH 199; monetary fines for commoner LH 198, 201)
	inadvertent direct	30 shekels (LH 207)	[20 shekels for commoner, LH 208; if own slave, no penalty; if slave of another, perhaps payment of less than 20 shekels]	payment for recuperation (LH 206)	[payment for recuperation?]
	indirect (ox) negligent	30 shekels (H 251)	20 shekels (LH 252)		
	indirect (ox) ad hoc	no claim (LH 250)	[no claim]		
	killing burglary at day	[some guilt implied in LE 13]	[??]		
	killing burglar at night	no penalty (LE 13)	[no penalty]		

Table 5.5: Summary penalties for injury and homicide in LH (with LE 13)

source	modality	homicide		injury	
		free person	slave	free person	slave
CC	intentional direct	capital punishment, no vicarious option (21.12-14)	capital punishment if death is immediate and caused by owner (21.20-21)	payment of lost wages (= disability payment; 21.18-19) and payment for recuperation	release of permanently injured slave, debt-cancelled (21.26-27)
	inadvertent direct	talion payment ('life for life', indemnification 21.23b)	no penalty at all if death is delayed (21.20-21)	talion payment = payment of lost wages (= disability payment; 21.18-19, 23b-25) and payment for recuperation	[release of permanently injured slave, (debt-cancelled) (21.26-27)]
	indirect (ox) negligent	stoning ox and capital punishment or indemnification (21.29-30)	stoning ox and 30 shekels (21.32)		
	indirect (ox) ad hoc	stoning ox (21.28)	[stoning ox?]		
	killing burglary at day	capital punishment	[??]		
	killing burglar at night	no penalty	[no penalty]		

Table 5.6: Summary of CC's penalties for injury and homicide

THE DEATH OF THE HERO AND THE VIOLENT DEATH OF JESUS

Lawrence M. Wills

1. *Introduction*

Although there are a number of ways in which one could approach the death of Jesus in the gospels, I would like to discuss here an approach that is comparative. The death of Jesus in early Christian texts is often likened by scholars to the death and sacrifice of the hero in Greek and Roman culture, but with mixed results.[1] Some comparisons of Jesus with heroes have focused on the birth instead of the death, but in 1997 and 1998 Adela Yarbro Collins and I both independently published comparisons to hero cults that focused on the death of Jesus.[2] At the meeting of the Society of Biblical Literature in 2005 a session was initiated on Jesus and the death of the hero organized by Ellen Aitken and Jennifer Maclean,[3] who are pursuing a research project on this topic. The idea is thus being revived. I would also mention the historical continuation of this question in the work of David Frankfurter on the death of saints as sacrifice and Joan Branham on the relationship between menstrual blood and sacrificial

---

1. Studies of the hero relevant to the gospels include: Moses Hadas and Morton Smith, *Heroes and Gods: Spiritual Biographies in Antiquity* (London: Routledge & Kegan Paul, 1965); Charles H. Talbert, *What Is a Gospel? The Genre of the Canonical Gospels* (Philadelphia: Fortress, 1977); David Aune, 'The Problem of the Genre of the Gospels: A Critique of C.H. Talbert's *What Is a Gospel?*', in R.T. France and David Wenham (eds.), *Gospel Perspectives II* (Sheffield: JSOT Press, 1981), pp. 9-60; 'Heracles and Christ: Heracles Imagery in the Christology of Early Christianity', in David L. Balch, Everett Ferguson and Wayne A. Meeks (eds.), *Greeks, Romans, and Christians: Essays in Honor of Abraham J. Malherbe* (Minneapolis: Fortress Press, 1990), pp. 3-19.

2. Wills, *The Quest of the Historical Gospel: Mark, John and the Origins of the Gospel Genre* (London and New York: Routledge, 1997); Collins, 'Finding Meaning in the Death of Jesus', *JR* 78 (1998), pp. 175-96. See also her *The Beginning of the Gospel: Probings of Mark in Context* (Minneapolis: Fortress, 1992), pp. 137, 141; and 'The Signification of Mark 10:45 among Gentile Christians', *HTR* 90 (1997), pp. 371-82.

3. See their works to date: Ellen Aitken, *Jesus' Death in Early Christian Memory: The Poetics of the Passion* (Göttingen: Vandenhoeck & Ruprecht; Fribourg: Academic Press, 2004); Jennifer Maclean, 'Jesus as Cult Hero in the Fourth Gospel', in Ellen Aitken and Jennifer Maclean (eds.), *Philostratus's Heroikos: Religion and Cultural Identity in the Third Century C.E.* (Atlanta: SBL, 2004), pp. 195-218.

blood in ancient Judaism and Christianity, and in this conference by the presentation of Jennifer Knust.[4]

My book was entitled *The Quest of the Historical Gospel*, and in it I argued, first, that the death of Jesus in *some* early Christian texts, but not in others, is expressed in motifs analogous to the death of the hero in Greece and Rome. Second, as in the case of Greek and Roman heroes, the narrative of the life and death of the hero is recounted in cult; that is, in the language of the Lord's Supper, there is a parallelism of narrative and cult. Also, just as the death of the hero in Greece and Rome is sometimes understood as an analogy to an animal sacrifice, so also Jesus' death is sometimes likened to an animal sacrifice. Finally, the *Life of Aesop*, a text roughly contemporary to the gospels, presents the death of Aesop and the resulting cult as an example of the hero paradigm in a way very similar to the gospels. The implication of these four theses is that the violent death of Jesus must be contextualized in the pervasive hero-cult discourse of the ancient Mediterranean, even if it is not always a perfect fit. Since publishing this book, however, I have had a chance to examine more evidence both for and against a connection, and have become even more strongly convinced that the paradigm of the death of the hero informs early Christian discourse. Here I will present new evidence for this fit and address some of the apparent discrepancies as well.

2. *The Greek and Roman Hero Tradition*

I will begin with a brief description of the hero in Greek and Roman culture. Heroes are not born as eternal gods, but acquire immortality after death, and receive cult that is qualitatively different from that of the Olympian or sky gods. Different words for sacrifice are used—θύω for sky gods, versus ἐναγίζω or ἐντέμνω for heroes, and there is a raised altar in the one case (βωμός) and a low altar (ἐσχάρα) in the other, or even a pit (βόθρος). The

---

4. Frankfurter, 'On Sacrifice and Residues: Processing the Potent Body', in Brigitte Luchesi and Kocku von Stuckrad (eds.), *Religion im kulturellen Diskurs: Festschrift für Hans G. Kippenberg zu seinem 65. Geburtstag* (Berlin: W. de Gruyter, 2004), pp. 511-33; Branham, 'Bloody Women and Bloody Spaces: Menses and the Eucharist in Late Antiquity and the Early Middle Ages', *Harvard Divinity Bulletin* 30 (2002), pp. 15-22; 'Blood in Flux, Sanctity at Issue', *RES Anthropology and Aesthetics* 31 (1997), pp. 53-70; 'Women as *Objets de sacrifice*? An Early Christian "Chancel of the Virgins"', in *Sacrifice animal et offrande végétale dans les sociétés de la Méditerranée ancienne* (Bibliothèque de l'Ecole des Hautes Etudes, Sciences religieuses; Paris: Brepols, forthcoming). I have learned much from conversations with all of these scholars, as well as with Gregory Nagy, Laura Nasrallah, Joanna Dewey, Andrew McGowan, Kimberley Patton, Gregory Mobley, the Gospel of Mark group of the Society of Biblical Literature, the Critical Biblical Studies group of the Boston Theological Institute, and the colleagues whose efforts are collected in the present volume.

cult offerings for heroes are like those of the earth deities.[5] Like Jesus, heroes may be understood as having one divine parent, but not necessarily. Either way, it is the special virtues of the heroes that account for their extraordinary abilities and contributions. But these virtues were also often a part of their conflicts both with the gods—to whom they are inferior—and humans—to whom they are superior. Heroes are often associated with conflict, and they cannot integrate into society as normal humans would. The conflicted and generally unjust death of a hero is often emphasized. As Mary Lefkowitz says, 'Death assumes a curious priority in representing the significance of a man's life and works'.[6] It is the special, conflicted circumstances of their deaths that give rise to cult. This constitutes the main difference between 'heroization' and 'divinization'. A special mortal, such as Augustus Caesar, could be divinized upon his death, but without a conflicted death he would not be a hero. Immortality for the hero is thus a compensation for suffering, 'remembrance as atonement for an interrupted life'.[7]

Heroes were honored at the sites of their tombs, but sometimes the tombs were hidden or secret or even empty. The absence of the body was often an issue, and the establishment of their cult site was often problematized and a matter of tension (Strabo 9.2.11). Their cult was generally local, intended for a particular city, but there were at the same time some, such as Pyrrhos, who became panhellenic heroes. More important, heroes were not always warriors; they were often city founders or kings, but also philosophers or poets. The genre of 'lives' of poets was popular, with stories of the violent death of Hesiod, which gives rise to his cult, and also the violent death of Archilochus.[8] Heroes were prayed to, and effected cures—so Orestes, Theseus, Rhesus, and Protesilaus.[9] This is also true for poet-heroes; Hesiod's bones were moved to another site to cure a plague. There were some heroine cults as well,[10] and the slave Drimacus, who led a slave rebellion, was reconciled with the masters

---

5. On the distinction between eternal gods and heroized or divinized mortals, see Plutarch, *Pelopidas* 16; *On the Malice of Herodotus* 857d; Herodotus 2.145-46; Diodorus Siculus 6.1.2.

6. Lefkowitz, *The Lives of the Greek Poets* (Baltimore: The Johns Hopkins University Press, 1981), p. 10. On immortality as a compensation: Oedipus in Pindar, *Olympian Ode* 7.77, *Nemean Ode* 1.69-72; Euripides, *Hippolytus* 1423; see Robert Parker, *Miasma: Pollution and Purification in Early Greek Religion* (Oxford and New York: Clarendon Press, 1996), pp. 320-21.

7. Corinne Ondine Pache, 'After Rohde and Farnell: Developments in the Study of Greek Hero Cult', presentation at Society of Biblical Literature Annual Meeting, November 21, 2004.

8. Gregory Nagy, *Best of the Achaeans* (Baltimore: The Johns Hopkins University, 1979), pp. 251, 286, 296-97, 301-308; Todd Compton, 'The Trial of the Satirist: Poetic *Vitae* (Aesop, Archilochus, Homer) as Background for Plato's *Apology*', *American Journal of Philology* 111 (1990), pp. 330-47; Collins, 'Finding Meaning'.

9. On Protesilaus and an interesting later interpretation of this phenomenon, see Philostratus, *Heroicus* 9.141.6.

10. Jennifer Larson, *Greek Heroine Cults* (Madison: University of Wisconsin Press, 1995).

and then treacherously killed, could be revered as a hero by elites (Athenaeus 6.265c–266e). Even infants who had significant deaths could receive cult as heroes and could provide boons for the living.[11]

Many of the heroes were considered to be people from the ancient past, but in the Hellenistic and Roman periods a large number of figures from the recent past were also heroized, whether they supposedly had one divine parent (Alexander the Great, Apollonius of Tyana) or none (Empedocles, Lysander, Cleomenes of Sparta). The number of heroizations and divinizations was such that satirists such as Lucian could lampoon it, and Pseudo-Seneca, in *The Pumpkinification of Claudius* could say, 'Once it was a great thing to become a god; now you have made it into a farce'. But the satire by elite intellectuals indicates that on a popular level it was taken very seriously. Even behind Lucian's savage lampooning of the Christian-turned-Cynic Peregrinus, who had immolated himself to make a philosophical statement, we can imagine the straightforward story of a hero that Lucian has satirized. Peregrinus has a period of ministry, upbraiding of leaders, and after he kills himself, is supposedly resurrected to provide cures to his followers. At one point Lucian even allows himself to speak more directly in the voice of the dead philosopher, who claims that his actions 'benefit humankind by showing people the way in which one ought to despise death' (*Passing of Peregrinus* 33).

There is also a relationship between the *narrative* of the death or expulsion of the hero and the *sacrifice* or expulsion of an animal. The death of an animal or the scapegoating of a chosen person takes away the impurities of the city, and the conflicts and death of the hero are often described in this way. Thus there is a strong overlap of sacrifice in general and death of the hero. In the Greco-Roman world it is impossible to consider the death of the hero without seeing it as a sacrifice, nor the sacrifice of a person without the concept of hero.[12] And

---

11. On the cult of the infant Archemoros, who was killed by a snake, see Pache, *Baby and Child Heroes in Ancient Greece* (Urbana: University of Illinois Press, 2004).

12. It is crucial to note that although biblical scholars often distinguish an expelled scapegoat and a slain sacrificial victim, scholars of Greek religion are likely to see them as more closely related, *especially in narratives as opposed to ritual practice*. See also Parker, *Miasma*, pp. 258-59. It is deeply unfortunate that although René Girard's study of scapegoating has highlighted many important parts of the process of sacrifice, he retains a Christian triumphalism that renders some of his reflections suspect (*Things Hidden since the Foundation of the World* [Stanford: Stanford University Press, 1986]; *The Scapegoat* [Baltimore: The Johns Hopkins University Press, 1986], and *Violence and the Sacred* [Baltimore: The Johns Hopkins University Press, 1977]). He sees Christianity as unique and superior to other ancient patterns of sacrifice because it takes the point of view of the victim. However, this is a misreading of the sources. Walter Burkert, for instance (*Structure and History in Greek Myth and Ritual* [Berkeley: University of California Press, 1979], pp. 64, 70), notes that our data comes more from narratives in Greece and rituals in Rome. The narratives emphasize the victim's point of view, the rituals the community's. The gospels are no more oriented toward the victim's point of view than is the *Life of Aesop*. See also Wills, *Quest*, pp. 229-30.

while many scholars emphasize that the actual slaying of the sacrificial animal is not the most important part of the sacrificial ritual, it is interesting that in the *narrative* of the hero it clearly is. Although the slaying of a sacrificial animal is not depicted in Greek art, the death of the hero is.[13]

The classicist Gregory Nagy in the *Best of the Achaeans* describes the pattern of narrative and cult that is characteristic of the Greek heroes. The heroes are benefactors of humanity, but also head-strong and antisocial. The hero stands outside of his own people, cannot integrate, and is often even rejected and killed by his own people. In addition, the heroes are often abandoned or even killed by their patron-deity. There is hero/people antagonism, but also hero/god antagonism. Yet the conflict between the hero and his own people on one hand and the hero and his patron-deity on the other is ultimately resolved in the *cult* of the dead hero. As Nagy says, there is 'antagonism in myth, symbiosis in cult'. In death the hero ultimately *resolves* the conflict with his god and people. As Nagy puts it in regard to the hero Aesop:

> By losing his identification with a person or group and by identifying himself with a god who takes his life in the process, the hero effects a purification by transferring impurity... In such a hero cult, god and hero are...institutionalized as the respectively dominant and recessive members of an eternal relationship... [We] see from the *Life of Aesop* tradition that the poet[-hero's] death results in purification. The immediate result from the death itself is impurity [for the city], but the ultimate result is eternal purification by way of propitiating the hero in cult—as ordained by [the god] himself. Moreover, the mode of Aesop's death is itself a purification, in that he dies like a *pharmakos* [φαρμακός] 'scapegoat'.[14]

No one telling of a hero's story would contain all of the elements. Here, for instance, we focus more on the end of a hero's life than the beginning. The elements of the Greek and Roman hero paradigm can be summarized in this way:

---

13. Jean-Pierre Vernant, *Mortals and Immortals: Collected Essays* (Princeton, NJ: Princeton University Press, 1991), pp. 294-95. The fact that the sacrificial knife is concealed and the process of slaying is not depicted in art has led some to argue that the violent act of slaying is *not* central. However, these mystifying aspects, plus the woman's yodel-cry (ὀλολυγή) at the moment of slaying would seem to argue that the slaying *is* crucial. To be sure, various aspects of sacrifice can be highlighted: the fact that the animal is domesticated and not wild (Jonathan Z. Smith, 'The Domestication of Sacrifice', in *Relating Religion: Essays in the Study of Religion* [Chicago and London: University of Chicago Press, 2004], pp. 145-51), the animal's supposed assent to being offered up, the act of slaying, the distribution of meat, the burning of the animal ('a sweet smell in the nostrils of God'; see Christian Eberhart, *Studien zur Bedeutung der Opfer im Alten Testament: Die Signifikanz von Blut- und Verbrennungsriten im kultischen Rahmen* [Neukirchen–Vluyn: Neukirchener Verlag, 2002]). Sacrifice offers up an interrelated collection of symbols, any of which can be highlighted, but I doubt that any of them are ever effectively repressed, despite the best efforts of native informants.

14. Nagy, *Best of the Achaeans*, pp. 307-308; see also Parker, *Miasma*, pp. 320-21.

1. The hero is a revered figure who has generally earned the status of hero by some accomplishment.
2. The hero usually has a troubled, wrongful, or conflicted death that elevates the hero to immortality as compensation for sufferings.
3. The hero often dies for others.
4. The hero is venerated in cult by an identifiable group of people.
5. There is a parallelism between the narrative of the hero's life and death and actions in the cult.
6. The death of the hero is sometimes likened to the sacrifice of an animal.
7. The hero's death was often viewed as a sacrifice for the expiation of the sin incurred by the hero's people in executing him.
8. Hero/god antagonism is resolved through cult.
9. Hero/people antagonism is resolved through cult.
10. After death, the hero provides continuing benefits for the living.

Aside from this common pattern of conflict and resolution there are also various options for the Greek hero narrative. The hero as sacrificial victim is innocent—or guilty. The sacrificial victim is slain—or expelled. The hero is noble, the 'best of the Achaeans'—or despised. The victim is spotless—or grotesque. The hero has performed great deeds—or is an infant. The hero is beloved by God—or hunted down. But behind the variations is a drama of tension and resolution in the cult of heroes which can incorporate these contradictions.

3. *The Gospel of Jesus and the Life of Aesop*

We can imagine that in the larger Roman world Jesus could easily have been likened to such a hero, as Gregory Riley also suggested in 1997.[15] Justin Martyr even played up the parallels between Jesus and three heroes, Herakles, Perseus, and Asklepios. I will turn now to a specific example of a hero text, the *Life of Aesop*, because it is roughly contemporary with the gospels, and very similar in length and structure.[16] The gospels and the *Life of Aesop* belong to the same genre, a form of biography which is a cult narrative of the dead hero. Aesop is

---

15. Riley, *One Jesus, Many Christs: How Jesus Inspired Not One True Christianity, But Many: The Truth about Christian Origins* (San Francisco: HarperSanFrancisco, 1997).

16. On *Life of Aesop* see esp. Nagy, *Best of the Achaeans*, and *Pindar's Homer;* John Winkler, *Auctor and Actor: A Narratological Reading of Apuleius' Golden Ass* (Berkeley: University of California Press, 1985), pp. 276-91; Compton, 'Trial of the Satirist;' and Niklas Holzberg (ed.), *Der Äsop-Roman: Motivgeschichte und Erzählstruktur* (Tübingen: Gunter Narr, 1992). Translations of this text are available as an appendix to Wills, *Quest*, and in Lloyd Daly, *Aesop Without Morals* (New York: T. Yoseloff, 1961); selections in William Hansen, *Anthology of Ancient Greek Popular Literature* (Bloomington: Indiana University Press, 1998); and selections also in Wills, 'The Aesop Tradition', in Amy-Jill Levine, John Dominic Crossan and Dale Allison (eds.), *The Historical Jesus in Context* (Princeton Readings in Religions; Princeton, NJ: Princeton University Press, 2006), pp. 222-37.

one of the seven sages of Greek tradition, but with a difference. He begins life as a despised and ugly slave who cannot speak. But while sleeping in a peaceful grove, he is granted the power of speech by Isis and the Muses. This power he uses to the utmost—he never stops talking, but skewers the pretensions of his master, a famous philosopher, the master's wife, and his master's fellow philosophers, using his characteristic animal fables. Thus Aesop's experience with Isis inaugurates a period of a ministry of teaching. A similar inauguration by the Muses is found in Hesiod, *Theogony*, and in the *Life of Archilochus*, and this inauguration is parallel in literary position and function to Jesus' baptism in the gospels.

Just as Jesus is depicted as using characteristic forms for teaching, the parable and the pronouncement story, Aesop uses his characteristic animal fables. Aesop's message has been likened by scholars to Cynicism played out in narrative form: social distinctions are superficial, and true wisdom and boldness of speech are there for anyone with the proper philosophical courage, even a slave. The satirical and even scatological humor of *Life of Aesop* is what Annabel Patterson calls 'a test of civilized thought'.[17] Other scholars also defend the ribald style of this text. In addition, Aesop is a benefactor: 'My worthless body', he says, 'is an instrument by which I utter wise sayings to benefit the lives of mortals'. (Compare the central line of Peregrinus above: 'My actions benefit humankind by showing people the way in which one ought to despise death'.) Through his cleverness he helps both his master and the citizens of the island of Samos and gains his own freedom. But once he attains his freedom, he runs into trouble. The humorous and satirical episodes of the first half give way to the more serious tone of the second. Upon returning to Delphi, city of his patron-god Apollo, Aesop insults the citizens with his sharp-tongued fables, and antagonizes his patron-god Apollo as well. Aesop is then abandoned by Apollo in his hour of need. It is this hero/god antagonism that combines with the hero/people antagonism to bring about his death. After Aesop is forsaken by Apollo, the leading citizens conspire against him, condemn him to death on a trumped-up charge of blasphemy and execute him. When a plague strikes the city, the citizens consult an oracle of Zeus and learn that they must expiate the sin of killing Aesop by establishing a cult in his honor and sacrificing to him as a hero.[18]

---

17. Patterson, *Fables of Power: Aesopian Writing and Political History* (Durham/London: Duke University Press, 1991), pp. 15-16. Defenders of the literary style of *Aesop*: Winkler, *Actor & Auctor*, pp. 279–91; Holzberg, 'Der Äsop-Roman', in Holzberg (ed.), *Der Äsop-Roman*, pp. 41–42, 71–75. See also Mikhail Bakhtin, *Rabelais and his World* (Cambridge: MIT Press, 1968), p. 19, on the scatological and the carnivalesque.

18. Interestingly, there is an alternative version of the narrative of Aesop's end that differs in the particulars, but that also revolves around Aesop's withering criticism of his fellow-citizens, their execution of him, and the need for them to expiate the sin through cult; see Nagy, *Best of the Achaeans*, pp. 284-85. The alternative ending involves a critique of sacrificial practices that is structurally similar to Mark's temple protest.

The parallels to the gospels are obvious, and can be summarized thus:

1. Aesop has a lowly beginning, but has an experience of a deity that initiates him into a special status, an experience similar in placement and function to Jesus' baptism.
2. The wise hero begins a period of ministry using a distinctive kind of discourse, animal fables, similar in function to Jesus' parables and pronouncement stories.
3. Through this ministry Aesop brings a message rejecting established social convention and offering penetrating insights.
4. Aesop returns to the city that is the center of his god's worship (Delphi) and enrages the citizens by his criticism.
5. Aesop is executed on trumped-up charges, including blasphemy, by the leading citizens of the city.
6. Apollo punishes the people, vindicates the hero and establishes a cult to him in the city that condemned him.

Note especially that in *Aesop*, Mark and John, there is a distinctive discourse of the protagonist that provokes a conspiracy against him—fable in the case of Aesop, parable in Mark 12, and Johannine discourse in John 8. Further, there is a similar role for blasphemy as a *literary* motif in all three texts. In *Aesop* blasphemy appears as one of the trumped-up charges. In Mark Jesus is interrogated by the high priest and the Sanhedrin, and his implication that he himself is the Son of Humanity elicits the condemnation of death for blasphemy. In the Gospel of John the Jews also introduce the charge of blasphemy against Jesus, but because it is in a different location in the narrative (Jn 10.33), and because it is expressed in a slightly different way (Jesus 'makes himself God'), it is often considered irrelevant for the question of blasphemy in Mark. However, its dramatic function in John is quite similar both to Mark and to *Life of Aesop*, as it also is in the tradition concerning Archilochus.[19] Blasphemy divides the parties and creates the irony that the wise and righteous man who has some close relationship with God is charged with blasphemy by the leaders through treachery. Those who sin against a fellow human being condemn him of sinning against God. We may perceive a rough equivalence also in the charge of impiety in Plato's story of Socrates. That story is filled with the same irony as the gospels' passion story: how could the wisest and most righteous person who ever lived be condemned to death by his own people on the charge of blasphemy/impiety?

One theme of this article is that the *differences* between the Jesus cult and Greek and Roman hero cult exist more in the minds of New Testament scholars than in the minds of classicists. The objections to the comparison often arise from overly restrictive notions of the nature of hero cult in the Greek and Roman

---

19. Aristotle, *Rhetoric* 2.23.11 1398b; see Collins, 'Finding Meaning', p. 190.

context. Hans Dieter Betz and Helmut Koester, for instance, both insist that the similarity between heroes and Jesus breaks down because the hero paradigm requires a *local* cult.[20] However, as noted here there are exceptions—Asklepios and Pyrrhos come to mind—and we should also consider the literary *topos* as something that can escape the bounds of a particular location. In the Greek and Roman traditions of the hero, scholars have pointed out an important distinction between what happens in text and what is enacted in cult.[21] The textual tradition of the followers of Jesus is more similar to the textual tradition of heroes in Greek religion than it is to the enacted cults. Jonathan Z. Smith also describes the transition in this period from a locative notion of cult to the diasporic notion of a wandering sage.[22] The rise in this period of diasporic savior gods and goddesses (Yahweh, Isis, Wisdom, Asklepios) may have opened up the local nature of the hero as well. (More on this below.) However, having said that, I do not believe the hero paradigm was the only early Christology, nor necessarily the primal one. A variety of paradigms co-existed in the first decades of the movement that may have mutually influenced each other: Savior, Lord of Heaven, Prophet, Living Sage, Son of Humanity, Wisdom, and so on. Despite my insistence that the Greek and Roman hero paradigm is important for understanding Jesus, I do not believe that the Jesus cult was *identical* to its counterparts in Greek and Roman tradition. The following section will begin to supply other reasons for this conclusion.

4. *A Jewish Hero Tradition*

Having made this comparison to Greek and Roman heroes, another comparison should also be added: Jewish heroes. A general misconception is that any similarities between Jesus and the hero paradigm result from a direct infusion of Greek or Roman influences into early Christianity, the Tiber flowing into the Orontes. The answer is more complicated and much more interesting than that, but the evidence is often shockingly ignored. Contrary to the common assumption that in Judaism such notions as special reverence for the dead would be anathema, we find that there is evidence of this *in every period of ancient Judaism*.

I provide some relevant examples here in table 6:

---

20. Betz, 'Hero Worship and Christian Beliefs: Observations from the History of Religion on Philostratus's *Heroikos*', in Aitken and Maclean (eds.), *Philostratus's Heroikos*, pp. 25–47; Koester, 'On Heroes, Tombs, and Early Christianity: An Epilogue', in Ellen Aitken and Jennifer Maclean (eds.), *Flavius Philostratus: Heroikos* (Atlanta: SBL, 2001), pp. 257-64.

21. Burkert, *Structure and History*, pp. 64, 70.

22. *Map Is Not Territory: Studies in the History of Religions* (Leiden: E.J. Brill, 1978), pp. xiii–xiv, 98-102; see his recent nuancing of this theory in 'Here, There, and Anywhere', in Smith, *Relating Religion: Essays in the Study of Religion* (Chicago: University of Chicago Press, 2004), pp. 323-39.

	Revered	Death emphasized	Died for others	Accomplishments	Venerated in cult	Hero/god antagonism	Hero/people antagonism	Sacrifice as expiation	Continuing benefits
Texts or figures:									
Grave cult	x	x			x				?
Cave of Machpelah	x	x		x	x				x
Teraphim of Rachel	x	x		?	?				?
Near-sacrifice of Isaac	x	(x)			x				x
Jacob	x	x		x	?	x[23]	x		x
Moses	x	x		x	x	x[24]			x
Marzeach	x	x			x				?
Judges' graves	x	x		x	?		?		x
Jephthah's daughter	x	x	x	x	x				x
Samuel	x	x		x	?		x	?	x
Samson	x	x		x	x[25]		?		?
Sons of Saul (2 Sam. 21)		x	x	x	?		x	x	x
Elijah/Elisha	x	x		x	?		x		?
4th Servant Song	x	x	x	x	?			x	
Grave cult (Tob. 4.17)	x	x		x	x				x
Ben Sira: bones of judges	x	x		x	?				x
Maskilim in Daniel	x	x		x	?		?		
Prayer Azariah[26]	x	x		x	x		?		
Jeremiah (2 Macc.)	x			x			?	?	x
Onias III (2 Macc.)	x	x		x	?		x	?	x
Judith	x			x	x		?		x
Solomon (healing)[27]	x	x		x	?		x	x	x
4 Macc.	x	x		x	x		x		x
Wisd. 2–5	x	x		x					
Philo, *Life of Moses*	x	x		x	?				?
Honi the Circlemaker	x	x		x	?		x	?	?
Lives of Prophets	x	x		x	?		x		x

Table 6.1: *Elements of the cult of dead heroes in ancient Judaism*

23. See Gen. 32.22-30.
24. See Exod. 4.24-26.
25. See Judg. 16.20.
26. Even though God saves Azariah and his companions from the flames, Azariah speaks in vss 16–17 as though he may become a sacrifice; see Jan N. Bremmer, 'The Atonement in the Interaction of Greeks, Jews, and Christians', in Jan N. Bremmer and Florentino García Martínez (eds.), *Sacred History and Sacred Texts: A Symposium in Honor of A.S. van der Woude* (Kampen, Netherlands: Pharos, 1992), p. 79.
27. Dennis E. Duling, 'Solomon, Exorcism, and the Son of David', *HTR* 68 (1975), pp.

Some of these I will comment on briefly for our discussion, in approximately chronological order:

- In addition to early grave offerings to tribal ancestors and the מרזח festival for the residents of Sheol,[28] we find a strong emphasis on the Cave of Machpelah where the bones of the patriarchs are buried; compare also the תרפים—ancestor deities?—and the tomb of Rachel (Gen. 31.19; 35.4, 20). This may be understood as the *general* cult of ancestors rather than a cult of a *specific* hero, but it is often suggested that hero cult in Greece arose out of ancestor cult. We also do not know precisely what boons, fertility and healing powers were associated with these practices, although we might speculate.
- Veneration of the patriarchs and Moses is often mentioned, and in particular at Exodus 4 we note a vestigial reference to god/hero antagonism when God tries to kill Moses; Moses is saved from God by the blood of his foreskin.
- The burial places of the judges in the Book of Judges are often noted—for tomb cult?—and a better translation of שופטים (judges) is 'heroes'.[29]
- Samson dies when he is abandoned by God (Judg. 16.20). In addition, his death is perhaps like a sacrifice for others.
- The sacrifice of Jephthah's daughter, offered up like a sacrificial animal, is ritually re-enacted annually by young women, likely as a heroine cult for fertility. There is an almost exact Greek parallel at Pausanias 9.17.1.
- Samuel is venerated by the prophetic guilds: he has a miraculous birth and childhood, intervenes with God for his people, and speaks from the grave to Saul.[30]
- The prophetic guilds also honored Elijah and Elisha as a venerated pair. Elijah achieves a kind of special immortality when he ascends to

---

235-52; 'The Eleazar Miracle and Solomon's Magical Wisdom in Flavius Josephus's *Antiquities* 8.42–49', *HTR* 78 (1985), pp. 1-25.

28. Jeremiah 16.5-9, condemned at Amos 6.7; Lev. 19.28, 21.1-11. See the fuller discussion at Wills, *Quest*, pp. 38-43. On these issues in general, see Mark Smith and Elizabeth Bloch-Smith, 'Death and Afterlife in Ugarit and Israel', *JAOS* 108 (1988), pp. 277-84; Saul Olyan, *Asherah and the Cult of Yahweh in Israel* (Atlanta: Scholars Press, 1988); Theodore Lewis, *Cults of the Dead in Ancient Israel and Ugarit* (Atlanta: Scholars Press, 1989); Susan Ackerman, *Under Every Green Tree: Popular Religion in Sixth-Century Judah* (Atlanta: Scholars Press, 1992); and Alan Cooper and Bernard Goldstein, 'Cult of the Dead and Entry into the Land', *BibInt* 1 (1993), pp. 285-303.

29. See Gregory Mobley, *The Empty Men: The Heroic Tradition of Ancient Israel* (New York: Doubleday, 2005).

30. Joseph Blenkinsopp, *A History of Prophecy in Israel* (Philadelphia: Westminster Press, 1983), pp. 71-72.

God in a chariot of fire—like Herakles or Romulus—and is expected to return before the end. But *just as important, and often ignored*, Elisha's bones bring a dead man back to life on contact. It is the healing power of Elisha's bones that is the hallmark of a revered, dead hero—or a saint, which is so similar.[31]

- The fourth Servant Song of Isaiah 52–53 evokes the death of the unnamed hero as a sacrificial animal that expiates sins.
- Ben Sira (46.11-12, 49.10; cf. 48.11) praises the bones of the judges and the twelve prophets, which will bring new life where they lie.
- The משכלים (knowledgeable ones) in Daniel 11–12 *may* die for others, but the near-death of Daniel's three friends is definitely compared to a sacrifice in the Prayer of Azariah.
- Judith emerges from a withdrawn life to save her people by slaying Holofernes. She then withdraws again, is buried in her dead husband's tomb, and is proclaimed a benefactor who protected Israel *even after her death*. Although there is no obvious heroine/people antagonism, she does upbraid her people, and she is incapable of integrating into the normal life of her people, a common motif in heroic traditions. The story was probably understood as a fictitious and romanticized notion of her benefaction for others, but it still demonstrates the power of this motif.
- In 2 Maccabees the high priest Onias III is singled out as the 'benefactor of Jerusalem' (2 Macc. 4.2) but is treacherously killed. After his conflicted and unjust death, he appears in a dream-vision along with Jeremiah to inspire the Maccabees to defend their city and temple (15.12–16).
- In 2 Maccabees 6–7 the mother and seven sons die to expiate their sins and the sins of Israel, but it is stated only in passing. Fourth Maccabees, however, enlarges on the expiatory notion with the death of Eleazar; here he prays to God as he is about to die, 'Render my blood an expiation (καθάρσιον) for your people, and receive my life as a ransom (ἀντίψυχον) for theirs' (6.29). The Jewish martyrs are said to 'become as though a ransom (ἀντίψυχον) for the sins of the people. Through the blood of these pious ones and the expiation (ἱλαστήριον) of their death, divine Providence saved Israel' (17.21–22).[32]
- Honi the Circlemaker is often compared to Jesus because of his

---

31. Burkert, *Greek Religion* (Cambridge: Harvard University Press, 1985), p. 207; on the bones of the heroes, see Erwin Rohde, *Psyche: The Cult of Souls and Belief in Immortality Among the Greeks* (London: Kegan Paul, Trench, Trübner; New York: Harcourt Brace, 1925), p. 122.

32. In agreement, see Bremmer, 'Atonement', pp. 75-93. Sammy K. Williams, *Jesus' Death as Saving Event: The Background and Origin of a Concept* (Missoula, MT: Scholars Press, 1975), pp. 178-79 makes too fine a distinction between an expiatory death and a temporary sacrificial moment in appealing to God.

miracles, but it is almost universally ignored that there is a further parallel in Josephus, *Antiquities* 14.2.1-2, 22-28, where Honi is killed by one party in a Jerusalem dispute. God punishes the perpetrators by sending a year-long drought.
- The theme of prophets being persecuted and killed increases in the Hellenistic period, and grave sites of the prophets—along with their post-death benefits for the people—are noted carefully in *Lives of the Prophets*.[33]
- In the period after the gospels pilgrimages to the graves of rabbis furnished a segue to the pilgrimages to the graves of Christian saints.

To continue the list forward would take us beyond the period under discussion, but the conclusions should be obvious. To be sure, none of these examples of Jewish revered dead contains *every* element of the Greek hero model, but all of the elements are found *somewhere* among these examples, including motifs, such as god/hero antagonism and the hero 'dying for others', that are supposed to be non-existent in Israelite and Jewish tradition. In addition, some of the motifs may be literary only, but the persistence of the motifs is striking. These examples are ignored regarding the death of Jesus. Martin Hengel can even assert that 'there are no references to veneration or cultic and magical contact with the dead in the *official* religion of Ancient Israel'.[34] If Jesus were part of the *official* religion of Israel this statement might have some relevance, but it is the marginal practices that would be more applicable to Jesus. Further, most of these examples are found in the Bible, part of the official religion of Israel.

5. *Ambiguities in the Early Jesus Tradition*

One might object that the similarity of all this to Mark is still vague; Mark does not emphasize the sacrificial and expiatory death of the hero. David Seeley even argues that Mark and Paul choose to emphasize a different paradigm, that of the 'noble death' of the philosopher.[35] Indeed, Mark may be interested, even more

---

33. Although David Satran has argued that the text as a whole is late (*Biblical Prophets in Byzantine Palestine: Reassessing the Lives of the Prophets* [Leiden: E.J. Brill, 1995]), this is based on passages that appear to be interpolated. It is more likely a text from about the turn of the Common Era into which some later references are inserted; so Anna Maria Schwemer, *Studien zu den frühjüdischen Prophetenlegenden* Vitae Prophetarum (2 vols.; Tübingen: Mohr [Paul Siebeck], 1995), I, pp. 65-71.

34. Hengel, 'The Expiatory Sacrifice of Christ', *Bulletin of the John Rylands University Library of Manchester* 62 (1980), p. 455.

35. Seeley, *The Noble Death: Graeco-Roman Martyrology and Paul's Concept of Salvation* (Sheffield: Sheffield Academic Press, 1990). See also Collins, 'From Noble Death to Crucified Messiah', *NTS* 40 (1994), pp. 481-503.

interested in the noble death paradigm, but the two paradigms of the 'noble death of the philosopher' and the 'sacrificial death of the hero' are not mutually exclusive or even competing paradigms. I would note that Fourth Maccabees clearly and explicitly affirms both a sacrificial model and a noble death model. But the gospel tradition also contained references to the sacrificial and expiatory death of the hero, whether they are vestigial—and therefore from an *earlier* moment—or more integral.[36] Further, Nagy points out a similar vagueness in regard to the Homeric epics. Although they sing the stories of the heroes, they contain very few references to the cult of heroes. And yet at key points they imply a connection between the actions that are narrated and the sacrificial cult of heroes with which the audience would have been familiar. Patroklos is killed in a way that calls to mind the sacrifice of a bull, and at his funeral there are wine libations and honey and oil, used also in the cult of the heroes.[37]

Another difficulty is that the eucharist is not a meat sacrifice. Does the reenactment of a once-for-all sacrifice that had occurred in the past qualify as a *hero-like* observance? I think the answer is yes. There are various ways of 'protecting' the eucharist from sacrificial implications. While Catholic and Orthodox churches turned to a more sacrificial understanding of the eucharist, Protestants rejected both the continuing sacrificial understanding and the emphasis on the priest's role in performing the ritual.[38] Nils Dahl argued that in Christian practice the eucharist was a 'remembrance' (ἀνάμνησις) of sacrifice only, not a repeated sacrificial ritual.[39] But in the cult of Adonis rites are also performed 'in remembrance of his suffering' (μνήμην τοῦ πάθεος; Lucian, *Syrian Goddess* 6). 'Remembrance' of sacrifice is still a sacrificial motif. On another front, Bruce Chilton and Bernhard Lang intriguingly suggest that in the words of institution Jesus is not offering *his* body and blood but a substitute for the temple offering—'This bread is my (substitute for a sacrificial) body', 'This wine is my (substitute for sacrificial) blood'.[40] But even if this is true for the

---

36. Whether the notion of Jesus' death as a sacrifice that atones for sins is early (Hengel, *The Atonement: The Origins of the Doctrine in the New Testament* [Philadelphia: Fortress, 1981]) or late (Joel B. Green, *The Death of Jesus: Tradition and Interpretation in the Passion Narrative* [Tübingen: Mohr (Siebeck), 1988]) is of some interest, but is a secondary question to whether it is tangibly present in Mark. I would argue that it is present in Mark and at least pre-Markan.

37. Nagy, *Best of the Achaeans*, pp. 116, 134; 'Introduction', *The Iliad* (Everyman Library; London: Random Century, 1992), p. vii. The *Iliad* references are 16.791-92; 18.28-31, 175-77; 23.218-21, 170; cf. *Odyssey* 3.447-55.

38. Joseph Henninger, 'Sacrifice', in Mircea Eliade (ed.), *Encyclopedia of Religion* (16 vols.; New York: MacMillan, 1987), XVI, pp. 555-56.

39. Dahl, 'Memorial and Commemoration in Early Christianity', in Dahl, *Jesus in the Memory of the Early Church* (Minneapolis: Augsburg, 1976), pp. 11-29.

40. Chilton, *A Feast of Meanings: Eucharistic Theologies from Jesus through Johannine Circles* (Leiden: E.J. Brill, 1994); and Lang, 'The Roots of Eucharist in Jesus' Practice', *SBLSP* 1992, pp. 467-72.

historical Jesus—I do not address that question—it seems very unlikely for the gospel tradition, and this is certainly at odds with almost all of the New Testament references to Jesus and blood. I am more convinced by those who argue that the eucharist language inaugurates powerful metaphors: the death of Jesus gives rise to a meal that is *like* temple sacrifice, not a substitute but a dialogue between the sign and the signified.[41] At the same time, it is also possible that the remembrance aspect creates in the meal a resonance with the communal meals at the sites of heroes' tombs rather than the wholly burnt animal sacrifices offered to heroes.[42]

Having stated my larger thesis about the heroic paradigm in Mark, John, and Matthew (I will omit Luke), I do want to recognize some problem passages in the gospels, which may reflect a variety of views. I turn first to Mk 10.45, 'For indeed the Son of Humanity did not come to be served, but to serve, and to give his life as a ransom (λύτρον) for many'. The passage expresses a similar theme and occupies a similar place in Mark as John 11.49-50 occupies for that gospel:[43]

Mark 10.45	*John 11.49–50*
For indeed the Son of Humanity did not come to be served, but to serve, and to give his life as a ransom (λύτρον) for many.	Caiaphas said to them, 'You know nothing, nor do you realize that it is far better for you if one man dies for the people, so that the whole nation not be destroyed'.

'Ransom' in Mark is sometimes interpreted metaphorically as a sacrifice for sins, but I would grant that it may also be understood not as a sacrificial exchange with God but as a ransom paid to the powers, a buy-back.[44] On the literal level it does refer to a buy-back, but it is quite possible that the non-sacrificial ransom (λύτρον) was a metaphor for the resolution of conflict in sacrifice. The metaphorical use of ransom as a sacrifice for sin was known in this period. We saw above in 4 Macc. 6.29, 17.21-22 that a different word for ransom (ἀντίψυχος), is twice paired with a word for sacrifice: 'Render my blood an expiation (καθάρσιον) for your people, and receive my life as

---

41. Klawans, 'Interpreting the Last Supper: Sacrifice, Spiritualization, and Anti-Sacrifice', *NTS* 48 (2002), pp. 1-17.

42. Maclean, 'Jesus as Cult Hero'.

43. In Wills, *Quest*, I argued that John was composed independently of Mark, and therefore certain parallel motifs that relate to the death of Jesus as hero in these texts were not invented by Mark, and must reflect an earlier Christian tradition. Most of what I present here will not depend on this argument. It is not important for my main arguments whether John was independent of Mark or not. Parallels between Mark and John may still be significant, however, even if John was directly or indirectly familiar with Mark's gospel.

44. Compare *kipper* in Exod. 30.12, Lev. 17.11, and Isa. 43.3. Note, however, that the buy-back in these texts is paid to God, not the powers. It is an exchange with God.

a ransom (ἀντίψυχον) for theirs'. The Jewish martyrs 'become as though a ransom (ἀντίψυχον) for the sins of the people. Through the blood of these pious ones and the expiation (ἱλαστήριον) of their death, divine Providence saved Israel'. In addition, we note:

Titus 2.14
He gave himself for us that he might redeem (λυτρώσηται) us from all iniquity.

1 Peter 1.18-19
You know that you were ransomed (ἐλυτρώθητε) from the futile ways inherited from your ancestors…with the precious blood of Christ.

Diognetus 9.2
When our iniquity was filled up, …God gave his own son as a ransom (λύτρον) for us.

Even if ransom (λύτρον) in Mark 10 is not a sacrifice *for sin*, is it still an exchange or a reconciliation *with God*? Sharyn Dowd and Elizabeth Struthers Malbon argued that it is not; in Mark's view, Jesus is crucified by Roman and Jewish leaders, not by God.[45] Although I agree with much of the feminist critique of expiatory sacrifice, I am not convinced that it is absent from many of the texts of early Christianity. Still, Mark remains the most interesting of the uncertain cases. The disagreement between Dowd and Malbon on one hand and

---

45. Dowd and Malbon, 'Hearing Mark's Story of Jesus' Death: Overlapping Contexts', presentation at the Annual Meeting of the Society of Biblical Literature, San Antonio, Texas, November 16, 2004; see also Elisabeth Schüssler Fiorenza, *Jesus: Miriam's Child, Sophia's Prophet: Critical Issues in Feminist Christology* (New York: Continuum, 1994), p. 116. In addition, on the feminist critique of Christian sacrificial theology, see Rita Nakashima Brock, *Journeys by Heart: A Christology of Erotic Power* (New York: Crossroad, 1988), pp. 95, 98-99; and for a critique of the related doctrine of suffering, see Rosemary Radford Ruether, *To Change the World: Christology and Cultural Criticism* (New York: Crossroad, 1981), pp. 27-28. In feminist criticism, the sacrificial death of Jesus is a problem, first, of 'redemptive violence': Why should God *need* the violent death of his son? It is also a problem of a cure requiring a disease. If Jesus expiates the sin of the people, then sin has to be magnified. It becomes an overwhelming condition that requires an institutional dispensation in order to be liberated from it.

The modern critique should be seen also in the context of the ancient critique of sacrifice which was a strong counter-current from early on; see Burkert, *Homo Necans: The Anthropology of Ancient Greek Sacrificial Ritual and Myth* (trans. Peter Bing; Berkeley: University of California Press, 1983), pp. 7-8; Stanley K. Stowers, 'Greeks Who Sacrifice, and Those Who Do Not: Toward an Anthropology of Greek Religion', in L. Michael White and O. Larry Yarbrough (eds.), *The Social World of the First Christians: Essays in Honor of Wayne A. Meeks* (Minneapolis: Fortress Press, 1995), pp. 293-333. But Burkert, *Homo Necans*, p. 82, also assumes an expiatory and sacrificial aspect in the death of Jesus and the eucharist.

Collins on the other can be summed up by their answers to two questions. Is the ransom an exchange with the powers—Dowd and Malbon—or an exchange with God—Collins? Does the ransom free many from oppression—Dowd and Malbon—or sin—Collins? Although all three scholars emphasize the apocalyptic worldview of Mark (as I do), how it relates to *this* question is controverted.

A digression is necessary to contextualize this issue. The discussion of ancient sacrifice has taken different directions in different spheres of discourse. In Jewish and Christian tradition there has occurred a parting of the ways that has defined the function of sacrifice in two mutually exclusive directions. Much of Christian theology has—especially from the eleventh century on—emphasized the expiation of sin in the sacrifice of Jesus. Jewish tradition, on the other hand, has emphasized that Jewish temple sacrifice was not to expiate sins but to remove impurity from the temple precincts—so Jacob Milgrom, David Wright and Jonathan Klawans.[46] On the other hand, modern scholars of Greek and Roman sacrifice emphasize the *range* of negatives that sacrifice resolves, which are often interchangeable: sin, disorder, impurity, estrangement, or abandonment. Nagy, H.S. Versnel, Walter Burkert, Robert Parker, Nancy Jay and others would impose little distinction among these.[47] Versnel, for instance, has amassed a number of Greek and Roman literary parallels that would suggest that 'a ransom for many' is a sacrifice of self for others that also satisfies a god. 'Why do gods demand that?' asks Versnel. His answer: 'That's just the way gods are'.[48] Mark may not have been as concerned with the distinction among the kinds of estrangement as we are.

A similar question arises with the Lord's Supper. In Matthew we find: 'This is my blood of the covenant which is poured out for many *for the forgiveness of sins*'. In Mark simply: 'This is my blood of the covenant which is poured out for many'. Collins points out the association in Mark with the sacrifice of oxen to ratify the covenant in Exodus 24, but forgiveness of sins is missing in Mark, so how exactly is it understood? Is it an expiatory sacrifice, a substitu-

---

46. Milgrom, *Leviticus 1–16* (New York: Doubleday, 1991), pp. 42-51; Wright, 'Holiness in Leviticus and Beyond: Defining Perspectives', *Int* 53 (1999), pp. 351-64; Klawans, *Impurity and Sin in Ancient Judaism* (New York: Oxford University Press, 2000).

47. Versnel, 'Self-Sacrifice, Compensation and the Anonymous Gods', in Jean Rudhardt and Olivier Reverdin (eds.), *Le sacrifice dans l'antiquité: huit exposés suivis de discussions* (Geneva: Vandoeuvres, 1980), pp. 135-90; Versnel, 'Quid Athenis et Hierosolymis? Bemerkungen über die Herkunft von Aspekten des 'Effective Death'', in J.W. van Henten (ed.), *Die Entstehung der jüdischen Martyrologie* (Leiden: E.J. Brill, 1989), pp. 162-96; Burkert, *Homo Necans*, pp. 7-8, 82; Parker, *Miasma*, esp. pp. 10, 258-61; Jay, *Throughout your Generations Forever: Sacrifice, Religion, and Paternity* (Chicago and London: University of Chicago Press, 1992), p. 17; see also M.F.C. Bourdillon, 'Introduction', in Bourdillon and Meyer Fortes (eds.), *Sacrifice* (London: Academic Press, 1980), p. 23; Henninger, 'Sacrifice', pp. 549-50; E.E. Evans-Pritchard, *Nuer Religion* (Oxford: Clarendon Press, 1956), p. 281.

48. Versnel, 'Self-Sacrifice;' 'Quid Athenis'.

tionary sacrifice, or not a sacrifice at all? Dowd and Malbon note that blood and covenant only appear together in Exodus 24; blood is not a *constituent* of covenant. But the evidence is split: the covenant renewal at Joshua 24 lacks a sacrifice, while the one at Deuteronomy 27 includes one. The later covenant texts Ezra 9, Nehemiah 9, and Daniel 9 all lack sacrifice, but focus strongly on sin and confession. The New Testament texts surrounding Mark are also mixed: Matthew, John, Hebrews, and Revelation emphasize blood and expiation of sin, while Luke, Q, and the *Didache* eucharist do not. Paul is unclear. There are a few passages that emphasize blood and sin, but the blood and sin passages are generally downplayed by scholars such as Seeley because they are pre-Pauline.[49] However, for our discussion the fact that they are *pre*-Pauline renders them more informative for the breadth of the earliest known cult of Jesus.

If we move to the climax of Mark, the crucifixion with its myriad echoes of psalms of the righteous sufferer, we find also another connection to sacrifice: the scapegoat of the Yom Kippur ritual. In Leviticus 16 there are two goats, one of which is sacrificed and the other allowed to escape. (Note that in Leviticus the scapegoat actually escapes, while in *Mishnah Yoma* 6.6 it is thrown off a cliff.) Now, whereas B. Hudson McLean would see the two goats as distinct modes—sacrificial and apotropaic—with distinct origins,[50] the fact that they are joined in the Yom Kippur ritual indicates that they are 'twinned'. Their fates and functions are interrelated. Barabbas in Mark is allowed to escape, like the scapegoat, while Jesus is like the sacrificial goat of the Yom Kippur ritual.[51]

---

49. Rom. 3.25, 4.25, 5.9-10; 1 Cor. 5.7, 15.3; Gal. 1.4. Contrast with this the destruction of sin in Rom. 8.3. See also Stowers, *A Rereading of Romans* (New Haven and London: Yale University Press, 1994), pp. 206-13, for a negative appraisal of the influence of the sacrificial metaphor in Paul, but also Pamela Eisenbaum, 'A Remedy for Having Been Born of Woman: Jesus, the Gentiles, and Genealogy in Romans', *JBL* 123 (2004), pp. 671-702, for a strongly sacrificial reading of Paul. I am inclined to agree with Eisenbaum.

50. McLean, *The Cursed Christ: Mediterranean Expulsion Rituals and Pauline Soteriology* (Sheffield: Sheffield Academic Press, 1996), pp. 70, 75-81. Both McLean and Basil S. Davis (*Christ as Devotio: The Argument of Galatians 3:1-14* [Lanham, MD: University Press of America, 2003], pp. 82-104) have written very interesting books on aspects of sacrificial theology in the Greco-Roman world and early Christianity, but they both try to distinguish as irreconcilable different modes of sacrifice that are actually related. Certainly, differences between sacrifice and expulsion are often invoked by scholars—see Henninger, 'Sacrifice', p. 545—but *in the narrative of heroes,* as opposed to ritual practice, sacrifice and expulsion are related dynamics.

51. See Aitken, *Jesus' Death;* Koester, *Ancient Christian Gospels: Their History and Development* (Philadelphia: Trinity Press International, 1990), pp. 220-30; John Dominic Crossan, *The Cross That Spoke: The Origins of the Passion Narrative* (San Francisco: Harper & Row, 1988), pp. 117-20; *Who Killed Jesus? Exposing the Roots of Anti-Semitism in the Gospel Story of Jesus* (San Francisco: HarperSanFrancisco, 1995), pp. 12-26. The association of the Passion with the Yom Kippur is also reflected in *Barnabas* 5, 7 (cf. Justin, *Dialogue* 40). The scapegoat (φαρμακός) is also of course a very strong motif in Greek and Roman hero traditions, and a close parallel to Barabbas is found in the figure of the similar-sounding Carabas at Philo, *Flaccus*

The fact that Jesus is silent when interrogated by the high priest is often appropriately likened to the Suffering Servant, and the Suffering Servant in Isaiah is indeed likened to a sacrificial animal. In John the connection is made explicit by an *inclusio* at the beginning and end of the gospel. Jesus is the lamb of God who takes away the sin of the world (by being sacrificed), and is crucified precisely at the moment of the sacrifice of the Passover lambs.

Compared with Mark, Matthew increases the sacrificial language by including the controversial 'blood libel' passage: 'The people as a whole answered, "His blood be upon us and our children!"' (27.25), after which, it is immediately said that Barabbas, the scapegoat, is released. As horrifying as the effect of the blood libel has been *historically*, for Matthew the spilled blood may express a process of resolution within Israel. This possibility may seem shocking, but note that in *Gospel of Peter* the Jews and their leaders—but not the Romans—*repent* of their deed. Far from declaring a divorce between Jesus and Jews, the blood libel may have indicated in Matthew's mind a hero/people antagonism that is resolved in the death of the hero. The Jews *as a whole*, it is emphasized—not just the leaders—say, 'His blood be upon us'. At the Last Supper Jesus says, 'This is my blood'. The difference is slight. As T.B. Cargal has asked provocatively, 'What do Christians say but "His blood be upon us and upon our children"'?[52] The blood of the sacrifice in Matthew took away the sins of Jesus' followers and perpetrators alike, but only *after* the punishment of the destruction of the temple. This would be identical to the resolution at the end of *Life of Aesop*, and other texts as well.

This gives rise to a possible objection to my argument, or at least a continuing ambiguity. Heroes in Greece and Rome had cult sites associated with their bodily remains. But in the gospel tradition Jesus lacked a tomb cult of his remains—his body had been resurrected. However, as noted above, the 'absent body' is a strong motif in Greek and Roman hero traditions—witness Sophocles' *Oedipus at Colonus* where the missing body of Oedipus drives home his importance as a hero, or the 'secret cult site' motif of some heroes. In Lord Raglan's list of hero narratives, the body is missing or the burial place uncertain for eight of the nine Greek heroes analyzed.[53] What seems common to the variations is the emphasizing or problematizing of the site of the remains,

---

6.36-39. The Barabbas tradition thus resonates with both the scapegoat of Yom Kippur and the scapegoat of the Roman world.

52. T.B. Cargal, '"His blood be upon us and upon our children". A Matthean Double Entendre?', *NTS* 37 (1991), pp. 101-12. The quotation is a paraphrase of Cargal's overall point. Questions remain in Matthew as to what resolution would look like at the end of time, or how the 'nations' (28.19) are understood.

53. Raglan, 'The Hero: A Study in Tradition, Myth, and Drama, Part II', in Robert A. Segal (ed.), *In Quest of the Hero* (Princeton, NJ: Princeton University Press, 1990), pp. 89-175; Wills, *Quest*, pp. 48-49; Collins, *Beginning of the Gospel*, pp. 137, 141; Aune 'Problem of the Genre', pp. 47-48.

as Collins also notes. Corresponding to this, the classic hero paradigm involves a resolution of the hero with *his city*; the gospels are interpreted—by later tradition, at any rate—as narrating a break with the city. However, there are two responses to this. First, the role of followers of Jesus in Jerusalem, from James to Paul, indicates that there may well have been an identification of this group with Jerusalem that only changes with certain authors. Perhaps the early gospel tradition did see Jesus' death as a reconciliation with Israel, as I noted already in regard to Matthew. Some scholars have asserted that a tomb cult of Jesus existed in Jerusalem at the site of the empty tomb. It is difficult to rule out the possibility that at least one strand of the early cult of Jesus was localized at the empty tomb in Jerusalem and understood Israel as the 'many' who would be ransomed.[54] (Compare here also the focus on gathered Israel in Q, the *Didache* eucharist, and *Gospel of Peter*.) Recall that some resurrection appearances are located in Jerusalem, and it is Mark who may have moved the locus to Galilee. The Lord's Supper tradition may have originally been localized at the supposed site of resurrection in Galilee, as Mark suggests. Second, as I mentioned before, not all Greek heroes remained local. Some heroes, such as Pyrrhos, transcended the local setting and became panhellenic. And whereas the cult of Asklepios *the hero* was confined to the city of Epidauros, he, like Jesus, became a god who had a more universal range throughout the Roman Empire.

We may also turn again to the questions of hero/people antagonism and hero/god antagonism. The former is certainly found in the gospels; in addition to Matthew we may examine the ending of Mark. John Dominic Crossan suggests that people ($\check{o}\chi\lambda os$) is positive throughout Mark until chap. 15, when the *people* suddenly turn and ask for Barabbas's freedom instead of Jesus'. Jesus is now abandoned by those who had been so loyal: the disciples, the people, the women followers now at a distance, and also God?—'My Lord, why have you forsaken me?' Is hero/god antagonism also in evidence here? It is perhaps not sin that separates Jesus from God but simply, as Harold Remus suggests, 'general abandonment':

> Christians...were convinced that the very god-forsakenness of Jesus on the cross...meant their salvation. Death was the portal to a glorious afterlife, a hope and

---

54. Gottfried Schille, 'Das Leiden des Herrn. Die evangelische Passionstradition und ihr "Sitz im Leben"', *Zeitschrift für Theologie und Kirche* 52 (1955), pp. 161-205; and Ludger Schenke, *Auferstehungsverkündigung und leeres Grab: eine traditionsgeschichtliche Untersuchung von Mk. 16, 1-8* (Stuttgart: Katholisches Bibelwerk, 1968), pp. 11-30; Wills, *Quest*, pp. 171-74. Canonical Mark ends with a resurrection prediction in Galilee, but the Longer Ending lacks this. John 20 depicts a resurrection in Jerusalem, while John 21 recounts an appearance in Galilee. It is also possible, as Hengel has argued (*Atonement*, p. 472), that perhaps Mark thinks of the sin of executing Jesus as falling on Jews and Romans alike, and the reconciliation is with both groups. For Hengel ('Expiatory Sacrifice of Christ', p. 475), the precise difference between the death of Jesus and that of Greek and Roman heroes is the 'universality of atonement' of Jesus, but he exaggerates the difference.

an expectation that marked them off from their polytheist neighbors, as numerous Christian sources . . . and a comparison of Christian and polytheist epitaphs across class lines attests.[55]

The death effects a resolution with God and the followers, and the followers memorialize this in the continuing cultic meal. The hope of salvation from death could not come except *through* abandonment, but this theme was only expressed in Mark and Matthew, not in Luke and John.[56]

6. Conclusion

A comparative approach thus suggests that the gospels, like *Life of Aesop*, were composed as cult narratives to present the story of the death of the hero. There are at least two traditions of what the hero paradigm would look like, Greek/Roman and Israelite/Jewish, and there was also the mutual influence of other paradigms, such as Lord, Savior, and so on. But to my mind, the hero paradigm can certainly be traced in Matthew and in the traditions now found in Mark and in John, but Mark the redactor presents a more ambiguous text. How much of this paradigm Mark wanted to *emphasize*, or how much the audience would *supply*, is unclear. What does seem clear is that the connection could hardly have been missed in the first century.

---

55. Remus, 'Persecution', in Anthony J. Blasi, Jean Duhaime and Paul-André Turcotte (eds.), *Handbook of Early Christianity: Social Science Approaches* (Walnut Creek, CA: AltaMira Press, 2002), p. 440.

56. And we should be aware that hero/god antagonism, or at least alienation and abandonment, is not unknown in the Israelite tradition. Consider the early biblical tradition of Jacob wrestling with an angel at Gen. 32.22-32 or God trying to kill Moses in Exod. 4.24-26. As Ronald Hendel suggests, *The Epic of the Patriarch: The Jacob Cycle and the Narrative Traditions of Canaan and Israel* (Atlanta: Scholars Press, 1987), p. 108, these quizzical traditions may reflect an early notion that it is specifically the *heroes* Moses and Jacob who contend with God and escape. However, this is a rare motif in regard to Israelite heroes. It is possible that Greco-Roman polytheism gave rise to a patron-client relation among the gods and heroes that is consistently problematized, and this is less common in Jewish 'monotheism'.

ROASTING THE LAMB: SACRIFICE AND SACRED TEXT
IN JUSTIN'S DIALOGUE WITH TRYPHO

Jennifer Wright Knust

1. *Introduction*

Offering yet another example of typological exegesis and arguing once again that the Jewish scriptures are, in fact, 'about Christ', Justin Martyr calls to mind the image of a sacrificial lamb, roasting on a spit, and compares this image to that of a human/divine body hanging on a cross:

> [T]he lamb which you were ordered to roast whole was a symbol of Christ's passion on the cross. Indeed, the lamb, while being roasted, resembles the figure of the cross, for one spit transfixes it horizontally from the lower parts up to the head, and another pierces it across the back, and holds up its forelegs (Justin, *Dialogue with Trypho*, 40.2-3).[1]

Perhaps, in this post-sacrificial, juridical age, this identification no longer has the impact Justin desired.[2] Nevertheless, for Justin, the sacrificial, bloody death of Jesus served as a central metaphor in the *Dialogue with Trypho*. Justin presents the crucifixion as one of the key sticking points between himself and Trypho, his Jewish interlocutor. Trypho wonders that 'you', the Christians, 'place your hope in a crucified man, and still expect to receive favors from God when you disregard His commandments' (*Dialogue*, 10.3; cf. 32).[3] Of course we do, Justin counters, since, as the Jewish scriptures predicted, the Christ suffered and died in order to save sinners (e.g. *Dial.* 32, 43, 46, 54, 72, 73, 76, 89, 90, 96, 97); yet the obstinate, intractable sins of the Jews have prevented them from seeing this truth. Jews, Justin claims, have remained so determined to ignore or sup-

---

1. English translation by Thomas B. Falls, *Saint Justin Martyr* (Fathers of the Church, 6; Washington, DC: Catholic University of America Press, 1965), p. 209; Greek text edited, with commentary and introduction, by Miroslav Marcovich, *Iustini Martyris Dialogus cum Tryphone* (Patristische Texte und Studien, 47; Berlin and New York: W. de Gruyter, 1997), p. 137.

2. Girard has argued that sacrifice and the judicial system perform the same function: that of concealing and redirecting violence (René Girard, *Violence and the Sacred* [trans. Patrick Gregory; Baltimore: The Johns Hopkins University Press, 1977], esp. pp. 15-27; also see Michel Foucault, *Discipline and Punish: The Birth of the Prison* [trans. Alan Sheridan; New York: Vintage Books, 1979], esp. pp. 25-31, 73-75).

3. Marcovich (ed.), *Iustini Martyris*, p. 87; Falls (trans.), *Saint Justin Martyr*, p. 163.

press the obvious that they even have the audacity to delete key passages from scripture, two of which prove that the Christ would die on a cross.[4] Neither of these passages can be found in any known copy of the Septuagint, but Justin has made his point: The Jews not only misread their own scriptures, they do violence to them, cutting away passages that displease just as they had 'pierced' Christ (*Dial.* 32.2). Violence against Christ and against the scriptures, Justin asserts, go hand in hand.

A reconsideration of religion, violence, and the biblical heritage invites a reappraisal of Justin Martyr's twin theory of violence and the Bible. Efforts to fix the content and meaning of sacred scripture regularly involve attempts at social scripting and thus debates about 'what the scriptures mean', 'what the scriptures say', and 'what counts as scripture' expose fundamental tensions within and between communities, reflecting contests for authority and the control of truth.[5] The very act of developing and defining 'sacred text', or 'the (Christian) Bible'—Justin's principal aim in the *Dialogue*—involves a sort of violence, or at least a theory of violence. During Justin's time, there was no agreement among the followers of Jesus regarding the meaning or the content of the books and sayings he invokes as if they were solid ground,[6] nor could one readily identify who was a 'Christian' let alone who was a 'Jew'.[7] Therefore,

---

4. 'This Passover is our savior and our refuge. And if you have understood, and it has entered your hearts, that we are about to humiliate him on a cross, and afterwards hope in him, then this place will never be forsaken, saith the Lord of hosts' (*Dial.* 72.2-3; attributed to Esdras. Marcovich [ed.], *Iustini Martyris*, p. 194; Falls [trans.], *Saint Justin Martyr*, p. 263). 'Say ye to the Gentiles: The Lord hath reigned from a tree' (*Dial.* 73.1, attributed to Psalm 95; Marcovich [ed.], *Iustini Martyris*, p. 195; Falls [trans.], *Saint Justin Martyr*, p. 264).

5. My thinking here is inspired by the work of Vincent L. Wimbush. See esp. 'Introduction: Reading Darkness, Reading Scriptures', in Vincent L. Wimbush with the assistance of Rosamond C. Rodman (eds.), *African Americans and the Bible: Sacred Texts and Social Textures* (New York: Continuum, 2000), pp. 1-43.

6. See esp. Charles H. Cosgrove, 'Justin Martyr and the Emerging Christian Canon: Observations on the Purpose and Destination of the Dialogue with Trypho', *VC* 36 (1982), pp. 209-32.

7. Indeed, a growing body of scholarly literature demonstrates just how fluid and ambiguous these identity categories were. There was no 'parting of the ways' between Jews and Christians, there was no clear separation or divorce and firm boundaries did not exist. See David Frankfurter, 'Jews or Not? Reconstructing the 'Other' in Rev 2:9 and 3:9', *HTR* 94 (2001), pp. 403-425; Paula Fredriksen, 'What 'Parting of the Ways'? Jews, Gentiles and the Ancient Mediterranean City', in Adam H. Becker and Annette Yoshiko Reed (eds.), *The Ways That Never Parted: Jews and Christians in Late Antiquity and the Middle Ages* (Tübingen: Mohr [Siebeck], 2003), pp. 35-64; Daniel Boyarin, *Borderlines: The Partition of Judaeo-Christianity* (Philadelphia: University of Pennsylvania Press, 2004); Judith Lieu, *Christian Identity in the Jewish and Graeco-Roman World* (Oxford: Oxford University Press, 2004). Justin flags this situation himself. His interlocutor Trypho asks, 'If a person knows that what you say is true, and, professing Jesus to be the Christ, believes in and obeys him, yet desires also to observe the commandments of the Mosaic Law, shall he be saved?' To which Justin replies: 'In my opinion, I say such a person will be saved, unless he exerts every effort to influence other people...to practice the same rites as himself,

Justin's deployment of these terms should be understood as a discursive move on his part, not as a reflection of a widespread or universally acknowledged sense of difference.[8] In the *Dialogue*, Justin seeks to accomplish two goals at once: theorizing the Bible as a Christian text, he wrests shared scriptures away from those whom he identifies as 'Jews'; identifying acts of violence against Jews as divine punishment but acts of violence against Jesus and the Christians as sacrifice or divine fulfillment, he develops a theory of violence that excludes Jews from sympathy while emphasizing the unjust, and temporary, afflictions of those who follow Christ.

Earlier generations of scholars tended to interpret Justin's *Dialogue* as genuinely interested in converting Jews to Christianity and as rooted in an actual conversation between Justin, a philosopher-Christian, and Trypho, a Jew.[9] More recently, however, the *Dialogue* has been interpreted as an in-group document, directed at fellow Christian insiders, especially those with whom Justin disagrees.[10] According to this line of interpretation, historical or not Trypho serves as a straw man, introduced by Justin so that certain Christian figures and arguments can be discredited. Seeking to persuade a fictional or fictionalized Trypho that the scriptures point toward Christ, Justin actually seeks to combat Christians who have dared to argue that the God and sacred books of Israel

---

informing them that they cannot be saved unless they do so' (*Dial.* 47, Marcovich [ed.], *Iustini Martyris*, p. 146; Falls [trans.], *Saint Justin Martyr*, p. 218). In other words, Justin is quite willing to accept followers of Jesus who, for all practical purposes, are Jews, even as he rhetorically distances himself from those whom he labels 'the Jews', calling them 'you' and treating them as one, undifferentiated category.

8. Justin's confusion was shared by outsiders such as Lucian of Samosata, who described the Christians as some sort of pseudo-Jew. According to Lucian, the Christians worship a crucified Palestinian lawgiver, meet in synagogues, pour over special books, and reject the Greek gods (Lucian, *The Passing of Peregrinus*, 11-13 [LCL 302, pp. 12-15]). Justin confuses his own categories, asserting that there are some 'of your race (*genos*)' who acknowledge Jesus as Christ but consider him human. To Justin, such people remain 'Jews'. Perhaps Trypho, were he an actual historical figure, would disagree (*Dial.* 48.4; Trypho is said to be sympathetic to this view, 49.1).

9. For example, Theodore Stylianopoulos, *Justin Martyr and the Mosaic Law* (Missoula, MT: Society of Biblical Literature, 1975), pp. 33-44. For a more recent argument along these lines, see Timothy J. Horner, *Listening to Trypho: Justin Martyr's Dialogue Reconsidered* (Leuven: Peeters, 2001).

10. See Tessa Rajak, 'Talking at Trypho: Christian Apologetic as Anti-Judaism in Justin's *Dialogue with Trypho the Jew*', in Mark Edwards, Martin Goodman and Simon Price, in association with Christopher Rowland (eds.), *Apologetics in the Roman Empire: Pagans, Jews, and Christians* (Oxford: Oxford University Press, 1999), pp. 59-80 (79-80), and Michael Mach, 'Justin Martyr's *Dialogus cum Tryphone Iudaeo* and the Development of Christian Anti-Judaism', in Guy G. Stroumsa (ed.), *Contra Iudaeos: Ancient and Medieval Polemics between Christians and Jews* (Texts and Studies in Medieval and Modern Judaism 10; Mohr [Siebeck], 1996), pp. 27-47. Cosgrove also views the challenge of Marcion to be an important factor in the production of the *Dialogue* (pp. 218-21, 25).

ought to be rejected outright, particularly Marcion, his contemporary also living in Rome at the time. Justin's vociferous rhetoric against Jews, then, was actually designed as a vociferous argument against certain Christians. As Michael Mach explains: 'This system according to which the whole of the Jewish Bible becomes a Christian book exacts a high price: The polemics against the Jews'.[11] Moreover, Justin's re-situation of the Septuagint as a Christian book that is, in the end, all about Christ, together with his incorporation of the sayings of Jesus within a 'proof from prophecy' scheme, educates Christians regarding the content of the scriptures while consolidating his fledgling group as a group, distinct from 'the Jews'.

Still, there is more at stake in the *Dialogue* than intra-Christian polemic regarding the Bible and the nature of the Christian canon. While it seems true that the *Dialogue* could not have attracted an extra-Christian audience—it is simply too polemical and too historically inaccurate to convince knowledgeable or unsympathetic outsiders—Justin's rhetoric has larger consequences, particularly in the context of the late second century. The vehemence of his attack produces a 'Christian'[12] theory of violence that renders certain violence invisible as violence even as it brings other violence into sharp relief, most particularly, violence against Christ and the Christians.[13] Justin's reconfiguration of the devastating aftermath of the Second Jewish Revolt as an example of divine justice, his insistence that the death of Jesus was a bloody sacrifice prefigured by Israelite sacrificial traditions and prophesied by the prophets, and his apocalyptic speculation regarding the ultimate victory of both Christ and the Christians erect group boundaries where there were none, produce 'Jews' who are perpetrators rather than victims, and defend Christian honor such that the Christians, though temporarily victimized by shaming death and punishment, will rise, whole and inviolate, ruling over a Christian Jerusalem for 1,000 years. Defining Christians, Justin defines Jews; defending Christians, Justin attacks Jews whom, he asserts, deserve the disasters they experience. For Justin, sacred text provides both the framework and the ground upon which his theory can be developed and justified. In Justin's system, readers know how to interpret violence if they adopt his interpretation of divine history and they understand how to interpret divine history if they adopt his view of Bible.

11. Mach, 'Justin Martyr's *Dialogus*', p. 46.
12. I use this label with caution. The point is that Justin's theory of Christian identity and his theory of violence work together.
13. On the framing of violence, its visibilities and invisibilities, in a contemporary context, see Laura Wexler, *Tender Violence: Domestic Visions in an Age of US Imperialism* (Chapel Hill: University of North Carolina Press, 2000); Elizabeth A. Castelli, 'Feminists Responding to Violence', and Minoo Moallem, 'Violence of Protection', in Elizabeth A. Castelli and Janet R. Jakobsen (eds.), *Interventions: Activists and Academics Respond to Violence* (New York: Palgrave Macmillan, 2004), pp. 1-9, 47-51.

2. *Divine Justice against Jews*

Infamously, Justin's *Dialogue* argues that violence against Jews by Romans was both deserved and divinely ordained. Early in the work, he explains that circumcision was given to Jews by God as a signifying mark, so that they could be more easily identified and punished once, in fulfillment of divine prophecy, they had chosen to reject 'the Just One' (i.e. Jesus; *Dial.* 16). This, the true purpose of circumcision, was fulfilled during Justin's own time, or so he claims.

Setting the *Dialogue* during the aftermath of the Second Jewish Revolt (132–135 CE)[14] and representing his dialogue partner Trypho as a Jewish refugee from a recently defeated homeland,[15] Justin suggests that the Romans acted as God's instruments when destroying Judean cities, villages, farms and fields:

> The purpose [of circumcision] was that you and only you might suffer the afflictions that are now justly yours; that only your land be desolate, and your cities ruined by fire; that the fruits of your land be eaten by strangers before your very eyes; that not one of you be permitted to enter your city of Jerusalem (*Dial.* 16).[16]

Here Justin signals his specific knowledge of the situation in Judea following the revolt: Judean cities have burned, Roman legions stationed in Judea eat the fruits of the land 'before your very eyes',[17] and Jews are not permitted to enter Jerusalem, one of the punishments imposed by Hadrian when the city was re-founded as *Colonia Aelia Capitolina*.[18] This brief summary of the circumstances in Judea parallels the more complete description of these events by the ancient historian Cassius Dio (*c.* 164–229 CE). According to Dio, the Roman army razed fifty Jewish outposts, slaughtered 580,000 insurgents, set fire to cities and villages, and killed many others with fire and famine (69.14.1-3).[19] Dio's numbers are not reliable, but, by any count, the defeat was crushing.[20] Still, in Justin's estimation, everything the Jews suffered was entirely deserved.

---

14. Though it was written some thirty years later, *c.* 160 CE.

15. 'Who are you most excellent sir?' Justin asks. Trypho replies, 'I am a Hebrew of the circumcision, a refugee from the recent war, and at present a resident of Greece, especially of Corinth' (*Dial.* 1; Marcovich [ed.], *Iustini Martyris*, pp. 69-70; Falls [trans.], *Saint Justin Martyr*, p. 147).

16. Marcovich (ed.), *Iustini Martyris*, pp. 96-97; Falls (trans.), *Saint Justin Martyr*, p. 172.

17. On the impact of the legions and their locations in Syria–Palestine after the Second Revolt, see Benjamin Isaac, *The Limits of Empire: The Roman Army in the East* (Oxford: Clarendon Press, rev. edn, 2000), pp. 106-107.

18. See Mary T. Boatwright, *Hadrian and the Cities of the Roman Empire* (Princeton, NJ: Princeton University Press, 2000), pp. 196-203.

19. Menahem Stern, *Greek and Latin Authors on Jews and Judaism* (Jerusalem: Israel Academy of Sciences and Humanities, 1976–1984), II, no. 440.

20. On the unreliability of statistics provided by Dio and other ancient historians, see Tim J.

By interpreting circumcision as a mark, given by God to punish Jews during the Second Revolt and afterwards, Justin suggests that Christians had nothing to do with the rebellion, that Jewish defeat was planned by God, and that God works through the Romans to punish Jews, a punishment that will be more fully realized later, when Christ comes again. He also implies that Christians are not circumcised, for if they were, they too could be singled out for punishment. This claim can easily be overturned by Justin's own argument. Just a few chapters later, he acknowledges to Trypho that some Christians are circumcised:

> But if some, due to their instability of will, desire to observe as many of the Mosaic precepts as possible—precepts which we think were instituted because of your hardness of heart—while at the same time they place their hope in Christ, and if they desire to perform the eternal and natural acts of justice and piety, yet wish to live with us as Christians and believers, as I already stated, not persuading them to be circumcised like themselves, or to keep the Sabbath, or to perform any other similar acts, then in my opinion we Christians should receive them and associate with them in every way as kinsmen and brethren (*Dial.* 47).[21]

In other words, Justin is fully aware of Christians who are circumcised, keep the Sabbath and obey the 'Mosaic precepts', and he accepts them as 'brethren' so long as they do not insist that circumcision is necessary for the salvation of Gentile believers. A few lines later, he also indicates a willingness to tolerate Gentiles who decide to follow the practices of the Jews, presumably including circumcision, if they remain loyal to their faith in Christ. The boundary between Christian and Jew, circumcised and uncircumcised is much more fluid than Justin's association of circumcision and divine punishment seems to permit. Nevertheless, he continues to insist that scripture predicted the suffering of circumcised Jews.

Justin defends his interpretation of Jewish suffering and guilt by repeated proof-texting, both of Jewish scriptures and the sayings of Jesus. Prior to claiming that circumcision was designed by God to facilitate the slaughter of Jews, he cites Greek versions of Isa. 51.4-5, Jer. 31.31-32, Isa. 55.3-5, Isa. 6.10 (a passage mistakenly attributed to Jeremiah), Isa. 52.10-15, 53.1-12, 54.1-6, Isa. 55.3-13, and Isa. 58.1-12 in order to argue that God, through the prophets, predicted that the old covenant would be abrogated (*Dial.* 11), that the new covenant would be scorned by Jews (*Dial.* 12), that they would murder and despise the Just One (*Dial.* 13), and that they would habitually fail to understand the rituals God had imposed upon them (*Dial.* 14-15). Following this prophetically informed censure of the Jews, he cites sayings of Jesus, paraphrasing a series

---

Parkin, *Demography and Roman Society* (Baltimore: The Johns Hopkins University Press, 1992), pp. 58-66. For a helpful discussion of the situation in Judea/Palestine and Galilee after the revolt, see Seth Schwartz, *Imperialism and Jewish Society 200 BCE to 640 CE* (Princeton, NJ: Princeton University Press, 2001), pp. 105-61.

21. Marcovich (ed.), *Iustini Martyris*, p. 147; Falls (trans.), *Saint Justin Martyr*, p. 218.

of 'woes' now found in the Synoptic Gospels to add Jesus' own denunciations to those of the prophets (*Dial.* 18; compare Mt. 21.13, 23, 27; Lk. 11.13, 52). Justin brings the discussion of circumcision and suffering to a close by linking Jewish injustice against Christ to Jewish injustice against Christians, again citing Isaiah.[22] He concludes by re-emphasizing the main point: circumcision, the Sabbath, and all Jewish festivals 'were imposed upon you because of your sins and your hardness of heart'; therefore these provisions are neither relevant nor necessary for 'us', the Christians (*Dial.* 18-19).[23]

Throughout the *Dialogue*, Justin lays the blame for the death of Jesus, the persecution of Christians, and their own misfortunes squarely on the shoulders of Jews. As such, he defines Jewish suffering as outside of the realm of Christian concern, suggesting instead that 'the Christians' ought take some satisfaction that they are not 'Jews' and therefore liable neither to the commandments given by God in the first covenant nor for the punishments God imposed on wicked Jews. Given that 'Jew' and 'Christian' were not distinct categories, as Justin's own discussion reveals, his legitimization of Roman violence against Jews, reinterpreted as divinely ordained and prophetically predicted punishment, wrenches Christianity from Judaism in a striking way, redirecting sympathy away from Jews, who may well have been viewed as fellow-sufferers by some followers of Jesus, toward Christians, who are described as victims of Jewish violence.[24] Justin, no friend to Rome, here chose to disguise Roman participation in the devastation of Judea in order to emphasize Jewish culpability. Hidden behind such phrases as 'those who are in power' and 'strangers' who 'eat the fruit of the land' lie actual Roman legions and governors. In the *Dialogue*, violence against Jews becomes invisible as violence. Violence against Christ and the Christians, however, is highlighted as violence. The suffering of Jesus was divinely ordained, Justin argues, but not as punishment. Rather, Jesus died as a sacrifice.

3. *Scripture and the Sacrificial Death of the Christ*

Sacrifice, it should be emphasized, was largely understood as a positive and solemn act among ancient Israelites.[25] The same could be said for other ancient

---

22. 'Now, indeed, you cannot use violence against us Christians, because of those who are in power, but as often as you could, you did employ force against us. For this reason, God cries out to you...' (*Dial.* 16, citing Isa. 52.5; Marcovich [ed.], *Iustini Martyris*, p. 97; Falls [trans.], *Saint Justin Martyr*, p. 173.).

23. Marcovich (ed.), *Iustini Martyris*, pp. 99-101; Falls (trans.), *Saint Justin Martyr*, pp. 174-77.

24. Compare the stoning of Stephen (Acts 7.56–8.1), with discussion by Shelly Matthews, 'The Need for the Stoning of Stephen', in Shelly Matthews and E. Leigh Gibson (eds.), *Violence in the New Testament* (New York and London: T. & T. Clark, 2005), pp. 124-39 (124-25, 130-33).

25. Jonathan Klawans, 'Pure Violence: Sacrifice and Defilement in Ancient Israel', *HTR* 94 (2001), pp. 135-57.

peoples, including the Romans.[26] It is not surprising, then, that rather than rejecting sacrifice, Justin insisted upon it, reconfiguring the crucifixion of Christ such that it became the central event in God's plan, toward which the prophets, Moses, Abraham, the Passover, Yom Kippur and even nature point.[27] Justin refers to the crucifixion on numerous occasions, repeatedly associating the crucifixion with sacrifice. Without faith in the sacrificial death of Christ, Justin argues, one cannot be truly washed clean (*Dial.* 13, 44, 54, 110, 111). Thanks to the sacrifice of Christ, the Gentile Christians are now 'the true spiritual Israel, the descendants of Judah, Jacob, Isaac, and Abraham' since Christ has paid their penalty (*Dial.* 11).[28] The two goats sacrificed on Yom Kippur point to the sacrificial death of Christ: the first goat representing the first advent, 'in which your priests and elders sent him away as a scapegoat, seizing him and putting him to death'; the second goat representing his second coming because, at that time, in Jerusalem 'you [Jews] shall recognize him whom you had subjected to shame, and who was a sacrificial offering for all sinners who are willing to repent' (*Dial.* 40.4-5).[29] In other words, if one knows how to read sacred texts properly, one naturally concludes that Jesus is the Christ and that his death was a sacrifice.

In Justin's scheme, Christians do not perform literal sacrifices: They do not sacrifice in the manner of Jews because Christ made these sacrifices both irrelevant and unnecessary. They do not sacrifice in the manner of non-Jews because to do so would mean sacrificing to demons. Instead they partake in a ritual meal that memorializes the sacrifice of Christ, a meal prefigured by the first covenant (*Dial.* 41, 117). The Jews do not partake in sacrifice either, Justin notes through Trypho, but not because they correctly understand that their sacrifices are not longer efficacious. Rather, they fail to sacrifice simply because they cannot: Jerusalem has been destroyed.[30] By contrast, Christians recognize that animal sacrifice has been rendered obsolete, though they regularly remember Christ's sacrifice by eating his (metaphorical) body and drinking his (metaphorical) blood.

---

26. See, for example, the altar and friezes of the *Ara pacis*, celebrating solemn sacrificial ritual, with discussion by John Elsner, 'Cult and Sacrifice: Sacrifice in the Ara Pacis Augustae', *JRS* 81 (1991), pp. 50-61. For discussion of Greek sacrifice, see esp. Simon Price, *Religions of the Ancient Greeks* (Key Themes in Ancient History; Cambridge: Cambridge University Press, 1999), pp. 25-46.

27. For example: The tree of life was a symbol of the crucifixion (*Dial.* 86); Moses stood cruciform when he was praying for victory in battle (*Dial.* 90); Moses' serpent in the desert was designed to point to the death of Christ on a cross (*Dial.* 94).

28. Marcovich (ed.), *Iustini Martyris*, p. 89; Falls (trans.), *Saint Justin Martyr*, p. 165. On this topic, see Denise Buell, *Why This New Race: Ethnic Reasoning in Early Christianity* (New York: Columbia University Press, 2005), esp. pp. 94-115.

29. Marcovich (ed.), *Iustini Martyris*, p. 137; Falls (trans.), *Saint Justin Martyr*, p. 209.

30. Trypho acknowledges that the whole law can no longer be kept, for sacrifices can only take place in Jerusalem (*Dial.* 46).

Interpreting the crucifixion this way, Justin removes the taint of shame usually associated with such a violent death, a taint to which he refers, by means of Trypho, on several occasions. Trypho is represented as surprised that 'you [Christians] place your hope in a crucified man' (*Dial.* 10), horrified by the blasphemous claim that a crucified man spoke with Moses and Aaron in a cloud (*Dial.* 38), and concerned that God's Christ could be 'so shamefully crucified', since 'the Law declared that he who is crucified is to be accursed' (*Dial.* 89).[31] For Trypho, the crucifixion of the Christ is impossible on biblical grounds, though the disgrace associated with this peculiarly Roman punishment is rooted in Greco-Roman assumptions about status and bodily inviolability and not in biblical law. Reserved by Romans for low-status provincials, slaves, and brigands, crucifixion was designed to humiliate, degrade and expose.[32] Justin, aware of the degradation involved in crucifixion, seeks to overcome it by theorizing the death of Jesus as a sacrifice demanded by God and predicted by the Bible. Sacrifice, which involves ceremony, control, and divinely sanctioned killing, offers Jesus an honorable and solemn death rather than a shameful and tragic one. Justin asserts that only an enemy and a 'Jew' would imagine otherwise by placing the objection to a crucified Christ in Trypho's mouth and suggesting, once again, that Jews do not know how to read their scriptures properly. In fact, he argues, they are so stubbornly ignorant that they would rather delete key biblical passages regarding the Christ than accept the truth as it has been plainly revealed to them.

For Justin, the insolence of Jewish interpretation is found not only in a stubborn misinterpretation of shared scriptures but also in an intentionally wicked editorial procedure. He accuses Jews as a group of removing objectionable verses from the divinely-inspired Greek translation of the seventy elders, including the phrases 'we are about to humiliate him on a cross', attributed to Esdras (Pseudo-Ezra), and 'the Lord hath reigned from the tree', attributed to Psalm 95 (96) (*Dial.* 71–73). Justin's accusations seem to rely upon a collection

---

31. Marcovich (ed.), *Iustini Martyris*, pp. 86-87, 132, 224-25; Falls (trans.), *Saint Justin Martyr*, pp. 163, 204-205, 290.

32. Thus, Roman citizens found guilty of heinous crimes could only be executed by *damnatio ad bestias* if they were first designated as a 'slave of the punishment' (*servus poenae*) stripped of their citizenship and their freedom (*Digest of Justinian* 48.19.1, Ulpian; 48.19.8, Ulpian; 18.19.12, Macer). Callistratus explains the purpose of crucifixion: 'The practice approved by most authorities has been to hang notorious brigands on a gallows in the place which they used to haunt, so that by the spectacle others may be deterred from the same crimes, and so that it may, when the penalty has been carried out, bring comfort to the relatives and kin of those killed in that place where brigands committed their murders; but some have condemned these [criminals] to the beasts. Our ancestors, whatever the punishment, penalized slaves more severely than freemen, and notorious persons more than those of unblemished reputation' (*Digest of Justinian* 48.19.28, Callistratus, *Judicial Examinations*, 6.15-16; edited and translated by Alan Watson, *The Digest of Justinian* [Philadelphia: University of Pennsylvania Press, 1985], vol. 4).

of biblical proof-texts regarding the crucifixion circulating among the followers of Jesus and not upon a collection assembled by Justin himself.[33] Despite his confident assertions to the contrary, these verses are not found in any known copy of the Septuagint, though he may have heard them used by his Christian contemporaries. Nevertheless, these passages, whoever collected them, indicate to Justin that Jews like Trypho deny the obvious: 'that the Crucified One was foretold as God and man, and as about to suffer death on a cross' (*Dial.* 71).[34] If Trypho and his ilk would simply adopt the proper text and its true meaning, Justin asserts, they would have no choice but to conclude that the crucifixion took place in fulfillment of scripture and in response to the divine will. The crucifixion, then, neither humiliates the Christ nor violates biblical mandates, as Trypho supposes. Instead, the crucifixion indicts and shames the Jews, both for their refusal to honor God's Christ and for their denial of biblical truths about sacrifice and sin, truths they reject only by means of an offensive deletion of central passages.

Justin juxtaposes two sacrificial systems in the *Dialogue*: the first, given to Israel by God to prevent them from further sin, did not succeed, despite God's best efforts, and has now become both meaningless and impossible; the second, given by Christ when he died a sacrificial death on the cross, takes on 'the curses of the whole human race', overcoming sin and death (*Dial.* 95). In this way, Justin re-imagines Jesus' death as a once-for-all sacrifice rather than a gory degradation. Still, he does not shrink from the gore of Jesus' death, referring to Jesus' blood, his pierced body, and even to the roasting of the Passover lamb/Jesus. By describing Jesus' death as a sacrifice, predicted by the sacred scriptures and consecrated by God, Justin has utterly revised its significance. As a sacrificial death rather than a cruel punishment, the crucifixion is controlled: his death is fully in the control of God who both instigates the crucifixion and hangs on the cross. As such, the blood spilled is cleansing, since it is God who has authorized the violent act. Finally, Jesus' death/sacrifice saves, maintaining the divine presence among those who constitute 'true Israel', that is, the

---

33. See discussion in Oskar Skarsaune, *The Proof from Prophecy: A Study in Justin Martyr's Proof-Text Tradition: Text-Type, Provenance, Theological Profile* (NTSup, 61; Leiden: E.J. Brill, 1987), pp. 35-46; Pierre Prigent, *Justin et l'ancien testament: l'argumentaton scripturaire du traité de Justin contre toutes les hérésies comme source principale du Dialogue avec Tryphon et la première apologie* (Etudes Bibliques; Paris: Librairie Lecoffre, 1964), pp. 175, 191-94. The deletions Justin cites appear only in a few Christian writings authors and in no known copy of Esdras or the Septuagint Psalms. For example, Lactantius mentions the passage from Esdras (*Divine Institutes* 4.18). The author of the Epistle of Barnabas seems to know the tradition about the Christ reigning form the tree (*Ep. Barn.* 8.5: 'Why is the wool placed on a piece of wood? Because the kingdom of Jesus is on the tree, and because those who hope in him will live forever'. English translation by Bart D. Ehrman, *The Apostolic Fathers*, vol. 2 [LCL, 25, Cambridge: Harvard University Press, 2003], pp. 41-43).

34. Marcovich (ed.), *Iustini Martyris*, p. 193; Falls (trans.), *Saint Justin Martyr*, p. 262.

Christians.³⁵ Conflating sacrifice and crucifixion, Justin transformed what he knows to be shameful into an honor. Arguing that the sacred scriptures prove his point, Justin works to transform both sacrifice and scripture. The honor of the Christians, however, remains under threat.

4. *Christian Bodies Resurrected and Redeemed*

Recent discussions of the writings of Justin Martyr observe that Justin—and his fellow apologists—contributed to an effort on the part of some Christian authors to manufacture an image of persistent persecution.³⁶ They did so as a defensive measure, subverting the shame associated with condemnation to the beasts and other humiliating punishments by arguing that their endurance during torture was "manly" and therefore honorable. ³⁷ For example, in the *Dialogue*, Justin observes:

> Now it is obvious that no one can frighten or subdue us who believe in Jesus throughout the whole world. Although we are beheaded and crucified, and exposed to wild beasts and chains and flames, and every other means of torture, it is evident that we will not retract our profession of faith; the more we are persecuted, the more do others in ever-increasing numbers embrace the faith and become worshippers of God through the name of Jesus (*Dial*. 110.4).³⁸

This argument reverses some of the more traditional assumptions about "manliness" and status.³⁹ More often, bodily inviolability was imagined as a funda-

---

35. See Klawans, 'Pure Violence'. Klawans persuasively argues that sacrifice in Israel served neither as a negative, apotropaic turning away of violence nor as an 'empty vestige' that preserved forgotten, more primitive impulses, but as a positive imitation of God's action in the world intended to maintain God's presence among the people. Though Justin's Christians did not sacrifice, the regular participation in a Eucharistic meal offered another way of fulfilling this function. Indeed, the Eucharist provides a method for continuing participation in sacrifice by Christians, whereas Jews have lost that ability, a fact that Justin takes care to point out.

36. Keith Hopkins, 'Christian Number and its Implications', *JECS* 6 (1998), pp. 185-226; Judith Perkins, *The Suffering Self: Pain and Narrative Representation in the Early Christian Era* (London and New York: Routledge, 1995).

37. Therefore, female Christian martyrs were regularly described as becoming even more "manly" than their persecutors, enduring whatever tortures non-Christian men chose to inflict. See discussion in Elizabeth A. Castelli, *Martyrdom and Memory: Early Christian Culture Making* (Gender, Theory and Religion; New York: Columbia University Press, 2004), pp. 59-67.

38. Marcovich (ed.), *Iustini Martyris*, p. 259; Falls (trans.), *Saint Justin Martyr*, p. 318.

39. See Castelli, *Martyrdom*; Brent Shaw, 'Body/Power/Identity: Passions of the Martyrs', *JECS* 4 (1990), pp. 269-312; Daniel Boyarin, *Dying for God: Martyrdom and the Making of Christianity and Judaism* (Stanford: Stanford University Press, 1999), pp. 74-81; Virginia Burrus, 'Reading Agnes: The Rhetoric of Gender in Ambrose and Prudentius', *JECS* 4 (1995), pp. 25-46. On this phenomenon in Jewish sources, see also Tessa Rajak, 'Dying for the Law: The Martyrs' Portrait in Jewish-Greek Literature', in *The Jewish Dialogue with Greece and Rome: Studies in Cultural and Social Interaction* (Leiden: E.J. Brill, 2002).

mental characteristic of what it meant to be male and elite,[40] with the relative vulnerability or invulnerability of bodies to violation by others mapped onto a hierarchical, gendered scheme. The bodies of those who had achieved the highest status were sacrosanct, at least in theory, but the bodies of subordinates, especially slave bodies, were vulnerable to disciplinary intervention.[41] The more open the body to violation, the more degraded that body had become.[42] By contrast, Justin treats the bodily violation of Christians as a relative good. Christian endurance attracts outsiders to the faith, and proves that they are friendly:

> And we who delighted in war, in the slaughter of one another, and in every other kind of iniquity have in every part of the world converted our weapons of war into implements of peace ... and we cultivate piety, justice, brotherly charity, faith, and hope, which we derive from the Father through the Crucified Savior (*Dial.* 110.3)[43]

In other words, Christian suffering—unlike Jewish suffering—demonstrates and affirms their election as God's own people and their exceptional virtue. Christians, unlike Jews, do not deserve to suffer, but, when they do, they take their (temporary) afflictions like men.

However, Justin does not fully overturn the association between bodily inviolability and elite status, nor does he revoke the fundamental privilege of self-mastered men to control and violate the bodies of subordinates. Instead, he looks forward to the resurrection, a time when Christian bodies will rise again, intact and inviolable, but the bodies of their enemies will be torn apart and destroyed. As he explains in the *Dialogue*, "there will be a resurrection of the flesh, followed by a thousand years in the rebuilt, embellished, and enlarged city of Jerusalem, as was announced by the prophets Ezekiel, Isaiah, and the

---

40. Hence, as James Rives has argued, the decision of Hilarianus, the Roman procurator, to condemn Perpetua, the daughter of a Roman citizen family of decurial rank, to the beasts for refusing to recant her Christianity indicates how deeply offended he was at her revocation of her status and duty (James Rives, 'The Piety of a Persecutor', *JECS* 4 [1996], pp. 1-25). From Hilarianus's perspective, Perpetua's treason was so serious that she had effectively sold herself to slavery and revoked any claim of privilege she may have had. See further Kathleen M. Coleman, 'Fatal Charades: Roman Executions Staged as Mythological Enactments', *JRS* 80 (1990), pp. 44-73.

41. Jennifer Glancy, *Slavery in Early Christianity* (New York: Oxford University Press, 2002), pp. 10-27.

42. See, for example, the procedure adopted by Pliny the Younger when he decided to investigate the Christians in Bithynia. He tortured two female Christian slaves, not because he was interested in convincing *them* to recant their Christian "superstition," but because he hoped to discover the practices of their masters. Having gathered relevant evidence, he then asked free persons charged with Christianity to curse Christ, putting to death those who would not offer a small sacrifice to the gods (*Ep.* 10.96). In this way, he refrained from harming the physical bodies of free Christians until after he had first investigated their crimes by torturing the appropriate Christian "bodies," that is, Christian slaves.

43. Marcovich (ed.), *Iustini Martyris*, pp. 258-9; Falls (trans.), *Saint Justin Martyr*, p. 318.

others" (*Dial.* 80).⁴⁴ He further claims that "the followers of Christ [will] dwell in Jerusalem for a thousand years, and that afterwards the universal and, in short, everlasting resurrection and judgment [will] take place" (*Dial.* 81, probably referring to Rev. 20.4-6).⁴⁵ The suffering and torture of Christians, therefore, is envisioned as a temporary condition, to be overcome at the end of days. By contrast, the suffering and torture of Jews prefigures the final suffering they will experience on the judgment day, unless, of course, they repent and follow Jesus as Christ. Thus, while the Christians will be raised up "incorruptible, immortal, and free from pain in an everlasting and indissoluable kingdom" others will be banished "into the eternal torment of fire" (*Dial.* 117), including Jews who shall lament on the judgment day (*Dial.* 118.1).⁴⁶ Justin ceded bodily punishments to others for the time being, but, he promised, Christ would justly destroy all who reject him in the end. It was just a matter of time.

5. *Conclusion: Justin, Violence and the Bible*

Throughout the *Dialogue*, Justin invokes the authority of the Bible to defend his view that 'the Jews' have been rejected, that the death of Jesus was sacrificial, and that 'the Christians', having received the new covenant, would come to reign with Christ in Jerusalem. This proof-texting accomplishes two tasks at once: Citing and discussing various passages, Justin feigns an agreement regarding the content of authoritative scripture that was by no means secure. At the same time, providing an interpretation for each of these passages, he naturalizes the meanings he proposes for the passages he cites. These meanings are decidedly and pointedly 'Christian': they produce a 'Jew' who cannot fail to misinterpret and so is outside the community of God. Justin's arguments do more than generate a Christian Bible, however, they develop a system whereby certain violence is identified as just punishment while other violence is interpreted as efficacious sacrifice or a temporary lesson in manly endurance. In the process, the status of victim is denied to those whom Justin labels 'the Jews'. These 'Jews' brought their misery upon themselves. By contrast, the victimization of the followers of Jesus is clear: though peaceful and friendly, 'the Jews' conspire to have Christians killed and the Romans, enslaved to demons, fall victim to their plans.⁴⁷ In this way, Justin invites his audience to redirect

---

44. Marcovich (ed.), *Iustini Martyris*, pp. 209-10; Falls (trans.), *Saint Justin Martyr*, p. 277.
45. Marcovich (ed.), *Iustini Martyris*, p. 211; Falls (trans.), *Saint Justin Martyr*, p. 278.
46. Marcovich (ed.), *Iustini Martyris*, pp. 271-74; Falls (trans.), *Saint Justin Martyr*, pp. 328-30.
47. Jews 'have never evidenced any friendship or love either toward God, or toward the prophets, or towards one another, but you have shown yourselves always to be idolaters and murderers of the just' (*Dial.* 93; Marcovich [ed.], *Iustini Martyris*, pp. 231-32; Falls [trans.], *Saint Justin Martyr*, p. 296), yet Christians 'do not hate you [Jews], nor those who believed the wicked rumors you have spread against us; on the contrary, we pray that even now you may mend your

their sympathies away from Jews, who are identified as outside and guilty, and toward those followers of Jesus Justin identifies as 'true Christians'.[48] He does so at a time when many followers of Jesus were, after all, 'Jews'.

Justin's theory of violence is just that: a theory. He does not recommend that his audience injure those whom he identifies as enemy and outsider. Indeed, his arguments depend, in part, upon their refusal to do so, a refusal that he links with Christian friendliness. Nevertheless, by describing the actual violence associated with the Second Jewish Revolt in terms of divine punishment, the violent crucifixion of Jesus as a perfect sacrifice, and the deaths of followers of Jesus as only temporary tests of endurance, he situates victims of violence in such a way that some injuries and deaths become irrelevant or deserved while other injuries and deaths are condemned as violence, only to be overturned by a coming reversal to be effected by God. As such, his theory simultaneously conceals and reveals, assigning each death to a proper category and providing each injury with a divine reason. 'Sacred text' provides the framework upon which these assignments are made, making them appear inescapable and self-evidently true even though, as we have seen, sacred text may have been precisely what was at issue.

Justin may well have written the *Dialogue* with Marcion and other Christians in mind. He was also an important proponent of the effort to wrest the Jewish scriptures and certain aspects of Jewish identity from Jews in such a way that they could become newly 'Christian'. Even so, the invitation to identify and recognize only certain deaths as violent deaths and only certain punishments as deserved constructed what might then appear to be an insurmountable gap between Christian and Jew. The nearness of these categories, hinted at by Justin himself, only demonstrates, once again, the truism that the enemy within is always, in the end, the most dangerous enemy of all.[49]

---

ways and find mercy from God the Father of all' (*Dial.* 108; Marcovich [ed.], *Iustini Martyris*, p. 255; Falls [trans.], *Saint Justin Martyr*, p. 316). On 'violent Jews' as a rhetorical problem, see David Frankfurter, 'Violence and Religious Formation: An Afterword', in Shelly Matthews and E. Leigh Gibson (eds.), *Violence in the New Testament* (London: T. & T. Clark, 2005), pp. 140-44. The argument regarding the slavery of the Romans to demons is expressed most vividly in Justin's *Apologies*. For discussion, see Jennifer Knust, *Abandoned to Lust: Sexual Slander and Ancient Christianity* (Gender, Theory and Religion; New York: Columbia University Press, 2005), pp. 100-12 and 'Enslaved to Demons: Sex, Violence and the *Apologies* of Justin Martyr', in Todd Penner and Caroline Vander Stichele (eds.), *Mapping Gender in Ancient Religious Discourses* (Biblical Interpretation, 84; Leiden: E.J. Brill, 2007), pp. 431-55.

48. In addition to attacking 'Jews', Justin also argues against Christians he identifies as 'heretics', including Marcion. For further discussion, see Knust, *Abandoned to Lust*, pp. 143-63.

49. See, for example, Elaine Pagels, *The Origin of Satan* (New York: Random House, 1995), pp. 47-46; Bernard McGinn, *Antichrist: Two Thousand Years of the Human Fascination with Evil* (San Francisco: HarperSanFrancisco, 1994); Frankfurter, 'Violence and Religious Formation', pp. 146-50.

THE LEGACY OF SECTARIAN RAGE:
VENGEANCE FANTASIES IN THE NEW TESTAMENT[1]

David Frankfurter

1. *Introduction*

Scripture holds a complex, even secondary, relationship to acts of religious violence. In many of the most horrendous recent expressions of ritualized or religiously-sanctioned violence one is hard-pressed to find scripture of any sort (even if propaganda tracts, conspiracy legends, and ancient myths are freely invoked). On the other hand, in cases where violence is envisioned as expressing the will of God according to specific scripture—one thinks of David Koresh in Texas, Baruch Goldstein in Hebron, Shoko Asahara in Tokyo, and the Mormon fundamentalists profiled by Jon Krakauer—the interpretations and citations of that scripture are so utterly beholden to the larger vision and passions of the charismatic leader that the text serves as no more than a reference point. And some astoundingly violent religious rhetoric does not necessarily lead to violent action: 'We are under spiritual invasion!', preached Rod Parsley, an Ohio megachurch evangelist, to an enthusiastic crowd of three hundred at the 'War on Christians' gathering in Washington, DC, in March, 2006. 'Man your battle stations! Ready your weapons! Lock and load!' The threat was clear; the enemy defined; but violent mobilization did not follow.[2]

Ultimately, real religious violence emerges from a complex of social dynamics: first of all, group convictions in the necessity and holiness of the acts; second, the presence of one who can shape those convictions, some leader, who is granted clairvoyant authority over the interpretation of the times, the sacred texts, and the definition of meaningful action; third, an enclave environment that encourages a polarized worldview of group sanctity and worldly evil and that fosters mutual convictions in the divine necessity of violent acts; and fourthly, an overall mobilizing vision that can be justly called millennialist in

---

1. I am indebted to the Casablanca Group for helping me hone these arguments.
2. Source: 'Hysterical Females, Perverted Sodomites, and the Collapse of 'Christian America'' (PFAW Right-Wing Watch Online 2006 [http://www.pfaw.org/pfaw/general/default.aspx?oid=20904], accessed April 6, 2006), and Elizabeth Castelli, 'Notes from the War Room', *The Revealer* April 5, 2006 (http://www.therevealer.org/archives/main_story_002500.php, accessed April 6, 2006).

Norman Cohn's sense, bringing a transcendent order into terrestrial reality.[3] It is in this broad context that scripture can sanction religious violence, by framing the enclave experience, the methods of violence, and the vision of the millennial order.

This paper, however, looks not at how scripture continues to frame or shape sectarian experience in violent terms, but rather how several texts that came to be scripture arose out of enclave environments similarly consumed with polarization, vengeance fantasies, and eschatological scenarios. These texts reflect the perspective of the embattled enclave and thus preserve that perspective for future interpreters in the form of canonical scripture, to inspire or inflame ever new enclaves in new times.

The texts under examination—2 Thessalonians, 1 John, and Revelation—stand out in the New Testament canon for several reasons. All three texts are consumed with articulating group boundaries on a cosmic scale, laying out the purity, wisdom, and sanctity of insiders against a world both bent on *their* destruction and bound for *its own* by divine hands. They each reflect identifiably collective concerns—self-definition, boundaries, enemies, and models for perseverance—even if the language used to phrase those concerns cannot be clearly delimited to a time or a place in the first century CE. They also move quickly from the depiction of some sectarian rivalry or internecine crisis to the depiction of eschatological vengeance, triumph, and culmination, as if the crisis triggered eschatological fantasizing and prediction.

In these three texts one is confronted above all with visions of the way things are and will be—for those ancient apocalyptic enclaves and, through canonization, for their later heirs. And those visions revolve around, first, the demonization of outsiders; and secondly, fantasies of their destruction.[4]

2. *1 John*

1, 2, and 3 John, written in the decade after the final version of the Gospel of John (late first century CE), provide exciting evidence for the afterlife of the same social body that produced the Gospel of John. These brief letters develop much of the Gospel's unique terminology, including ἀγάπη (love), the opposition of light and darkness, and the enmity of the cosmos, while showing that

---

3. See Norman Cohn, *The Pursuit of the Millennium: Revolutionary Millenarians and Mystical Anarchists of the Middle Ages* (London: Temple Smith, rev. edn, 1970) and Yonina Talmon, 'Pursuit of the Millennium: The Relation Between Religious and Social Change', *Archives européennes de sociologie* 3 (1962), pp. 125-48. On enclave environment, see Emmanuel Sivan, 'The Enclave Culture', in Martin E. Marty and R. Scott Appleby (eds.), *Fundamentalisms Comprehended* (Chicago and London: University of Chicago Press, 1995), pp. 11-68.

4. Cf. Guy G. Stroumsa, 'Early Christianity as Radical Religion', in *Barbarian Philosophy: The Religious Revolution of Early Christianity* (Wissenschaftliche Untersuchungen zum Neuen Testament, 112; Tübingen: Mohr [Siebeck], 1999), pp. 8-26.

many of the crises over the nature of Jesus' body that the Gospel had explored (Jn 1.14; 19.34; 20.20-29) were causing actual schisms in the time of the letters (1 Jn 4.2; 5.6; 2 Jn 7; cf. *AcJn* 89–93, 97–102).

The discourse of 1 John—its representation of social experience—fundamentally reflects the polarized worldview of the enclave. Key juxtapositions of κόσμος (cosmos) to πατήρ (Father; 2.15), Truth to Lie (2.21-22), and God to Devil (3.8-10) follow in a historical trajectory from the insular social world of the Gospel of John.[5] But the boundaries have been widened: insiders possess a special discernment (2.20), a heavenly seed (3.9), and a χρίσμα (2.20, 27)—some unique ritual state or even talismanic substance;[6] while those who have left the enclave, and whose departure evidently triggered a crisis, must be viewed as of a different order entirely: 'They went out from us, but they did not belong to us, for if they *had* belonged to us, they would have remained with us' (2.19). The world thus seems to pose deception as its principal danger—'those who would deceive you' (2.26; 3.7)—rather than demons or Jews or Romans; and it is a social danger: the danger of contrary teachings, of the intimate enemy.[7] Indeed, as the Johannine scholar Georg Strecker pointed out, 1 John's 'conceptual world . . . is to a large extent formed by a conflict with [rival] teachers'.[8]

An enclave will inevitably cultivate an idiom, an insiders' argot, that affirms in daily speech and broader discussion the distinctiveness and wisdom of its members. All religious communities of even moderate group-boundaries possess an insiders' discourse, from Hasidim to Jehovah's Witnesses. In 1 John one finds the characteristics of the idiom in a number of different ways: in the language of polarity, like κόσμος and πατήρ; in the language of demonology, like διάβολος (Devil) rather than Σατάνας (Satan);[9] in the language of ἀγάπη for insiders' bonds, which curiously denies or displaces a powerful animosity towards outsiders;[10] and most importantly in the strange term ἀντίχριστος (antichrist):

---

5. Alan F. Segal, 'The Ruler of This World' [1981], in *The Other Judaisms of Late Antiquity* (Brown Judaic Studies, 127; Atlanta: Scholars Press, 1987), pp. 41-77.

6. Raymond E. Brown, *The Epistles of John* (AB, 30; Garden City, NY: Doubleday, 1982), pp. 341-42, 344; Georg Strecker, *The Johannine Letters* (Hermeneia; trans. Linda M. Maloney; Minneapolis: Fortress Press, 1996), pp. 64-66.

7. Brown, *Epistles of John*, p. 374; Strecker, *Johannine Letters*, pp. 63-64, 69-70; cf. David Frankfurter, *Elijah in Upper Egypt: The Coptic Apocalypse of Elijah and Early Egyptian Christianity* (Studies in Antiquity and Christianity, 7; Minneapolis: Fortress Press, 1993), pp. 103-106.

8. Georg Strecker, 'Chiliasm and Docetism in the Johannine School', *Australian Biblical Review* 38 (1990), pp. 45-61 (59). Strecker convincingly proposes that these rival teachers are specifically promoting a docetic christology.

9. 1 Jn 3.8-10. The preference is clear in comparison to 2 Thess. 2.9, where the cosmic force behind the ἄνομος (lawless one) is identified as Satan. See Segal, 'Ruler of This World', pp. 65-67.

10. This topic of animosity couched in terms of ἀγάπη is taken up in Shelly Matthews, *Perfect Martyrs: Jews, Christians, and Death in Acts* (in preparation).

(2.18) Children, it is the last hour! As you have heard that antichrist is coming, so now many antichrists have come. From this we know that it is the last hour. (19) They went out from us, but they did not belong to us; for if they had belonged to us, they would have remained with us. But by going out they made it plain that none of them belongs to us. (20) But you have been anointed by the Holy One, and you know all things. (21) I write to you, not because you do not know the truth, but because you know it, and you know that no lie comes from the truth. (22) Who is the liar but the one who denies that Jesus is the Christ? This is the antichrist, the one who denies the Father and the Son [1 Jn 2.18-22 NRSV].

Inextricably linked to 'those who went out from us' (as the potential subject of the verbs in v. 19), the word *antichrist/s* refers to the cumulative force of rival teachings or false prophecy in the current experience of the enclave, *not* to some beast or End-tyrant as later authorities sought to clarify it (cf. 4.1-6). But it is a term and a semantic field unique to the social world of this particular audience—'as *you have heard* that antichrist is coming' (2.18; 4.3)—invented in the time since the Gospel of John for an eschatology that was consumed with deception.[11]

Indeed, it is worth noting the character of 1 John's eschatology. Missing from its scenario are angels battling demons, terrestrial cataclysms, falling stars, and heathen armies. The focus lies entirely on the onset of false teachings. We should not be surprised, of course, for this is the quintessential anxiety of the sectarian enclave. Indeed, numerous early Christian texts reflect how the disruptions of schism and ideological rivalry *within* a religious community repeatedly are negotiated by moving into a state of millennial anticipation.[12] 'So now many antichrists have come: *from this we know* it is the last hour' (2.18), when the cosmos 'is passing away' (2.17). This eschatology is not particularly violent or advocating of violence, and yet the world itself presents a broad sense of danger, posed especially by ex-comrades now deemed apostates and rivals: the danger posed by intimate enemies. Historically and sociologically, this worldview does lie perilously close to that in which violence plays an expressive role in resolving eschatological danger, and so it is useful to examine some of the theory that has developed around it. As Georg Simmel put it, 'the degeneration of a difference in convictions into hatred and fight ordinarily occurs *only when there were essential, original similarities between the parties*'.[13] That is to say,

---

11. L.J. Lietaert Peerbolte, *The Antecedents of Antichrist: A Traditio-Historical Study of the Earliest Christian Views on Eschatological Opponents* (JSJSup, 49; Leiden: E.J. Brill, 1996), pp. 96-103; Brown, *Epistles of John*, p. 333; Bernard McGinn, *Antichrist: Two Thousand Years of the Human Fascination with Evil* (San Francisco: Harper, 1994), pp. 55-56; *pace* Strecker: 'The mythological figure of the antichrist belongs to the oldest layer of the traditions of the Johannine circle' (*Johannine Letters*, p. 63).

12. *Apoc. Pet., Asc. Isa., Apoc. Elij.*

13. Georg Simmel, *Conflict and the Web of Group-Affiliations* (trans. Kurt H. Wolff and

the self-idealization and -mythologization of the sectarian group forbids the slightest division. Hence, the slightest division or differences are experienced as an affront to the *entirety* of the group, and by extension to the divine sanction that the group represents. The deviant, the heretic, the rival is an affront to God himself, a monster or the tentacle of a monster, and thus signifies a danger of cosmic proportions. It is in this spirit that a community could start talking about *antichrists*.[14]

Simmel's point also offers an historically cogent interpretive principle for examining other cases of harsh vilification in ancient texts. That is to say, the most violent recriminations we find should be understood as responses *not* to heathen or non-christocentric Jewish neighbors, who were not experienced as constituting the larger, presumptive body of the in-group, but to *other* Jesus-believers—others imagined as members of the principal enclave.[15] (The principle becomes more clear in subsequent uses of texts like 1 John, as when the fourth-century heresiographer Epiphanius of Salamis recycles the warning of antichrists [2.18-19] to drive as wide as possible a wedge between his own 'holy church of God' and the proponents of the Christian New Prophecy movement [*Panarion* 58.5].)

3. *2 Thessalonians*

Almost all scholarship on this text concerns its claim to Pauline authorship, for the eschatological timetable of ch. 2 (which even includes an antichrist-like character) seems to contradict the ostensibly prior letter of Paul's hand, 1 Thessalonians. In this paper I am skeptical of Pauline authorship but do not depend on one position or the other. What concerns me in this text is its explicit imagery of vengeance against the audience's 'afflictors (τοῖς θλίβουσιν)':

Reinhard Bendix; New York: Free Press, 1955), p. 48 (emphasis mine). See also Lewis A. Coser, *The Functions of Social Conflict* (New York: Free Press, 1956), p. 70, and Jonathan Z. Smith, 'Differential Equations: On Constructing the Other', in *Relating Religion: Essays in the Study of Religion* (Chicago and London: University of Chicago Press, 2004), pp. 230-50.

14. And it is in this spirit that the term would retain value: as the seventh-century CE Egyptian monk Samuel of Kalamun was supposed to have called an emissary of the Chalcedonian church, saying, 'It is better to obey God and our father the archbishop Benjamin, than to obey you and your demonic teaching, you son of Satan and deceiving Antichrist' (*Life of Samuel of Kalamun* [tr. Anthony Alcock; Warminster: Aris & Phillips, 1983], ch. 11, p. 85).

15. John G. Gager, *Kingdom and Community: The Social World of Early Christianity* (Englewood Cliffs, NJ: Prentice–Hall, 1975), pp. 80-88; David Frankfurter, 'Jews or Not? Reconstructing the 'Other' in Revelation 2:9 and 3:9', *HTR* 94 (2001), pp. 403-25 (410-16), and 'Violence and Religious Formation: An Afterword', in Shelly Matthews and E. Leigh Gibson (eds.), *Violence in the New Testament* (New York: T. & T. Clark, 2005), pp. 140-52 (142-44).

(1.6) For it is indeed just of God to repay with affliction those who afflict you, (7) and to give relief to the afflicted as well as to us, when the Lord Jesus is revealed from heaven with his mighty angels (8) in flaming fire, inflicting vengeance on those who do not know God and on those who do not obey the gospel of our Lord Jesus. (9) These will suffer the punishment of eternal destruction from the face of the Lord and from the glory of his might... [2 Thess. 1.6-9 adjusted from NRSV].

Does the writer respond here to a real civic persecution—a riot or pogrom of sorts—behind the reference to 'affliction'? More precisely, *must* the term θλῖψις refer to a historical persecution? In general, historians of early Christianity have rushed far too uncritically to assume or even invent real persecutions on the basis of vague and overdetermined insiders' language. In the case of 2 Thessalonians, the details of 'affliction' remain entirely vague, so there seems little reason to contrive some civic persecution behind the word.[16] Rather, all the text's indications point to *internecine* conflict in the world of the author: new apocalyptic teachings that 'shake' and 'alarm' insiders (2.1-2);[17] the wisdom of insiders versus the 'deception' and 'delusion' of outsiders vis-à-vis the signs of the Lawless One (2.5-6, 10-12); and a reference to the afflictors themselves as 'those who do *not* obey the gospel of our Lord Jesus' (1.8)—that is, those who presumably *ought* to do so. 'Not obeying the gospel', we know from Paul, serves as an absolutist insider's term for rival believers who, as it were, do not hew to *our* interpretation of Jesus-tradition (cf. Gal. 1.6-9). Here again we have indications that the apocalyptic worldview the author is spinning out has been triggered by some experience of rival teachers.

It is not atypical for enclaves in crisis to envision rival teachings or internecine schism as 'affliction' or persecution.[18] The 'affliction' that the insiders

---

16. *Pace* Lars Hartman, 'The Eschatology of 2 Thessalonians as Included in a Communication', in Raymond Collins (ed.), *The Thessalonian Correspondence* (BETL, 87; Leuven: Leuven University Press, 1990), pp. 470-85 (484), who relates the affliction to 'local harassment' by neighbors, and Todd D. Still, who offers an elaborate scenario for persecution by heathen family members (*Conflict at Thessalonica: A Pauline Church and its Neighbours* [JSNTSup, 183; Sheffield: Sheffield Academic Press, 1999], pp. 208-85).

17. Helmut Koester astutely proposes that the teachings of the *parousia*'s arrival pertained not to theological matters but to an adjustment in ritual practices ('From Paul's Eschatology to the Apocalyptic Schemata of 2 Thessalonians' in Collins [ed.], *The Thessalonian Correspondence*, pp. 441-58 [455-56]).

18. The perception of affliction as a necessary enclave experience probably goes back to Paul himself: 1 Thess. 2.14; 3.3-4. It is never clear what kind of 'affliction' (θλῖψις) any of these communities would actually have experienced. Gerhard Krodel suggests that the opponents of 2.1-2 were interpreting the affliction in ch. 1 as proof of the eschaton's arrival ('2 Thessalonians', in Krodel [ed.], *The Deutero-Pauline Letters* [Minneapolis: Fortress, rev. edn, 1993], pp. 39-58 [44]); but this would require a primary and actual persecution. More likely is Koester's observation that the separation of the affliction from the eschatological timetable of ch. 2 indicates that the former has not been systematically integrated into the latter (Helmut Koester, *History and Literature of Early Christianity* [Philadelphia: Fortress Press, 1982], p. 245).

are supposed to envision here is a social, not supernatural or institutional phenomenon: *those who* afflict, *those who* do not obey (or conform to our) gospel of our Lord Jesus, *those who* will be repaid with affliction and suffer punishment. But it is important to see how rapidly the word 'affliction' is turned *against* these unnamed opponents. In 2 Thessalonians they are themselves consigned to immediate, painful vengeance. The *parousia* itself—usually a glorious theophany that initiates resurrection (1 Thess. 4.15-17) or gathers in the Elect (Mk 13.26-27)—is here conceived in exclusively vengeful terms: 'when the Lord Jesus is revealed from heaven with his mighty angels in flaming fire, inflicting vengeance on those who do not know God and on those who do not obey the gospel of our Lord Jesus. These will suffer the punishment of eternal destruction from the πρόσωπον [appearance or face] of the Lord and the *glory of his might*' (2 Thess. 1.7-9; cf. 2.8). Like an apotropaic Medusa head, the very face of Christ is invoked as a devastating weapon—a scene given vivid narrative nuance in the latest volume of the popular Christian fiction series *Left Behind* :

> Tens of thousands of foot soldiers dropped their weapons, grabbed their heads or their chests, fell to their knees, and writhed as they were invisibly sliced asunder. Their innards and entrails gushed to the desert floor, and as those around them turned to run, they too were slain, their blood pooling and rising in the unforgiving brightness of the glory of Christ...

> And Jesus said, in that voice like a trumpet and the sound of rushing waters, 'I AM WHO I AM'. ...The soldiers screamed and fell, their bodies bursting open from head to toe at every word that proceeded out of the mouth of the Lord as He spoke to the captives within Jerusalem.[19]

Thus 2 Thessalonians is reimagined for a twenty-first-century audience with similar concerns about the boundaries of the righteous and God's chastisement of outsiders.[20] So also in the ancient author's world the opponents ('afflictors') are cursed as *God's*—not just the enclave's—enemies, a logic we have already seen with 1 John and thus likewise indicative of an *intimate* enemy.

In 2 Thessalonians, then, violent vengeance fantasies stem from a situation of bitter internecine sectarian rivalry: 'us' against 'those who afflict us', who seem to be identical with 'those who do not obey (our) gospel'. There are, of course, no indications that the violence extended from ritual speech to ritual *gestures*, as if the author's partisans were actually to *embody* the wrath of Lord Jesus. Yet the combination of vengeful fantasy and the construction of the opponent as *afflictor*, as persecutor, has historically often called forth violent acts, which are

---

19. Tim Lahaye and Jerry B. Jenkins, *Glorious Appearing: The End of Days* (Left Behind, 12; Wheaton, IL: Tyndale House, 2004), pp. 226, 286.

20. See Glenn W. Shuck, 'Marks of the Beast: The *Left Behind* Novels, Identity, and the Internalization of Evil', *Nova religio* 8 (2004), pp. 48-63, and Amy Johnson Frykholm, *Rapture Culture:* Left Behind *in Evangelical America* (New York: Oxford University Press, 2004).

conceived as preemptive and defensive. Early and contemporary fundamentalist Mormons offer especially vivid examples of this pattern: a discourse of persecution inciting a combative attitude to the world and especially to rivals and apostates.[21] So also in 2 Thessalonians, θλῖψις (affliction) is met initially with a kind of appropriation or engagement for the purposes of martyrdom (1.5); but joy in martyrdom quickly turns to invocations of reversal and revenge.

4. Revelation

The Book of Revelation offers the most violent imagery of the three texts in its visions of the fate of outsiders to John's particular enclave—and of the world in general. Much recent scholarship has sought to rationalize John's violence as directed either to spark revolutionary justice for the subaltern or to rail against a tyrannical Roman empire—reading the text in either case as advocating justice, equality, and hope rather than brutality, misogyny, and vengeance.[22] Unfortunately, besides a kind of canonical special-pleading for a very problematic text, these lines of interpretation have seriously neglected the sectarian, internecine, and devoutly Jewish character of the text.[23]

The clearest evidence of this social context emerges in John's initial polemic against the woman prophet he typologically labels 'Jezebel' (2.20). Immediately, before we even enter the teachings at issue, we understand the immediate religious context to be dominated by prophet-figures—charismatic channelers of otherworld beings. This is a social context with little internal 'grid' but enormous concern for sacred identity, boundary markers, and authority. Suspicion, polarity, and anxiety to preserve the borders of purity within the group and beyond the group preoccupy prophet-dominated movements. Altogether the reliance on prophets can make for a highly unstable social order, as other Christian documents show.[24] And here we see a typical struggle between prophets within the larger enclave over points of practice and purity. Indeed,

---

21. Jon Krakauer, *Under the Banner of Heaven: A Story of Violent Faith* (Garden City, NY: Doubleday, 2003).

22. Adela Yarbro Collins, *Crisis and Catharsis: The Power of the Apocalypse* (Philadelphia: Westminster Press, 1984), pp. 167-75, and Elizabeth Schüssler Fiorenza, *Revelation: Vision of a Just World* (Minneapolis: Fortress Press, 1991). Cf. Tina Pippin, *Death and Desire: The Rhetoric of Gender in the Apocalypse of John* (Louisville, KY: Westminster Press, 1992), pp. 49-53.

23. See Frankfurter, 'Jews or Not?', and compare more innovative engagements with the violence of the text by John Marshall, *Parables of War: Reading John's Jewish Apocalypse* (Waterloo, ON: Wilfrid Laurier University Press, 2001), and Christopher A. Frilingos, *Spectacles of Empire: Monsters, Martyrs, and the Book of Revelation* (Philadelphia: University of Pennsylvania Press, 2004).

24. *Didache* 11; *Asc. Isa.* Cf. 1 Cor. 12–14. See in general on the social dynamics of prophet movements Talmon, 'Pursuit of the Millennium', and Mary Douglas, *Natural Symbols: Explorations in Cosmology* (New York: Pantheon, 1973), pp. 111-22.

more than 1 John or 2 Thessalonians, the Apocalypse actually gives the points of contention, albeit in the language of moral monstrosity: to wit, *porneia* and eating non-kosher food. It takes little imagination to see these immoralities as precisely those areas where Paul himself had loosened halakhic rules (1 Cor. 7–8). The prophetess, it would seem, was an advocate of Pauline views of marriage and food-laws rather than practicing *porneia* or eating *treif* victuals. What we read in 2.19-23 are John's accusations, worded in such a way as to cast the Paulinists' deviance in gross terms and hopefully protect an enclave he viewed as his own and subject to high purity standards. Depicting opponents in pornographic terms was hardly unusual in antiquity and gained a particular intensity in early Christianity.[25] So also the 'blasphemy' he decries from those he calls 'so-called Jews' (2.9, 3.9), as I have argued elsewhere, must indicate the disruptive presence of Pauline Gentile God-fearers in the larger collective—an affront to John's sense of Jewish halakhic and enclave purity.[26] In all these ways, Revelation offers a further glimpse of the dynamics of internecine strife among the Jesus movements of the later first century.

So what about violence? Most of the vengeance fantasies we find in this text—linked particularly to the heavenly liturgy and its trumpets and bowls (9.4-6; 16.10-21; 19.17-21)—seem directed at a vague assortment of outsiders:

> (9.4) [The locusts] were told not to damage the grass of the earth or any green growth or any tree, but only those people who do not have the seal of God on their foreheads. (5) They were allowed to torture them for five months, but not to kill them, and their torture was like the torture of a scorpion when it stings someone. (6) And in those days people will seek death but will not find it; they will long to die, but death will flee from them.
>
> (16.10) The fifth angel poured his bowl on the throne of the beast, and its kingdom was plunged into darkness; people gnawed their tongues in agony, (11) and cursed the God of heaven because of their pains and sores, and they did not repent of their deeds... (21) and huge hailstones, each weighing about a hundred pounds, dropped from heaven on people, until they cursed God for the plague of the hail, so fearful was that plague.

If there is a distinctive identity to those imagined as victims here, it revolves around three elements: their association with alternative kingdoms, their lack of the seal of God (9.4; cf. 7.3-4), or their possession of the seal of the Beast (13.16). Their 'cursing (ἐβλασφήμησαν)' of God underlines their separateness: they are not victims but blasphemers! And yet those wrongly-sealed, blaspheming outsiders are also constructed in relation to the obstinate impurity they bring to divine space: 'As for the cowardly, the faithless, the polluted, the murderers, the fornicators, the sorcerers, the idolaters, and all liars, their *place* will be in

---

25. See J. Rives, 'The Blood Libel against the Montanists', *VC* 50 (1996), pp. 117-24, and Jennifer Wright Knust, *Abandoned to Lust: Sexual Slander and Ancient Christianity* (New York: Columbia University Press, 2006), pp. 113-19.

26. Frankfurter, 'Jews or Not?'.

the *lake* that burns with fire and sulphur' (21.8; cf. 21.27, 22.15). Thus it seems that divine vengeance is meant to hit those who pollute halakhically—through ritual impurity—the purity represented by the enclave.

'Jezebel' herself—the quintessential intimate enemy for her association with *porneia*—is also the declared object of violence, in the form of a curse: John (as Christ) declares that he will 'throw her on a bed', conveying not rape but the prophetess's consignment to a wasting illness.[27] In fact, it is her *followers* who copulate (μοιχεύοντας) with her, John claims, and Christ will consign them to great tribulation (θλῖψις; 2.22). So internecine rivalry leads to cosmic or typological demonization—'Jezebel!'—and then to threats or declarations of imminent divine vengeance.

Consequently, this Jezebel, promoter of *porneia*, reappears in cosmic scope as the very icon of *porneia*: a giant woman in red, riding a beast and holding a cup of 'the abominations and impurities of her *porneia*' (17.4). Following Paul Duff's insightful analysis, we can understand this figure as 'Jezebel' and Pauline teachings in nightmarish hyperbole, the very inversion of John's heavenly male celibacy (14.4).[28] Intimate enemies become but the faces of cosmic enemies, so violent and painful ends must be envisioned for the whole cosmos of polluted peoples.[29] The lurid details of their destruction encourage insiders, who anticipate transcendence and angelization through their purity. The larger population becomes in some respects an extension of sectarian dispute and the vengeance it incites: the fantasy extends to people in such pain from giant stinging locusts that they try to kill themselves (9.3-6); people crushed by giant hailstones (16.21); and an enormous avian feast on the human flesh of 'kings and captains...free and slave, both small and great' (19.17-18, 21).

Let us remember too that John is not simply assembling a pastiche of biblical allusions in these vengeance fantasies. He means the images to be *declarations*—on heavenly authority—against the full force of opposition against true purity.[30] He means them to carry *illocutionary* force, like the swords or fire that come out of the mouths of heavenly beings (Rev. 1.16; 11.5; 19.16).

---

27. David E. Aune, *Revelation* (Word Biblical Commentary, 3 vols.; Nashville: Nelson, 1997–98), I, p. 205.

28. Paul B. Duff, *Who Rides the Beast? Prophetic Rivalry and the Rhetoric of Crisis in the Churches of the Apocalypse* (New York: Oxford University Press, 2001), pp. 83-112, with Pippin, *Death and Desire*, pp. 57-68.

29. See 2 Thess. 2 and 1 Jn 4.3: Satan and the spirit of antichrist are active through current deceivers.

30. E.g., Rev. 18 is an ironic dirge, a pseudo-mournful description of misfortune past (Adela Yarbro Collins, 'Revelation 18: Taunt-Song or Dirge?', in J. Lambrecht [ed.], *L'apocalypse johannique et l'apocalyptique dans le Nouveau Testament* [BETL, 53; Leuven: Leuven University Press, 1980], pp. 185-204). Yet a mourning over Rome would only be wishful in the later first century CE. As Yarbro Collins herself observes, 'there are literary and historical indications that the desire for revenge played a role in the composition of the passage' ('Taunt-Song or Dirge?', p. 204).

What is the afterlife of these graphic fantasies of vengeance? Interestingly, witnesses to the use of Revelation in the second and third centuries do not mention the violent features of the text. Early documents of the New Prophecy movement of Asia Minor, for example, suggest that its prophets would declare their divine authority much as John does in the letter incipits in Revelation 2–3 (§§1, 5, 7, 15-16), that they promoted celibacy as John does (Rev. 2.14, 20; 14.4; §24[31] [Apollonius, *apud* Eusebius, *H.E.* 5.18.2]) and possibly also Jewish meal purity (in the form of fasts [*ibid.*]), and perhaps most significantly, they regard their intimate opponents as προφητοφόντας—'prophet-murderers' (§23 [Anonymous, *apud* Eusebius, *H.E.* 5.16.12]). If polemical and eschatological violence pervaded the discourse of New Prophecy, as we would historically expect it to have, the materials that come down to us through its detractors concern simply the legitimacy of their leaders.

Two witnesses from third-century upper Egypt show divergent readings of the Apocalypse's vengeance fantasies. Dionysius of Alexandria describes a religious movement in Arsinoë that was focused entirely on the concrete and imminent arrival of 'a kind of millennium devoted to bodily indulgence', based exegetically—Dionysius implies—on Revelation (*apud* Eusebius, *H.E.* 7.24.1-3). The *Apocalypse of Elijah*, from about the same period, draws on Revelation not only to frame the triumph of the righteous (ch. 1) but also as an inspiration for the elevation of graphic martyrdoms (ch. 4) and the judgment of enemies (ch. 5).[32]

This tendency to draw violent scenarios out of the Apocalypse, either as vengeance fantasies or to envision the holy sufferings of insiders, does indeed characterize much of the history of the use of the text, as Judith Kovacs and Christopher Rowland have recently documented.[33] And if second- and third-century prophet-movements lacked the power to exert more than the fantasy and anticipation of violence, medieval times found Revelation's scenes of apocalyptic vengeance to be just warrant to exterminate.[34] Concern for the saints' ritual purity gave way to the anxious purging of the countryside.

5. *Conclusions: Vengeance Fantasy and Violence*

What then do these texts teach us about violence and scripture, both in antiquity and today? First of all, they provide intimate, graphic evidence of sectarian con-

---

31. Paragraph (§§) references from Ronald E. Heine, *The Montanist Oracles and Testimonia* (Patristic Monograph Series, 14; Macon, GA: Mercer University Press, 1989). On New Prophecy's celibacy and fasting traditions in relation to Revelation see Christine Trevett, 'Apocalypse, Ignatius, Montanism: Seeking the Seeds', *VC* 43 (1989), pp. 313-38.

32. See Frankfurter, *Elijah in Upper Egypt*, pp. 37-38, on use of Revelation, and pp. 270-78 on links between *Apoc. Elij.* and the millennialist movement in Arsinoë.

33. Judith Kovacs and Christopher Rowland, *Revelation: The Apocalypse of Jesus Christ* (Blackwell Bible Commentaries; Oxford: Blackwell, 2004).

34. See Cohn, *Pursuit of the Millennium*, pp. 32-33, 75-81, and *passim*.

flict and its propensity for extraordinary hatred and vilification. Second, they show us how the enclave in internecine conflict will mythologize that conflict as the resurgence of ancient typologies—combat myths, icons of aggressive impurity—or according to an insider's discourse—ἀντίχριστος, θλῖψις, ἄνομος (lawless one)—that offers group-members the experience of unique discernment into the nature of things. Elevating and mythologizing sectarian conflict will transmogrify the intimate enemy—the apostate or heretic or charismatic rival—as monstrous, as perversely impure, and often as a cruel and overwhelming persecutor: the great πόρνη (whore) of Babylon, for example, who is 'drunk with the blood of the holy ones and the blood of the witnesses' (Rev. 17.6).[35]

A third feature that emerges in these texts, especially when one faction does find itself on the losing end in a crisis of sectarian leadership, is the leaders' move to conjure apocalyptic scenarios of ultimate triumph. With the growing dominance of Paulinism in Asia Minor, those who (like John of Patmos) rejected Pauline teachings would certainly have felt that this-worldly debate could no longer withstand those advocates of *porneia* and heathen food. Only the heavenly world could clarify the justice of things. And in such situations—which pervade early Christian texts—we see a tendency both to transvalue frustration in terms of persecution and affliction, on the one hand, and to lay out lurid vengeance fantasies as a channel for aggression. But the word 'fantasy' should be clarified: in the discourse forms in which we find them, they are not idle musings in the spirit of *Schadenfreude* on the way things might go for one's enemies, but rather prophetic *declarations*—speech-acts, curses—that for some enthusiastic or anxious audience render those lurid scenes of revenge efficacious and real: that Rome, as Babylon, *has* fallen (Rev. 18); that afflictors *are* being incinerated (2 Thess. 1); or in the lurid second-century *Apocalypse of Peter*, that sexual sinners *are* being tortured in exotic punishments.

Now, it must be clarified that we have not a whit of evidence for actual physical violence in the immediate milieux of these texts (and, indeed, far less physical violence from outside forces than once was assumed).[36] What does this mean for the subject of violent vengeance fantasies in these materials from the early Jesus movement? For one thing, isolating this tendency to vengeance fantasy in the social context of internecine conflict can lead us to consider alternative routes to negotiating rage—alternative forms of 'violence'—in the early Roman empire. The eastern Mediterranean of the first century CE was a violent world, as Josephus and Acts show quite clearly. And yet, physical violence was

---

35. Cf. McGinn, *Antichrist*, p. 78, on uses of antichrist ideas against rivals and heretics in the centuries following the original proof-texts.

36. See Leonard L. Thompson, *The Book of Revelation: Apocalypse and Empire* (New York: Oxford University Press, 1990), pp. 95-132; and Mary Beard, John North, and Simon Price, *Religions of Rome*. I. *A History* (Cambridge: Cambridge University Press, 1998), pp. 236-45.

not often a viable form of expression, especially for subaltern groups. But the corpora of magical texts give certain evidence that, in many (if not most) cases of social conflict, *curses*—both private and public—could go far in *displacing* violence through hostile declarations: 'Lady [Goddess], Destroy Eleutheros. If you vindicate me, I will make a silver palm, if you destroy him utterly from the human race!'; 'You holy letters, cause there to fall on [— insert victim's name here—] fire and fever and groaning and may he be cast down on a sickbed and may he have no healing for as long as I desire!'[37] The curse is a speech act, a performative utterance, that involves the performer in establishing efficacious authority (by this ritual—these series of gestures and components—action *will* occur), in articulating the constraints or demise he wishes upon an enemy or rival, and certainly in gaining some vicarious satisfaction in the proper completion of the curse rite. The curse 'works' through its properly articulated (and often socially transparent) performance: the rival is declared vanquished or bound through authoritative word and gesture.[38] Taking this aspect of Mediterranean social life back to the articulation of vengeance fantasies and the rhetorical forms to which these fantasies extended, we can imagine that the formulation of a curse could sometimes mean that the author would foreswear actual assault. John of Patmos, speaking in the authoritative voice of Christ, declares that 'I am throwing her on a (sick-)bed and [her devotees] into great affliction…and I will strike her children dead' (Rev. 2.22-23); and later, 'I warn everyone who hears the words of the prophecy of this book: if anyone adds to them, God will add to that person the plagues described in this book' (22.18), and even the aggressive declarative woe-utterance, '*Outside* [ἔξω, meant to parallel μακάριοι (blessed) in the previous declaration] are the dogs and the sorcerers and fornicators and murderers and idolaters, and everyone who loves and practices falsehood' (22.15). Words, curses and blessings, are the means of dividing the insiders from the outsiders, of sanctifying the insiders sealed by the Lamb, and of condemning to dreadful fates the outsiders.

Yet the goal of this paper has not been simply to discuss images of religious violence in ancient texts but also to identify *sources* for violence and

---

37. Sicilian defixio tablet (first century CE), from John G. Gager, *Curse Tablets and Binding Spells from the Ancient World* (New York: Oxford University Press, 1992), no. 93 (pp. 192-93); Geniza spell manual 6 (medieval Egyptian Jewish), from Gager, *Curse Tablets*, no. 113 (pp. 210-11).

38. In general on curses in the ancient Mediterranean world, see Gager, *Curse Tablets*, pp. 21-23; David Frankfurter, 'Curses, Blessings, and Ritual Authority: Egyptian Magic in Comparative Perspective', *Journal of Ancient Near Eastern Religion* 5 (2005), pp. 159-87, and Frankfurter, 'Fetus Magic and Sorcery Fears in Roman Egypt', *Greek, Roman, and Byzantine Studies* 46 (2006), pp. 37-62. For examples of cursing sectarian rivals in late antiquity see Gideon Bohak, 'Magical Means for Handling Minim in Rabbinic Literature', in P. Tomson and D. Lambers-Petry (eds.), *The Image of the Judaeo-Christians in Ancient Jewish and Christian Literature* (Tubingen: Mohr [Siebeck], 2003), pp. 267-79.

combative self-definition in texts that have been—conveniently or inconveniently—determinative of Christian identity for two thousand years. Thus the question becomes, how *might* groups—medieval millennialists, early modern radical Protestants, contemporary fundamentalists—use canonical vengeance fantasies as sanction for violence? And this question poses a problem. Taking, for example, 2 Thessalonians, we might ask, is it not Christ and his angels who are supposed to fry 'our' afflictors? Or in the lurid bowl-visions of the Apocalypse, aren't there angels up there to take care of stinging, crushing, infecting, or otherwise wasting the masses wallowing in sin? Whence the arrogance, the *temerity*, of any religious group to take divine vengeance into its own hands?

The social dynamics laid out in the beginning of this paper would suggest that any religious enclave confronting such texts as Revelation or 2 Thessalonians—for more routinized congregations are not the topic here—would *already* be committed to cultivating a conviction in its own divine sanction, involving a tangible sense of (a) immediacy to the supernatural world; (b) insiders' purity and righteousness, with an insiders' discourse to encourage this transcendent self-conception; (c) opposition to an outer world of darkness and confusion; and often (d) some narrative scenario to encourage perseverance and triumph in the world. Any religious enclave will therefore bring these dispositions *to* a text they deem canonical or authoritative.

Moreover, before the historian even considers matters of content, it can be understood that the texts will intrinsically offer typological frameworks—myths, legends, language—for comprehending both conflict and sanctity in any crisis situation. We are persecuted by the dark forces of society *as the prophets were*, reveal the authors of Q and the *Ascension of Isaiah*; the Romans descend upon the house of our God *as the Babylonians did*, pronounce the authors of *4 Ezra* and *2 Baruch*; we are persecuted by the world *as Jesus was*, preaches the author of the Gospel of John.[39] All these authors produced new documents to clarify that typological interpretation; and so on for later times into modernity. Thus certain apocalyptic enclaves already consumed with scripture typology—with the authority of scripture over the interpretation of current times—will cultivate a sense of the *realization* of scripture narrative, *especially narratives of conflict*. Mark Juergensmyer has pointed out the central experience of being in a state of war for the most violent religious sects—that this experience is cultivated and embraced enthusiastically through all aspects of life; and many now-canonical texts, especially those produced in situations of internecine conflict, lay out scenarios, terminology, and triumphal ends for just such a state of war.[40] An

---

39. On Q, see Melanie Johnson-DeBaufre, 'The Blood Required of This Generation: Interpreting Communal Blame in a Colonial Context', in Matthews and Gibson (eds.), *Violence in the New Testament*, pp. 22-34. On *Ascension of Isaiah*, see Robert G. Hall, 'The *Ascension of Isaiah*: Community, Situation, Date, and Place in Early Christianity', *JBL* 109 (1990), pp. 289-306.

40. Mark Juergensmyer, *Terror in the Mind of God: The Global Rise of Religious Violence*

enclave that has already come to imagine itself in this state of war (and that has formed itself in dynamic relationship with scripture) will come inevitably to insert itself *into* scripture, as the saints or the righteous or the martyrs, and thus find a script for themselves as *actors*, not just discerners of God's plan.

It is in this phase of transforming canonical scripture from encouraging narrative to a script for action that violent acts can seem like divinely legitimate, even necessary, responses. Perhaps the saints must fight for their lives to survive the Tribulation, as the Branch Davidians felt in 1993.[41] Perhaps there is the understanding that the divine realm—God, Michael, or Christ—will enter the fray only in the pitch of battle against the forces of darkness—a point easily drawn from Daniel 12 (and now rationalized as 'mid-tribulationist' theology). Or perhaps the scenes of vengeance decreed in scripture are *so* inevitable, the fate of the sinful or perverse sealed *so* securely, that initiating God's vengeance oneself involves no arrogance whatsoever. We (as it were) are merely setting the ball rolling. We are the sword of God against those whom he has decreed for punishment. In these first blows we are *initiating* a process that will culminate in the in-rushing of the heavenly host.[42]

For these scenarios, texts describing the advent of antichrist, the burning vengeance of the Lord Jesus, or rains of divine affliction and lurid massacres of the people of the Beast all have a remarkable convenience.

(Berkeley: University of California Press, 3rd edn, 2003), pp. 148-66. See also Stroumsa, 'Early Christianity as Radical Religion', pp. 15-18.

41. Thomas Robbins and Dick Anthony, 'Sects and Violence: Factors Enhancing the Volatility of Marginal Religious Movements', in Stuart A. Wright (ed.), *Armageddon in Waco: Critical Perspectives on the Branch Davidian Conflict* (Chicago and London: University of Chicago Press, 1995), pp. 236-59 (239-40), and Dick Anthony and Thomas Robbins, 'Religious Totalism, Exemplary Dualism, and the Waco Tragedy', in Thomas Robbins and Susan J. Palmer (eds.), *Millennium, Messiahs, and Mayhem* (New York and London: Routledge, 1997), pp. 261-84 (272-74).

42. See Juergensmyer, *Terror in the Mind of God*, pp. 110-11, on Aum Shinrikyo.

CONCLUDING REFLECTIONS ON RELIGION AND VIOLENCE:
CONFLICT, SUBVERSION, AND SACRIFICE

Stephen A. Marini

1. *Introduction*

Our volume has captured a rich discourse on the topic of 'Religion and Violence: the Biblical Heritage'. My concluding task is to gather together the strands of our conversation that seem to have been most pertinent to our subject and to place them in a perspective that will evoke still more questions about this fatefully important issue. At the risk of egregious overgeneralization, I see three main strands of the heritage presented as most relevant to us here and now.

2. *Conflict*

One strand of our conversation has concerned conflicts between different cultural groups expressed in religious texts about violence. David Wright's careful analysis of the rationale of talion and homicide laws in Exodus 20–23 raises a large question about the Israelite appropriation of legal norms from their Babylonian adversaries and conquerors. If, as he argues, the Laws of 'that Old Babylonian king' Hammurabi were in fact the template for the Covenant Collection in Exodus, then Israelite ideas of justice were, as he suggests, a symbolic reconfiguration of political ideology in face of international domination. Put more pointedly, his evidence suggests that in the biblical world, the justice of the oppressor of God's people could sometimes become the justice of God's people themselves. Notions of justice, here in the form of casuistic and apodictic laws, can and did transfer from oppressor to oppressed despite, or even because of, the bond of violence that joined them together. In a similar vein, for Lawrence Wills the formation of Mark's passion narrative entails literary borrowings about the death of sages, specifically Aesop, from the Greek cultures that opposed and resisted Christianity's construction of new mythic formulations.

For both the Israel of the Exodus account and the early Christians, the development of religious narratives was an act that overcame antecedent cultural alienation by incorporating part of an old, foreign, and oppressive religious order into a new, indigenous, and liberating one. The emphasis here is on the fact of cultural alienation, often accompanied by violence, as a situation out of which new mythic narratives can emerge. Cultural conflict, then, is built into the very nature of religious texts, even when they seem to share specific teachings across religious traditions. These papers suggest the troubling premise that within the biblical horizon, violence and peace are related to each other dialectically, as are oppression and justice. Peace and justice, it seems, do not, and perhaps cannot, exist without violence and oppression. The former do not simply oppose the latter, moreover, they also borrow from or even require their opposites.

In this sense, conflict and violence between cultures seem to mediate the production of new scriptural texts, to be one of their important, perhaps even necessary, preconditions. Such a premise has the uncomfortable ring of human truth to it, replete with the irony, paradox, limitation, and inevitability that moral experience brings. But it also seems to foreclose some essential moral qualities of religious affirmation: hope, purity, transcendence, categorical good. It therefore raises a fundamental question about how the historical formation of religious traditions stands in tension with the highest moral aspirations that those traditions proclaim.

3. Subversion

A second strand of this volume has addressed the intra-religious tensions that inform religious texts concerning violence. A number of the papers have pointed out conceptual and literary inconsistencies in biblical texts that subvert their own explicit agendas. Tamar Kamionkowski suggests that while Isa. 2.2-4 offers a vision of universal peace so perennially alluring that it has been used as an inscription at the United Nations, it comes at the price of universal submission to a divine sovereign. Applying Johan Galtung's thoughtful analysis of violence to this text, she concludes that while the prophet's vision may indeed reject all actual and structural violence, it still relies on the cultural violence of Zion's royal domination to maintain God's peace. Isaiah's vision of universal peace requires a divine sovereignty grounded in power and the threat of violent judgment, incorporating a constituent element of violence into even the most sublime biblical vision of peace. In an analogous fashion, Stephen Geller argues that the very agenda of prophecy itself, which he does not hesitate to identify with 'biblical religion' *per se*, is marked by an ineluctable conflict between the prophets' quest for sacred experience and their mission to interpret that experience in multiple social contexts. Geller concludes that this tension has developed into the irreconcilable alternatives of interpretation and literalism that continue to bedevil scriptural and cultural hermeneutics to this day.

Concerning the New Testament and Patristic writings, David Frankfurter and Jennifer Knust have raised a complementary issue about violence within religious traditions. They focus on 'the enemy within' and 'the embattled enclave' as perspectives informing violent and judgmental texts from New Testament apocalyptic and from Justin Martyr respectively. Frankfurter argues that the 'vengeance fantasies' in 1 John, 2 Thessalonians, and Revelation derive not from antipathy toward non-Christians but rather toward rival Christians. The 'embattled enclave' mentality of these writers imagined the gravest threats of impurity, disobedience, and betrayal to lie with those Christians whose practice most directly resembled and therefore challenged their own, rather than with more distant Romans and Jews. Knust makes a similar interpretation of Justin's *Dialogue with Trypho*, understanding it not as the anti-Jewish polemic it purports to be, but rather as an indexing text designed to describe true believers and exclude marginal or false ones. The source of these violent and influential early Christian texts, they both conclude, is not persecution but internecine strife.

This viewpoint makes a great deal of sense to me from the perspective of sectarian studies. At moments of religious crisis, centralized institutional authority is not effective, as in the Israel of the prophets, or does not exist at all, as in the early Christian case. This vacuum leaves geographical and ideological communities free to articulate alternative worldviews which express the social and psychological qualities of their crisis situation. Where conflict ensues between sectarian rivals, especially in metropolitan centers, the new worldviews absolutize into categorical condemnation of all believers outside one's own sect. Conflict among variants of a religious tradition combines with the urgency to define and defend the true religious path, thereby justifying violent language and even violent acts against coreligionists.

4. Sacrifice

A third theme of this conversation, more muted but no less important than the other two, has been that of sacrifice. I want to bring it forward along with the others, because it brings us closer to the heart of the problem as I understand it. Among the respective chapters, Jennifer Knust's on Justin Martyr's *Dialogue with Trypho* addresses sacrifice most directly. Knust draws our attention to how Justin recast the shameful crucifixion of Christ into a redemptive sacrifice, then deployed it against the repudiated and abandoned practice of Jewish temple sacrifice. In her discussion, Knust also notes approvingly the interpretation of Jonathan Klawans, that for Israel, temple sacrifice served 'as a positive imitation of God's action in the world intended to maintain God's presence among the people'.

What strikes me most about this brief consideration of sacrifice is the centrality of killing as the essential ritual act in both in Israelite religion and early Christianity. Whether we agree with Knust and Klawans or with other interpreters of sacrifice is not the issue. My concern is, rather, to point out the obvious fact that for both biblical faiths, sacrifice was not simply propitiation or obedience to divine command, but rather the defining act of relationship between humans and the divine. If the intention of religion is to gain an efficacious bond between the human and the sacred, then the essential way attain it, for both of these biblical traditions, is to kill something or someone. The intentional ritual killing of God's most perfect creatures, or of God himself, constitutes the primal phenomenology of the divine-human relationship itself.

It seems to me that this inherently violent conceptual and performative definition of how humans relate to God must inform our discourse here, which has primarily focused on how violence between and among cultural groups can be inscribed onto sacred texts. To reconstruct how rival communities wrote and interpreted violent biblical texts to manipulate historic conflicts is a valuable and vital work of scholarship, which has been admirably demonstrated here. But to carry on such work without acknowledging the essential message of those texts that violence mediates the divine and the human is to miss much of the power that such manipulation possessed. A number of our papers have asked how such social and literary strategies could have been successful, but they have not hazarded an answer. An important part of the answer, I suggest, is that those societies and cultures required an objective correlate of violence embedded in the nature of the human-divine relationship itself. The biblical texts of sacrifice provided precisely that requisite articulation of primal sacred violence.

5. Religion and Violence

To summarize all of this as succinctly as I can, we have learned from these papers that biblical texts express violence in at least three ways. They borrow and contest teachings from political conquerors or cultural oppressors and make them their own. On the other hand they can articulate 'the enemy within' or the 'embattled enclave' mentality of sectarian strife to demonize fellow believers. And thirdly, they contain an inherent element of sacred violence, especially of sacrifice, that constitutes the divine-human relationship itself and thereby can legitimate appeals to violence against enemies or fellow believers.

One unavoidable consequence of this evidence is a critique of religion itself. Our students always ask why religion seems to be such a cause of violence, when it proclaims universal values of peace and harmony. The biblical evidence presented here about conflict, subversion, and sacrifice does not so much answer the question as invalidate it. We may well be profoundly mistaken in assuming that religion has a peaceful or just or humanitarian element at its core. From a cultural and historical perspective, it is certainly difficult to deny that religion is indeed a major source of human violence.

The papers in this volume suggest one reason why: biblical religion, at least, seems rooted in concepts of power, not of love or even of justice. And power as the prime reality of the divine must, it seems, be manifested in acts of communal righteousness, social violence, and ritual sacrifice that validate the authority of the divine and thereby of the religious order. The assumption, whether explicit or tacit, of all of our papers has been the Durkheimian one that the problem of religious violence lies in the incorporation of political power and social conflict into religious myth and ritual. I have suggested that we also need to include the power of violence inherent in the sacred itself, rendered by biblical texts about sacrifice, in order to explain more adequately how the process works.

But the reality of human conflict is not going to change, nor will it be easy to mitigate the violence that seems to lie at the heart of biblical sacrality itself. The most plausible way out seems to be to remove human conflict and violence from God's agenda. Tamar Kamionkowski has challenged us to think in these terms, but we must first ask if such a move can be made without severing the connection between sacrality and the human situations of conflict that religion quintessentially addresses. In other words, to the extent that we remove violence from the divine, we also seem to remove religion's relevance to the social conflicts in which it is inextricably imbedded.

Such a strategy has in fact been attempted. Indeed, it is characteristic of modern liberal religious thought from Moses Mendelssohn and Søren Kierkegaard to Abraham Joshua Heschel and Reinhold Niebuhr. Such thinkers challenged the cultural violence of their religious traditions and concluded that the most effective antidote was the individual who reinterprets religion in the corrosive but morally superior light of reason and the Enlightenment values of freedom and justice. The fate of this liberal project, however, has not been encouraging. While liberals have tried over the past two centuries to persuade the West of their religious corrective, the forces of religious violence have run rampant and now engulf the world. Liberals can of course continue to assert their project and hope that the world will learn its truth. But the central cultural potency of religion—its ability to mythicize and ritualize social conflict into sacred justifications of violence—will not thereby be confronted.

Is it then the case that violence is categorically ingredient in religion, and the world is therefore condemned to endemic and violent religious conflict? Perhaps so. And if so, one valid response certainly would be to reject religion entirely as a hopelessly manipulative cultural medium that inevitably serves political power and produces inhumane treatment of others. One is sorely tempted to do precisely that in light of the results of our symposium. But there still may be an alternative. It would be to re-center biblical religious traditions around the visions of peace that they contain without succumbing either to the violence so central to their depiction of the divine-human relationship, or to the violent socio-political agendas they so often foster. The challenge of this alternative is to recast religion as a vehicle for a sacrality that genuinely articulates notions of universal peace and justice. This is an inherently liberal task, requiring immense energy and patience to interpret and live out sacrality in unprecedented ways. Unlike historic liberalism, however, any such effort to renew the religious traditions of Judaism and Christianity cannot be content with a merely individualistic critique and agenda. It must not ignore or dismiss social and cultural conflict, lest it lose contact with the human side of the religious equation. The task is not to condemn or deny violence, but to heal it.

Such a renewal must confront the realities of religious conflict and sacred violence directly and explicitly, and it must require collective, faithful, and categorical commitment from all who seek the paths of peace. To excise violence from biblical faiths demands that divine righteousness be proclaimed against those who profane the name of God with claims of violent reprisal against non-believers; that peace be proclaimed against those who would rend God's community with sectarian division and strife; and that the metaphors and rituals of violence be utterly effaced from the teaching and worship of God's peoples.

Whether such a renovation can in fact retain either the Jewish or the Christian religious template is quite uncertain. If violence—committed against one another and with God—is the sin against which authentic religious renewal must be directed, it is unlikely that such a strategy would include substantive fidelity to two religious traditions so utterly informed by violence itself. Yet new religious forms, as we have learned, come out of precisely the experience of violence and conflict. Perhaps the world has finally gotten so violent and hateful as actually to trouble the sort of people who sponsor, organize, participate in, and attend conferences like the one that engendered the present volume. I think it likely that our situation will only get worse, calling those who know that religion thrives in conflicted and threatened communities to act as if they, too, were part of such a community, but one that has a remedy to proclaim. That community needs to ask new questions, think new thoughts, dream new dreams, and do new things to deploy the symbolic mechanisms of religion against its own inherent violence. Failure to try is not only to betray the responsibility of our knowledge, but also to miss the urgent opportunity of this moment.

BIBLIOGRAPHY

Ackerman, Susan, *Under Every Green Tree: Popular Religion in Sixth-Century Judah* (Atlanta: Scholars Press, 1992).
Aitken, Ellen, *Jesus' Death in Early Christian Memory: The Poetics of the Passion* (Göttingen: Vandenhoeck & Ruprecht; Fribourg: Academic Press, 2004).
Anthony, Dick and Thomas Robbins, 'Religious Totalism, Exemplary Dualism, and the Waco Tragedy', in Thomas Robbins and Susan J. Palmer (eds.), *Millennium, Messiahs, and Mayhem* (New York: Routledge, 1997), pp. 261-84.
Aune, David E., 'Heracles and Christ: Heracles Imagery in the Christology of Early Christianity', in David L. Balch, Everett Ferguson and Wayne A. Meeks (eds.), *Greeks, Romans, and Christians: Essays in Honor of Abraham J. Malherbe* (Minneapolis: Fortress Press, 1990), pp. 3-19.
—'The Problem of the Genre of the Gospels: A Critique of C.H. Talbert's *What Is a Gospel?*', in R.T. France and David Wenham (eds.), *Gospel Perspectives II* (Sheffield: JSOT Press, 1981), pp. 9-60.
—*Revelation* (Word Biblical Commentary; 3 vols.; Nashville: Nelson, 1997–98).
Avalos, Hector, *Fighting Words: The Origins of Religious Violence* (Amherst, NY: Prometheus Books, 2005).
Bakhtin, Mikhail, *Rabelais and his World* (Cambridge, MA: MIT Press, 1968).
Barmash, Pamela, *Homicide in the Biblical World* (Cambridge: Cambridge University Press, 2005).
Beard, Mary, John North, and Simon Price, *Religions of Rome*. I. *A History* (Cambridge: Cambridge University Press, 1998).
Bernat, David A., 'Circumcision', in John J. Collins and Daniel Harlow (eds.), *Dictionary of Early Judaism* (Grand Rapids, MI: Wm B. Eerdmans [forthcoming]).
Betz, Hans Dieter, 'Hero Worship and Christian Beliefs: Observations from the History of Religion on Philostratus's *Heroikos'*, in E. Aitken and J. Maclean (eds.), *Philostratus' Heroikos: Religion and Cultural Identity in the Third Century C.E.* (Atlanta: Society of Biblical Literature, 2004), pp. 25-47.
Blenkinsopp, Joseph, *A History of Prophecy in Israel* (Philadelphia: Westminster Press, 1983).
Boatwright, Mary T., *Hadrian and the Cities of the Roman Empire* (Princeton, NJ: Princeton University Press, 2000).
Bohak, Gideon, 'Magical Means for Handling Minim in Rabbinic Literature', in P. Tomson and D. Lambers-Petry (eds.), *The Image of the Judaeo-Christians in Ancient Jewish and Christian Literature* (Tubingen: Mohr [Siebeck], 2003), pp. 267-79.
Bourdillon, M.F.C., and Meyer Fortes (eds.), *Sacrifice* (London: Academic Press, 1980).
Boyarin, Daniel, *Borderlines: The Partition of Judaeo-Christianity* (Philadelphia: University of Pennsylvania Press, 2004).
—*Dying for God: Martyrdom and the Making of Christianity and Judaism* (Stanford: Stanford University Press, 1999).
—*A Radical Jew: Paul and the Politics of Identity* (Berkeley: University of California Press, 1994).

Branham, Joan, 'Blood in Flux, Sanctity at Issue', *RES Anthropology and Aesthetics* 31 (1997), pp. 53-70.
—'Bloody Women and Bloody Spaces: Menses and the Eucharist in Late Antiquity and the Early Middle Ages', *Harvard Divinity Bulletin* 30 (2002), pp. 15-22.
—'Women as Objects of Sacrifice? An Early Christian "Chancel of the Virgins"', in Stella Georgoudi, Renée Koch Piettre and Francis Schmidt (eds.), *La cuisine et l'autel: les sacrifices en question dans les sociétés de la Méditerranée ancienne* (Bibliothèque de l'Ecole des Hautes Etudes, Sciences religieuses; Turnhout: Brepols, 2005), pp. 371-86.
Bremmer, Jan N., 'The Atonement in the Interaction of Greeks, Jews, and Christians', in J. Bremmer and Florentino García Martinez (eds.), *Sacred History and Sacred Texts: A Symposium in Honor of A.S. van der Woude* (Kampen: Kok Pharos, 1992), pp. 75-93.
Brock, Rita Nakashima, *Journeys by Heart: A Christology of Erotic Power* (New York: Crossroad, 1988).
Brown, Raymond E., *The Epistles of John: A New Translation with Introduction and Commentary* (AB, 30; Garden City. NY: Doubleday, 1982).
Buell, Denise, *Why This New Race: Ethnic Reasoning in Early Christianity* (New York: Columbia University Press, 2005).
Burkert, Walter, *Greek Religion* (Cambridge, MA: Harvard University Press, 1985).
—*Homo Necans: The Anthropology of Ancient Greek Sacrificial Ritual and Myth* (trans. Peter Bing; Berkeley: University of California Press, 1983).
—*Structure and History in Greek Myth and Ritual* (Berkeley: University of California Press, 1979).
Burrus, Virginia, 'Reading Agnes: The Rhetoric of Gender in Ambrose and Prudentius', *JECS* 4 (1995), pp. 25-46.
Cardellini, Innocenzo, *Die biblischen 'Sklaven'-Gesetze im Lichte des keilschriftlichen Sklavenrechts* (Bonner biblische Beiträge, 55; Königstein: Peter Hanstein, 1981).
Cargal, Timothy B., '"His blood be upon us and upon our children': A Matthean Double Entendre?', *NTS* 37 (1991), pp. 101-12.
Carr, David M., *Writing on the Tablet of the Heart: Origins of Scripture and Literature* (New York: Oxford University Press, 2005).
Carrasco, Davíd, *City of Sacrifice: The Aztec Empire and the Role of Violence in Civilization* (Boston: Beacon Press, 1999).
Castelli, Elizabeth A., 'Feminists Responding to Violence', in Elizabeth Castelli and Janet R. Jakobsen (eds.), *Interventions: Activists and Academics Respond to Violence* (New York: Palgrave Macmillan, 2004), pp. 1-9.
—*Martyrdom and Memory: Early Christian Culture Making* (Gender, Theory and Religion; New York: Columbia University Press, 2004).
Chilton, Bruce, *A Feast of Meanings: Eucharistic Theologies from Jesus through Johannine Circles* (Leiden: E.J. Brill, 1994).
Chirichigno, Gregory C., *Debt-Slavery in Israel and the Ancient Near East* (JSOTSup, 141; Sheffield: JSOT Press, 1993).
Cohn, Norman, *The Pursuit of the Millennium: Revolutionary Millenarians and Mystical Anarchists of the Middle Ages* (London: Temple Smith, rev. edn, 1970).
Coleman, Kathleen, M., 'Fatal Charades: Roman Executions Staged as Mythological Enactments', *JRS* 80 (1990), pp. 44-73.
Collins, Adela Yarbro, *The Beginning of the Gospel: Probings of Mark in Context* (Minneapolis: Fortress Press, 1992).
— *Crisis and Catharsis: The Power of the Apocalypse* (Philadelphia: Westminster Press, 1984)

—'Finding Meaning in the Death of Jesus', *JR* 78 (1998), pp. 175-96.
—'From Noble Death to Crucified Messiah', *NTS* 40 (1994), pp. 481-503.
—'Revelation 18: Taunt-Song or Dirge?', in J. Lambrecht (ed.), *L'apocalypse johannique et l'apocalyptique dans le Nouveau Testament* (BETL, 53; Leuven: Leuven University Press, 1980), pp. 185-204.
—'The Signification of Mark 10:45 among Gentile Christians', *HTR* 90 (1997), pp. 371-82.
Collins, John J., 'The Zeal of Phinehas: The Bible and the Legitimation of Violence', *JBL* 122 (2003), pp. 3-21.
Collins, Raymond F. (ed.), *The Thessalonian Correspondence* (BETL, 87; Leuven: University Press, 1990).
Compton, Todd, 'The Trial of the Satirist: Poetic *Vitae* (Aesop, Archilochus, Homer) as Background for Plato's *Apology*', *American Journal of Philology* 111 (1990), pp. 330-47.
Cooper, Alan and Bernard Goldstein, 'Cult of the Dead and Entry into the Land', *BibInt* 1 (1993), pp. 185-303.
Coser, Lewis A., *The Functions of Social Conflict* (New York: Free Press, 1956).
Cosgrove, Charles H., 'Justin Martyr and the Emerging Christian Canon: Observations on the Purpose and Destination of the Dialogue with Trypho', *VC* 36 (1982), pp. 209-32.
Crossan, John Dominic, *The Cross That Spoke: The Origins of the Passion Narrative* (San Francisco: Harper & Row, 1988).
—*Who Killed Jesus? Exposing the Roots of Anti-Semitism in the Gospel Story of Jesus* (San Francisco: HarperSanFrancisco, 1995).
Dahl, Nils, 'Anamnesis: Memory and Commemoration in Early Christianity', in his *Jesus in the Memory of the Early Church* (Minneapolis: Fortress Press, 1976), pp. 11-29.
—*Jesus in the Memory of the Early Church* (Minneapolis: Fortress Press, 1976).
Daly, Lloyd, *Aesop without Morals* (New York: T. Yoseloff, 1961).
Davies, Eryl W., 'The Morally Dubious Passages of the Hebrew Bible: An Examination of Some Proposed Solutions', *Currents in Biblical Research* 3 (2005), pp. 197-228.
Davis, Basil S., *Christ as Devotio: The Argument of Galatians 3:1-14* (Lanham, MD: University Press of America, 2003).
Delaney, Carol, *Abraham on Trial: The Social Legacy of a Biblical Myth* (Princeton, NJ: Princeton University Press, 1998).
Dever, Willam B., *Who Were the Early Israelites and Where Did They Come from?* (Grand Rapids, MI: Wm B. Eerdmans, 2003).
Douglas, Mary, *Natural Symbols: Explorations in Cosmology* (New York: Pantheon, 1973).
Dowd, Sharyn and Elizabeth Struthers Malbon, 'Hearing Mark's Story of Jesus' Death: Overlapping Contexts', presentation at the Annual Meeting of the Society of Biblical Literature, San Antonio, TX, November 16, 2004.
Duff, Paul B., *Who Rides the Beast? Prophetic Rivalry and the Rhetoric of Crisis in the Churches of the Apocalypse* (New York: Oxford University Press, 2001).
Duling, Dennis E., 'The Eleazar Miracle and Solomon's Magical Wisdom in Flavius Josephus's *Antiquities* 8.42-49', *HTR* 78 (1985), pp. 1-25.
—'Solomon, Exorcism, and the Son of David', *HTR* 68 (1975), pp. 235-52.
Eagleton, Terry, *Ideology: An Introduction* (London: Verso, 1991).
Eberhart, Christian, *Studien zur Bedeutung der Opfer im Alten Testament: Die Signifikanz von Blut- und Verbrennungsriten im kultischen Rahmen* (Neukirchen–Vluyn: Neukirchener Verlag, 2002).
Eilberg-Schwartz, Howard, *God's Phallus and Other Problems for Men and Monotheism* (Boston: Beacon Press 1994).
Eisenbaum, Pamela, 'A Remedy for Having Been Born of Woman: Jesus, the Gentiles and Genealogy in Romans', *JBL* 123 (2004), pp. 671-702.

Ellens, J. Harold (ed.), *The Destructive Power of Religion: Violence in Judaism, Christianity, and Islam* (4 vols.; Westport, CT: Praeger, 2003).

Elsner, John, 'Cult and Sacrifice: Sacrifice in the Ara Pacis Augustae', *JRS* 81 (1991), pp. 50-61.

Ember, Carol R. and Melvin Ember, 'Issues in Cross-Cultural Studies of Interpersonal Violence', in R. Barry Ruback and Neil A. Weiner (eds.), *Interpersonal Violent Behaviors: Social and Cultural Aspects* (New York: Springer Publishing, 1995), pp. 25-42.

Evans-Pritchard, E.E., *Nuer Religion* (Oxford: Clarendon Press, 1956).

Falls, Thomas B. (trans.), *Saint Justin Martyr* (Fathers of the Church, 6; Washington, DC: Catholic University of America Press, 1965).

Feldman, Louis H., *'Remember Amalek!' Vengeance, Zealotry and Group Destruction in the Bible according to Philo, Pseudo-Philo, and Josephus* (Monographs of Hebrew Union College, 31; Cincinnati: Hebrew Union College Press, 2004).

Finkelstein, J.J., *The Ox That Gored* (Transactions of the American Philosophical Society, 70/2; Philadelphia: American Philosophical Society, 1981).

Fiorenza, Elisabeth Schüssler, *Revelation: Vision of a Just World* (Minneapolis: Fortress Press, 1991).

—*Jesus: Miriam's Child, Sophia's Prophet: Critical Issues in Feminist Christology* (New York: Continuum, 1994).

Foucault, Michel, *Discipline and Punish: The Birth of the Prison* (trans. Alan Sheridan; New York: Vintage Books, 1979).

Frankfurter, David, 'Curses, Blessings, and Ritual Authority: Egyptian Magic in Comparative Perspective', *Journal of Ancient Near Eastern Religion* 5 (2005), pp. 159-87.

—'Early Christian Apocalypticism: Literature and Social World', in John J. Collins (ed.), *Encyclopedia of Apocalypticism*. I. *Jewish and Christian Origins of Apocalypticism* (New York: Continuum, 1998), pp. 415-53.

—*Elijah in Upper Egypt: The Coptic Apocalypse of Elijah and Early Egyptian Christianity* (Studies in Antiquity and Christianity, 7; Minneapolis: Fortress Press, 1993).

—'Fetus Magic and Sorcery Fears in Roman Egypt', *Greek, Roman, and Byzantine Studies* 46 (2006), pp. 37-62.

—'Jews or Not? Reconstructing the "Other" in Revelation 2:9 and 3:9', *HTR* 94 (2001), pp. 403-25.

—'On Sacrifice and Residues: Processing the Potent Body', in Brigitte Luchesi and Kocku von Stuckrad (eds.), *Religion im kulturellen Diskurs: Festschrift für Hans G. Kippenberg zu seinem 65. Geburtstag* (Berlin: W. de Gruyter, 2004), pp. 511-33.

—'Violence and Religious Formation: An Afterword', in Shelly Matthews and E. Leigh Gibson (eds.), *Violence in the New Testament* (London: T. & T. Clark, 2005), pp. 140-52.

Fredriksen, Paula, 'What "Parting of the Ways"? Jews, Gentiles and the Ancient Mediterranean City', in Adam H. Becker and Annette Yoshiko Reed (eds.), *The Ways That Never Parted: Jews and Christians in Late Antiquity and the Middle Ages* (Tübingen: Mohr [Siebeck], 2003), pp. 35-64.

Fretheim, Terence, 'God and Violence in the Old Testament', *Word and World* 24 (2004), pp. 18-28.

—'"I Was Only a Little Angry": Divine Violence in the Prophets', *Interpretation* 58 (2004), pp. 365-75.

Frilingos, Christopher A., *Spectacles of Empire: Monsters, Martyrs, and the Book of Revelation* (Philadelphia: University of Pennsylvania Press 2004).

Frykholm, Amy Johnson, *Rapture Culture:* Left Behind *in Evangelical America* (New York: Oxford University Press, 2004).

Gager, John G., *Curse Tablets and Binding Spells from the Ancient World* (New York: Oxford University Press, 1992).
—*Kingdom and Community: The Social World of Early Christianity* (Englewood Cliffs, NJ: Prentice–Hall, 1975).
Galtung, Johan, 'Cultural Violence', *Journal of Peace Research* 27 (1990), pp. 291-305.
—'Violence, Peace, and Peace Research', *Journal of Peace Research* 6 (1969), pp. 167-91.
Geller, Stephen A., *Sacred Enigmas: Literary Religion in the Hebrew Bible* (New York: Routledge, 1996).
Girard, René, *The Scapegoat* (trans. Yvonne Freccero; Baltimore: The Johns Hopkins University Press, 1986).
—*Things Hidden since the Foundation of the World* (trans. Stephen Bann and Michael Metteer; Stanford: Stanford University Press, 1986).
—*Violence and the Sacred* (trans. Patrick Gregory; Baltimore: The Johns Hopkins University Press, 1977).
Glancy, Jennifer, *Slavery in Early Christianity* (New York: Oxford University Press, 2002).
Green, Joel B., *The Death of Jesus: Tradition and Interpretation in the Passion Narrative* (Tübingen: Mohr [Siebeck], 1988).
Greenberg, Moshe, *Biblical Prose Prayer as A Window to the Popular Religion of Ancient Israel* (Berkeley: University of California Press, 1983).
—'More Reflections on Biblical Criminal Law', *Scripta hierosolymitana* 31 (1986), pp. 1-17.
—'Some Postulates of Biblical Criminal Law', in Menahem Haran (ed.), *Yehezkel Kaufman Jubilee Volume* (Jerusalem: Magnes Press, 1960), pp. 5-28.
Hadas, Moses and Morton Smith, *Heroes and Gods: Spiritual Biographies in Antiquity* (London: Routledge & Kegan Paul, 1965).
Hall, Robert G., 'The *Ascension of Isaiah*: Community, Situation, Date, and Place in Early Christianity', *JBL* 109 (1990), pp. 289-306.
Hallo, William W. (ed.), *The Context of Scripture*. II. *Monumental Inscriptions from the Biblical World* (Leiden: E.J. Brill, 2000).
Hamerton-Kelly, Robert G., *The Gospel and the Sacred: Poetics of Violence in Mark* (Minneapolis: Fortress Press, 1994).
—*Sacred Violence: Paul's Hermeneutic of the Cross* (Minneapolis: Fortress Press, 1992).
—(ed.), *Violent Origins: Walter Burkert, René Girard, and Jonathan Z. Smith on Ritual Killing and Cultural Formation* (Stanford: Stanford University Press, 1987).
Hansen, William, *Anthology of Ancient Greek Popular Literature* (Bloomington: Indiana University Press, 1998).
Hartman, Lars, 'The Eschatology of 2 Thessalonians as Included in a Communication', in Raymond Collins (ed.), *The Thessalonian Correspondence* (Leuven: Leuven University Press, 1990), pp. 470-85.
Hauerwas, Stanley, and John Berkman, 'Violence', in Paul Barry Clark and Andrew Linzey (eds.), *Dictionary of Ethics, Theology and Society* (New York: Routledge, 1996), pp. 866-70.
Hayes, Christine E., *Gentile Impurity and Jewish Identities: Intermarriage and Conversion from the Bible to the Talmud* (New York: Oxford University Press, 2002).
Heine, Ronald E., *The Montanist Oracles and Testimonia* (Patristic Monograph Series, 14; Macon, GA: Mercer University Press, 1989).
Hendel, Ronald S., *The Epic of the Patriarch: The Jacob Cycle and the Narrative Traditions of Canaan and Israel* (Atlanta: Scholars Press, 1987).
Hengel, Martin, *The Atonement: The Origins of the Doctrine in the New Testament* (Philadelphia: Fortress Press, 1981).

—'The Expiatory Sacrifice of Christ', *Bulletin of the John Rylands University Library of Manchester* 62 (1980), pp. 454-75.
Henninger, Joseph, 'Sacrifice', in Mircea Eliade (ed.), *Encyclopedia of Religion* (16 vols.; New York: MacMillan, 1987), XII, pp. 544-57.
Heschel, Abraham Joshua, *The Prophets* (Philadelphia: Jewish Publication Society, 1962).
Hoffman, Yair, 'The Deuteronomistic Concept of the Herem', *ZAW* 111 (1999), pp. 196-210.
Hoffmann, R. Joseph (ed.), *The Just War and Jihad: Violence in Judaism, Christianity, and Islam* (Amherst, NY: Prometheus Books, 2006).
Holzberg, Niklas (ed.), *Der Äsop-Roman: Motivgeschichte und Erzählstruktur* (Tübingen: Gunter Narr Verlag, 1992).
Hopkins, Keith, 'Christian Number and its Implications', *JECS* 6 (1998), pp. 185-226.
Horner, Timothy J., *Listening to Trypho: Justin Martyr's Dialogue Reconsidered* (Leuven: Peeters, 2001).
Hostetter, Edwin C., 'Prophetic Attitudes toward Violence in Ancient Israel', *Criswell Theological Review* 7 (1994), pp. 83-89.
Hunter, Alistair G., '(De)Nominating Amalek: Racist Stereotyping in the Bible and the Justification of Discrimination', in Jonneke Bekkenkamp and Yvonne Sherwood (eds.), *Sanctified Aggression: Legacies of Biblical and Post-Biblical Vocabularies of Violence* (JSOTSup, 400; London: T. & T. Clark, 2003), pp. 92-108.
Isaac, Benjamin, *The Limits of the Empire: The Roman Army in the East* (Oxford: Clarendon Press, rev. edn, 2000).
Jackson, Bernard, *Wisdom-Laws: A Study of the* Mishpatim *of Exodus 21:1–22:16* (Oxford: Oxford University Press, 2006).
Japhet, Sara, *I and II Chronicles* (OTL; Louisville, KY: Westminster/John Knox Press, 1993),
Jay, Nancy, *Throughout your Generations Forever: Sacrifice, Religion, and Paternity* (Chicago: University of Chicago Press, 1992).
Jensen, Joseph, *The Use of Tora by Isaiah: His Debate with the Wisdom Tradition* (CBQMS, 3; Catholic Bible Association, 1973).
Johnson, Allan Chester, Paul Robinson Coleman-Norton, and Frank Card Bourne (eds.), *Ancient Roman Statues* (Austin: University of Texas Press, 1961).
Johnson-DeBaufre, Melanie, 'The Blood Required of This Generation: Interpreting Communal Blame in a Colonial Context', in Shelly Matthews and E. Leigh Gibson (eds.), *Violence in the New Testament* (New York: T. & T. Clark, 2005), pp. 22-34.
Juergensmyer, Mark, *Terror in the Mind of God: The Global Rise of Religious Violence* (Berkeley: University of California Press, 3rd edn, 2003).
Kimball, Charles, *When Religion Becomes Evil: Five Warning Signs* (New York: HarperCollins, 2002).
Klawans, Jonathan, *Impurity and Sin in Ancient Judaism* (New York: Oxford University Press, 2000).
—'Interpreting the Last Supper: Sacrifice, Spiritualization, and Anti-Sacrifice', *NTS* 48 (2002), pp. 1-17.
—'Pure Violence: Sacrifice and Defilement in Ancient Israel', *HTR* 94 (2001), pp. 133-55.
—*Purity, Sacrifice and the Temple: Symbolism and Supersessionism in the Study of Ancient Judaism* (New York: Oxford University Press, 2005).
Knust, Jennifer, *Abandoned to Lust: Sexual Slander and Ancient Christianity* (Gender, Theory and Religion; New York: Columbia University Press, 2005).
—'Enslaved to Demons: Sex, Violence and the *Apologies* of Justin Martyr', in Todd Penner and Caroline Vander Stichele (eds.), *Mapping Gender in Ancient Religious Discourses* (Biblical Interpretation, 84; Leiden: E.J. Brill, 2007), pp. 431-55.

Koester, Helmut, *Ancient Christian Gospels: Their History and Development* (Philadelphia: Trinity Press International, 1990).
—'From Paul's Eschatology to the Apocalyptic Schemata of 2 Thessalonians', in Raymond Collins (ed.), *The Thessalonian Correspondence* (Leuven: University Press, 1990), pp. 441-58.
—*History and Literature of Early Christianity* (Philadelphia: Fortress Press, 1982).
—'On Heroes, Tombs, and Early Christianity: An Epilogue', in E. Aitken and J. Maclean (eds.), *Philostratus' Heroikos: Religion and Cultural Identity in the Third Century C.E.* (Atlanta: Society of Biblical Literature, 2004), pp. 257-64.
Kovacs, Judith, and Christopher Rowland, *Revelation: The Apocalypse of Jesus Christ* (Blackwell Bible Commentaries; Oxford: Blackwell 2004).
Krakauer, Jon, *Under the Banner of Heaven: A Story of Violent Faith* (Garden City, NY: Doubleday, 2003).
Krodel, Gerhard, '2 Thessalonians', in Gerhard Krodel (ed.), *The Deutero-Pauline Letters* (Minneapolis: Fortress Press, rev. edn, 1993), pp. 39-58.
Kroeber, Alfred Louis, and Clyde Kluckhohn, *Culture: A Critical Review of Concepts and Definitions* (New York: Vintage Books, 1963 [1952]).
Lahaye, Tim, and Jerry B. Jenkins, *Glorious Appearing: The End of Days* (Left Behind, 12; Wheaton, IL: Tyndale House, 2004).
Landy, Francis, 'Torah and Anti-Torah: Isaiah 2:2-4 and 1:10-26', *BibInt* 11 (2003), pp. 317-34.
Lang, Bernhard, 'The Roots of Eucharist in Jesus' Practice', *SBLSP* (1992), pp. 467-72.
Larson, Jennifer, *Greek Heroine Cults* (Madison: University of Wisconsin Press, 1995).
Lefkowitz, Mary, *The Lives of the Greek Poets* (Baltimore: The Johns Hopkins University Press, 1981).
Levinson, Bernard M., *Deuteronomy and the Hermeneutics of Legal Innovation* (New York: Oxford University Press, 1998).
—'Is the Covenant Code an Exilic Composition? A Response to John Van Seters', in John Day (ed.), *In Search of Pre-Exilic Israel* (JSOTSup, 406; London: T. & T. Clark, 2004), pp. 272-325.
Lewis, Theodore, *Cults of the Dead in Ancient Israel and Ugarit* (Atlanta: Scholars Press, 1989).
Lietaert Peerbolte, L.J., *The Antecedents of Antichrist: A Traditio-Historical Study of the Earliest Christian Views on Eschatological Opponents* (JSJSup, 49; Leiden: E.J. Brill, 1996).
Lieu, Judith, *Christian Identity in the Jewish and Graeco-Roman World* (Oxford: Oxford University Press, 2004).
Limburg, James, 'Swords to Ploughshares: Text and Contexts', in Craig C. Broyles and Craig A. Evans (eds.), *Writing and Reading the Scroll of Isaiah: Studies of an Interpretive Tradition* (VTSup, 70/1; Leiden: E.J. Brill, 1997), I, pp. 279-93.
Lind, Millard C., *Yahweh Is a Warrior: The Theology of Warfare in Ancient Israel* (Scottdale, PA: Herald Press, 1980).
Lorenz, Konrad, *On Aggression* (trans. Marjorie Kerr Wilson; San Diego: Harcourt Brace Jovanovich, 1966).
Mach, Michael, 'Justin Martyr's *Dialogus cum Tryphone Iudaeo* and the Development of Christian Anti-Judaism', in Guy G. Stroumsa (ed.), *Contra Iudaeos: Ancient and Medieval Polemics between Christians and Jews* (Texts and Studies in Medieval and Modern Judaism, 10; Mohr [Siebeck], 1996), pp. 27-47.
Machinist, Peter, 'Assyria and its Image in the First Isaiah', *JAOS* 103 (1983), pp. 719-37.
Maclean, Jennifer, 'Jesus as Cult Hero in the Fourth Gospel', in E. Aitken and J. Maclean (eds.), *Philostratus' Heroikos: Religion and Cultural Identity in the Third Century C.E.* (Atlanta: Society of Biblical Literature, 2004), pp. 195-218.

Malul, Meir, *The Comparative Method in Ancient Near Eastern and Biblical Legal Studies* (AOAT, 227; Kevelaer: Butzon & Bercker; Neukirchen–Vluyn: Neukirchener Verlag, 1990).

Marcovich, Miroslav, *Iustini Martyris Dialogus cum Tryphone* (Patristische Texte und Studien, 47; Berlin: W. de Gruyter, 1997).

Marshall, John, *Parables of War: Reading John's Jewish Apocalypse* (ESCJ, 10; Waterloo, OT: Wilfrid Laurier University Press, 2001).

Matthews, Shelly, 'The Need for the Stoning of Stephen', in Matthews and Gibson (eds.), *Violence in the New Testament*, pp. 124-39.

Mattews, Shelly, and E. Leigh Gibson (eds.), *Violence in the New Testament* (New York: T. & T. Clark, 2005).

McGinn, Bernard, *Antichrist: Two Thousand Years of the Human Fascination with Evil* (San Francisco: HarperSanFrancisco, 1994).

McKenna, Andrew J. (ed.), *René Girard and Biblical Studies* (Semeia, 33; Atlanta: Scholars Press, 1985).

McLean, B. Hudson, *The Cursed Christ: Mediterranean Expulsion Rituals and Pauline Soteriology* (Sheffield: Sheffield Academic Press, 1996).

Milgrom, Jacob, *Leviticus 1–16: A New Translation with Introduction and Commentary* (AB, 3; New York: Doubleday, 1991).

—*Leviticus 17–22: A New Translation with Introduction and Commentary* (AB, 3a; New York: Doubleday, 2000).

Moallem, Minoo, 'Violence of Protection', in Elizabeth Castelli and Janet R. Jakobsen (eds.), *Interventions: Activists and Academics Respond to Violence* (New York: Palgrave Macmillan, 2004), pp. 47-51.

Mobley, Gregory, *The Empty Men: The Heroic Tradition of Ancient Israel* (New York: Doubleday, 2005).

Morrow, William, 'Comfort for Jerusalem: The Second Isaiah as Counselor to Refugees', *Biblical Theology Bulletin* 34 (2004), pp. 80-86.

—'Post-Traumatic Stress Disorder and Vicarious Atonement in the Second Isaiah', in J. Harold Ellens and Wayne G. Rollins (eds.), *Psychology and the Bible: A New Way to Read the Scriptures* (Westport, CT: Praeger, 2004), pp. 168-83.

Nagy, Gregory, *Best of the Achaeans* (Baltimore: The Johns Hopkins University, 1979).

—'Introduction', *The Iliad* (Everyman Library; London: Random Century, 1992), pp. v-xviii.

—*Pindar's Homer* (Baltimore: The Johns Hopkins University Press, 1990).

Nelson-Pallmeyer, Jack, *Is Religion Killing Us? Violence in the Bible and the Quran* (New York: Continuum, 2003).

Niditch, Susan, *War in the Hebrew Bible: A Study in the Ethics of Violence* (New York: Oxford University Press, 1993).

Olyan, Saul, *Asherah and the Cult of Yahweh in Israel* (Atlanta: Scholars Press, 1988).

Orlinsky, Harry M., 'The Situational Ethics of Violence in the Biblical Period', in Salo W. Baron and George S. Wise (eds.), *Violence and Defense in the Jewish Experience* (Philadelphia: Jewish Publication Society, 1977), pp. 37-62.

Otto, Eckart, 'Aspects of Legal Reforms and Reformulation in Ancient Cuneiform and Israelite Law', in Bernard M. Levinson (ed.), *Theory and Method in Biblical and Cuneiform Law* (JSOTSup, 181; Sheffield: Sheffield Academic Press, 1994), pp. 160-96.

—'Town and Rural Countryside in Ancient Israelite Law: Reception and Redaction in Cuneiform and Israelite Law', *JSOT* 57 (1993), pp. 3-22.

—*Wandel der Rechtsbegründungen in der Gesellschaftsgeschichte des antiken Israel* (Studia biblica, 3; Leiden: E.J. Brill, 1988).

Pache, Corinne Ondine, 'After Rohde and Farnell: Developments in the Study of Greek Hero Cult', presentation at Society of Biblical Literature Annual Meeting, November 21, 2004.

—*Baby and Child Heroes in Ancient Greece* (Urbana, IL: University of Illinois Press, 2004).
Pagels, Elaine, *The Origin of Satan* (New York: Random House, 1995).
Parker, Robert, *Miasma: Pollution and Purification in Early Greek Religion* (Oxford: Clarendon Press, 1996).
Parkin, Tim J., *Demography and Roman Society* (Baltimore: The Johns Hopkins University Press, 1992).
Patterson, Annabel, *Fables of Power: Aesopian Writing and Political History* (Durham: Duke University Press, 1991).
Paul, Shalom M., *Studies in the Book of the Covenant in Light of Cuneiform and Biblical Law* (VTSup, 18; Leiden: E.J. Brill, 1970).
Perkins, Judith, *The Suffering Self: Pain and Narrative Representation in the Early Christian Era* (New York: Routledge, 1995).
Pippin, Tina, *Death and Desire: The Rhetoric of Gender in the Apocalypse of John* (Louisville, KY: Westminster Press, 1992).
Price, Simon, *Religions of the Ancient Greeks* (Key Themes in Ancient History; Cambridge: Cambridge University Press, 1999).
Prigent, Pierre, *Justin et l'ancien testament: l'argumentation scripturaire du traité de Justin contre toutes les hérésies comme source principale du Dialogue avec Tryphon et la première apologie* (Etudes Bibliques; Paris: Librairie Lecoffre, 1964).
Pyper, Hugh S., *An Unsuitable Book: The Bible as Scandalous Text* (The Bible in the Modern World, 7; Sheffield: Sheffield Phoenix Press, 2005).
Raglan, Lord, 'The Hero: A Study in Tradition, Myth, and Drama, Part II', in Robert A. Segal (ed.), *In Quest of the Hero* (Princeton, NJ: Princeton University Press, 1990), pp. 89-175.
Rajak, Tessa, 'Dying for the Law: The Martyrs' Portrait in Jewish-Greek Literature', in Tessa Rajak (ed.), *The Jewish Dialogue with Greece and Rome: Studies in Cultural and Social Interaction* (Leiden: E.J. Brill, 2002), pp. 99-133.
—'Talking at Trypho: Christian Apologetic as Anti-Judaism in *Justin's Dialogue with Trypho the Jew*', in Mark Edwards, Martin Goodman, Simon Prise and Christopher Rowland (eds.), *Apologetics in the Roman Empire: Pagans, Jews, and Christians* (Oxford: Oxford University Press, 1999), pp. 59-80.
Remus, Harold, 'Persecution', in Anthony J. Blasi, Jean Duhaime and Paul-André Turcotte (eds.), *Handbook of Early Christianity: Social Science Approaches* (Walnut Creek, CA: AltaMira Press, 2002), pp. 431-52.
Riccobono, Salvator, *Fontes iuris romani antejustiniani. I. Leges* (Florence: S.A.G. Barbèra, 1941).
Richardson, M.E.J., *Hammurabi's Laws* (London: T. & T. Clark, 2002).
Riley, Gregory, *One Jesus, Many Christs: How Jesus Inspired Not One True Christianity, But Many: The Truth about Christian Origins* (San Francisco: HarperSanFrancisco, 1997).
Rives, James, 'The Piety of a Persecutor', *JECS* 4 (1996), pp. 1-25.
Robbins, Thomas, and Dick Anthony, 'Sects and Violence: Factors Enhancing the Volatility of Marginal Religious Movements', in Stuart A. Wright (ed.), *Armageddon in Waco: Critical Perspectives on the Branch Davidian Conflict* (Chicago: University of Chicago Press, 1995), pp. 236-59.
Rofé; Alexander, *Deuteronomy: Issues and Interpretations* (London: T. & T. Clark, 2002).
Rohde, Erwin, *Psyche: The Cult of Souls and Belief in Immorality among the Greeks* (London: Kegan Paul, Trench, Trübner; New York: Harcourt Brace, 1925).
Roth, Martha, *Law Collections from Mesopotamia and Asia Minor* (Atlanta: Scholars Press, 2nd edn, 1997).

Rothenbusch, Ralf, *Die kasuistische Rechtssammlung im 'Bundesbuch' (Ex 21,2-11.18–22, 1)* (AOAT, 259; Münster: Ugarit-Verlag, 2000).
Ruether, Rosemary Radford, *To Change the World: Christology and Cultural Criticism* (New York: Crossroad, 1981).
Samuel, Maurice, *You Gentiles* (New York: Harcourt, Brace, & Company, 1924).
Sarna, Nahum, *Understanding Exodus* (New York: Schocken, 1986).
Satran, David, *Biblical Prophets in Byzantine Palestine: Reassessing the Lives of the Prophets* (Leiden: E.J. Brill, 1995).
Schade, Aaron, 'New Photographs Supporting the Reading *ryt* in Line 12 of the Mesha Inscription', *IEJ* 55 (2005), pp. 206-207.
Schenke, Ludger, *Auferstehungsverkündigung und leeres Grab: eine traditionsgeschichtliche Untersuchung von Mk. 16, 1-8* (Stuttgart: Katholisches Bibelwerk, 1968).
Schille, Gottfried, 'Das Leiden des Herrn. Die evangelische Passionstradition und ihr "Sitz im Leben"', *Zeitschrift für Theologie und Kirche* 52 (1955), pp. 161-205.
Schwartz, Baruch J., 'Torah from Zion: Isaiah's Temple Vision [Isaiah 2:1-4]', in Alberdina Houtman, Marcel Poorthuis and Joshua Schwartz (eds.), *Sanctity of Time and Space in Tradition and Modernity* (Jewish and Christian Perspectives Series, 1; Leiden: E.J. Brill, 1998), pp. 11-26.
Schwartz, Regina M., *The Curse of Cain: The Violent Legacy of Monotheism* (Chicago: University of Chicago Press, 1997).
Schwartz, Seth, *Imperialism and Jewish Society: 200 BCE to 640 CE* (Princeton, NJ: Princeton University Press, 2001).
Schwemer, Anna Maria, *Studien zu den frühjüdischen Prophetenlegenden* (Vitae prophetarum; 2 vols.; Tübingen: Mohr [Siebeck], 1995).
Schwienhorst-Schönberger, Ludger, *Das Bundesbuch (Ex 20, 22–23, 33)* (BZAW, 188; Berlin: W. de Gruyter, 1990).
Seeley, David, *The Noble Death: Graeco-Roman Martyrology and Paul's Concept of Salvation* (Sheffield: Sheffield Academic Press, 1990).
Segal, Alan F., 'The Ruler of This World', in *The Other Judaisms of Late Antiquity* (Brown Judaic Studies, 127; Atlanta: Scholars Press, 1987), pp. 41-77.
Shaw, Brent, 'Body/Power/Identity: Passions of the Martyrs', *JECS* 4 (1990), pp. 269-312.
Shuck, Glenn W., 'Marks of the Beast: The *Left Behind* Novels, Identity, and the Internalization of Evil', *Nova religio* 8 (2004), pp. 48-63.
Simmel, Georg, *Conflict and the Web of Group-Affiliations* (trans. Kurt H. Wolff and Reinhard Bendix; New York: Free Press, 1955).
Sivan, Emmanuel, 'The Enclave Culture', in Martin E. Marty and R. Scott Appleby (eds.), *Fundamentalisms Comprehended* (Chicago: University of Chicago Press, 1995), pp. 11-68.
Skarsaune, Oskar, *Proof from Prophecy: A Study in Justin Martyr's Proof Text Tradition: Text-Type, Provenance, Theological Profile* (NTSup, 61; Leiden: E.J. Brill, 1987).
Smart, Ninian, review of *Violence and the Sacred*, by René Girard (Baltimore: The Johns Hopkins University Press, 1977), *Religious Studies Review* 6 (1980), pp. 173-77.
Smith, Brian K. 'Monotheism and its Discontents: Religious Violence and the Bible' (Review of *The Curse of Cain* [Chicago: University of Chicago Press, 1997] by Regina Schwartz), *JAAR* 66 (1998), pp. 403-11.
Smith, Jonathan Z., 'Differential Equations: On Constructing the Other', in Jonathan Z. Smith, *Relating Religion: Essays in the Study of Religion* (Chicago: University of Chicago Press, 2004), pp. 230-50.
—'The Domestication of Sacrifice', in his *Relating Religion*, pp. 145-51.
—'Here, There, and Anywhere', in his *Relating Religion*, pp. 323-39
—*Map Is Not Territory: Studies in the History of Religions* (Leiden: E.J. Brill, 1978).

Smith, Mark S., review of *The Religions of Ancient Israel: A Synthesis of Parallactic Approaches* (London: Continuum, 2001) by Z. Zevit, *Maarav* 11 (2004), pp. 145-218.
Smith, Mark S., and Elizabeth Bloch-Smith, 'Death and Afterlife in Ugarit and Israel', *JAOS* 108 (1988), pp. 277-84.
Speiser, E., 'The Stem PLL in Hebrew', *JBL* 82 (1963), pp. 301-306.
Sprinkle, Joe M., *'The Book of the Covenant': A Literary Approach* (JSOTSup, 174; Sheffield: JSOT Press, 1994).
Stackert, Jeffrey, 'Why Does Deuteronomy Legislate Cities of Refuge? Asylum in the Covenant Collection (Exodus 21:12-14) and Deuteronomy (19:1-13)', *JBL* 125 (2006), pp. 23-49.
Stern, Menahem (ed.), *Greek and Latin Authors on Jews and Judaism* (3 vols.; Jerusalem: Israel Academy of Sciences and Humanities, 1976–1984).
Stern, Philip D., *The Biblical Herem: A Window on Israel's Religious Experience* (Brown Judaic Studies, 21; Atlanta: Scholars Press, 1990).
Still, Todd D., *Conflict at Thessalonica: A Pauline Church and its Neighbours* (JSNTSup, 183; Sheffield: Sheffield Academic Press, 1999).
Stowers, Stanley K., 'Greeks Who Sacrifice, and Those Who Do Not: Toward an Anthropology of Greek Religion', in L. Michael White and O. Larry Yarbrough (eds.), *The Social World of the First Christians: Essays in Honor of Wayne A. Meeks* (Minneapolis: Fortress Press, 1995), pp. 293-333.
—*A Rereading of Romans* (New Haven: Yale University Press, 1994).
Strecker, Georg, 'Chiliasm and Docetism in the Johannine School', *Australian Biblical Review* 38 (1990), pp. 45-61.
—*The Johannine Letters* (Hermeneia; ed. Harold Attridge; trans. Linda M. Maloney; Minneapolis: Fortress Press, 1996).
Strenski, Ivan, *Religion in Relation: Method, Application, and Moral Location* (Columbia: University of South Carolina Press, 1993).
Stroumsa, Guy G., 'Early Christianity as Radical Religion', in Guy G. Stroumsa, *Barbarian Philosophy: The Religious Revolution of Early Christianity* (Wissenschaftliche Untersuchungen zum Neuen Testament, 112; Tübingen: Mohr [Siebeck], 1999), pp. 8-26.
Stylianopoulos, Theodore, *Justin Martyr and the Mosaic Law* (Missoula,, MT: Society of Biblical Literature, 1975).
Sweeney, Marvin A., 'The Book of Isaiah as Prophetic Torah', in Roy F. Melugin and Marvin A. Sweeney (eds.), *New Visions of Isaiah* (JSOTSup, 214; Sheffield: Sheffield Academic Press, 1996), pp. 50-67.
—'Micah's Debate with Isaiah', *JSOT* 93 (2001), pp. 111-24.
Talbert, Charles H., *What Is a Gospel? The Genre of the Canonical Gospels* (Philadelphia: Fortress Press, 1977).
Talmon, Yonina, 'Pursuit of the Millennium: The Relation Between Religious and Social Change', *Archives européennes de sociologie* 3 (1962), pp. 125-48.
Thompson, Leonard L., *The Book of Revelation: Apocalypse and Empire* (New York: Oxford University Press, 1990).
Tigay, Jeffrey H., *The JPS Torah Commentary: Deuteronomy* (Philadelphia: Jewish Publication Society, 1996).
Trevett, Christine, 'Apocalypse, Ignatius, Montanism: Seeking the Seeds', *VC* 43 (1989), pp. 313-38.
Ussishkin, David, *The Conquest of Lachish by Sennacherib* (Tel Aviv: Tel Aviv University, The Institute of Archaeology, 1982).
Van Seters, John, *A Law Book for the Diaspora: Revisions in the Study of the Covenant Code* (New York: Oxford University Press, 2003).

Vernant, Jean-Pierre, *Mortals and Immortals: Collected Essays* (Princeton, NJ: Princeton University Press, 1991).
Versnel, H.S., 'Quid Athenis et Hierosolymis? Bemerkungen über die Herkunft von Aspekten des "Effective Death"', in Jan W. van Henten (ed.), *Die Entstehung der jüdischen Martyrologie* (Leiden: E.J. Brill, 1989), pp. 162-96.
—'Self-Sacrifice, Compensation and the Anonymous Gods', in Jean Rudhardt and Olivier Reverdin (eds.), *Le sacrifice dans l'antiquité: huit exposés suivis de discussions* (Geneva: Vandoeuvres, 1981), pp. 135-94.
Watson, Alan (ed. and trans.), *The Digest of Justinian* (4 vols.; Philadelphia: University of Pennsylvania Press, 1985).
Weinfeld, Moshe, *Deuteronomy 1–11: A New Translation with Introduction and Commentary* (AB, 5; New York: Doubleday, 1991).
Westbrook, Raymond, 'Lex talionis and Exodus 21, 22-25', *Revue biblique* 93 (1986), pp. 52-69.
Wexler, Laura, *Tender Violence: Domestic Visions in an Age of US Imperialism* (Chapel Hill: University of North Carolina Press, 2000).
Wildberger, Hans, *Isaiah 1–12: A Commentary* (trans. Thomas H. Trapp; Minneapolis: Fortress Press, 1991).
Williams, James G., *The Bible, Violence, and the Sacred: Liberation from the Myth of Sanctioned Violence* (San Francisco: HarperSanFrancisco, 1991).
Williams, Sammy K., *Jesus' Death as Saving Event: The Background and Origin of a Concept* (Missoula, MT: Scholars Press, 1975).
Willis, John T., 'Isaiah 2:2-5 and the Psalms of Zion', in Craig C. Broyles and Craig A. Evans (eds.), *Writing and Reading the Scroll of Isaiah: Studies of an Interpretive Tradition; Volume 1* (VTSup, 70/1; Leiden: E.J. Brill, 1997), pp. 295-316.
Wills, Lawrence M., 'The Aesop Tradition', in Amy-Jill Levine, John Dominic Crossan, and Dale Allison (eds.), *The Historical Jesus in Context* (Princeton Readings in Religions; Princeton, NJ: Princeton University Press, 2006), pp. 222-37.
—*The Quest of the Historical Gospel: Mark, John and the Origins of the Gospel Genre* (New York: Routledge, 1997).
Wilson, Robert, *Prophecy and Society in Ancient Israel* (Philadelphia: Fortress Press, 1980).
Wimbush, Vincent L., 'Introduction: Reading Darkness, Reading Scriptures', in Vincent L. Wimbush and Rosamond C. Rodman (eds.), *African Americans and the Bible: Sacred Texts and Social Textures* (New York: Continuum, 2000), pp. 1-43.
Winkler, John, *Auctor and Actor: A Narratological Reading of Apuleius' Golden Ass* (Berkeley: University of California Press, 1985).
Wrangham, Richard and Dale Peterson. *Demonic Males: Apes and the Origins of Human Violence* (Boston: Houghton Mifflin, 1996).
Wright, David P., 'The Compositional Logic of the Goring Ox and Negligence Laws in the Covenant Collection (Ex 21:28-36)', *Zeitschrift für altorientalische und biblische Rechtsgeschichte* 10 (2004), pp. 93-142.
—'The Fallacies of Chiasmus: A Critique of Structures Proposed for the Covenant Collection', *Zeitschrift für altorientalische und biblische Rechtsgeschichte* 10 (2004), pp. 143-68.
—'Holiness in Leviticus and Beyond: Defining Perspectives', *Interpretation* 53 (1999), pp. 351-64.
—'The Laws of Hammurabi as a Source for the Covenant Collection (Exodus 20:23–23:19)', *Maarav* 10 (2003), pp. 11-87.
— 'The Laws of Hammurabi and the Covenant Code: A Response to Bruce Wells', *Maarav* 13.2 (2006), pp. 209-58.

—Review of *A Law Book for the Diaspora: Revision in the Study of the Covenant Code* (New York: Oxford University Press, 2003), by John Van Seters, in *JAOS* 124 (2004), pp. 129-31.

Yee, Gale A., *Poor Banished Children of Eve: Woman as Evil in the Hebrew Bible* (Minneapolis: Fortress Press, 2003).

Zevit, Ziony, 'Archaeological and Literary Stratigraphy in Joshua 7-8', *BASOR* 251 (1983), pp. 23-35.

—*The Religions of Ancient Israel: A Synthesis of Parallactic Approaches* (London: Continuum, 2001).

INDEXES

INDEX OF REFERENCES

OLD TESTAMENT

Genesis		11.4-8	21	21.13	70, 71
1.26-27	66	11.5	21	21.14	68, 73
4.2-16	19	11.8	22	21.16	58
4.13-15	20	12.29-32	19	21.17	59
6.9-17	19	13.1	21	21.18-21	69, 70
9.4-5	66	13.15	21	21.18-19	59, 68, 70, 71, 78
9.5-6	20	14.30	21		
10.15-18	31	15.1-21	36	21.18	71
14.7	33	15.3	47	21.19	68, 71
15.16	27	17.8	33	21.20-21	59, 65, 70-72, 78
19.23-24	19	17.14-16	33		
22	5	17.14	19	21.20	72, 73
22.1-14	19, 23	20–23	129	21.21	73
31.19	89	20.23–23.19	57	21.22-25	58, 67
32.22-32	99	20.23-26	59, 61, 68	21.22-23	59
32.22-30	88	20.23-24	61	21.22	66, 68
34.1-31	19	20.23	61	21.23-27	59
35.4	89	20.24-26	68	21.23-25	68, 71, 78
35.20	89	20.24	61	21.23	65, 68, 70, 78
36.12	33	20.25-26	61		
49.5	18	21.1-2	58	21.26-27	72, 73, 78
		21.1	62	21.28-32	59, 64, 65
Exodus		21.2–22.19	58	21.28	65, 66, 78
1.22	19	21.2-11	59, 74	21.29-30	71, 78
2.11-12	19	21.2-6	59	21.29	65, 66, 68, 73
4	89	21.2	68, 72-74		
4.22-23	21	21.5	59	21.30	68
4.24-26	88, 99	21.6	58, 70	21.31	65
5.1	21	21.7-11	59	21.32	65, 66, 68, 72, 78
5.3	21	21.7	74		
7.16	21	21.12-32	74	21.33-34	58, 59
8.16	21	21.12-25	71	21.35-36	59
9.13	21	21.12-21	69	21.35	58, 65
10.3	21	21.12-14	59, 68-71, 78	21.36	66
11.1-10	19			21.37	59, 74
11.1-6	21	21.12	71, 73	22.1-2	58, 75, 76

22.1	75	17.4	66	7.17-24	30
22.2-3	59, 74	17.11	93	12	22, 32
22.4	58	18	27	12.2-7	25
22.5	58	18.3	27	13	32
22.6-8	59, 74	18.25	27	13.1-9	32
22.6	58, 74, 75	18.27-30	27	13.16-18	26
22.7	70, 75	19.18	34	13.17	26
22.8	70	19.28	89	15.12-18	74
22.9-12	59	21.1-11	89	17	43
22.10	70	24.19-20	71	17.8	19
22.13-14	58, 59	25.39-46	74	17.10	43
22.15-16	58	27.26-29	29	19.4	71
22.17-19	60	27.28-29	29	19.16	18
22.19	27	27.28	29	19.21	71
22.20–23.19	59	27.29	29	20	24
22.20–23.8	61			20.10-14	34
22.20-30	60	*Numbers*		20.10-11	34
22.20-23	60, 61	16.31-33	19	20.16-18	19, 25
22.23-25	67	21.1-3	23	21.5	19
22.24-26	61	21.4	20	25.17-19	19, 33
22.24	60	21.11-13	20	25.18	33
22.25-26	60	21.16	20	27	96
22.26-27	73	21.21-25	20	32.42	47
22.27	60, 61, 64	21.23-25	19		
22.28-30	60, 61	21.33-35	19, 20	*Joshua*	
22.30	66	25.1-9	25	6–11	10
23.1-8	59, 62	25.6-14	19	6.1-22	8
23.9-19	60, 61	25.16-19	23	6.20-26	19
23.9	60, 61	31.1-54	19	7.1	24
23.10-12	61	31.2-54	22	7.11-26	24
23.10-11	60, 72	31.2	23	9.1-26	29
23.12	60	31.8	23	9.27	29, 30
23.13	60-62	31.16	23	15.63	29
23.14-19	61	31.17	22	16.10	29
23.27	31	35.25-28	71	17.12-13	29
23.28	31			19.47	29
23.29-30	30	*Deuteronomy*		24	96
24	95, 96	2.30-32	20		
30.12	93	2.33	20	*Judges*	
32.25-29	19	2.34	20	1.27-36	29
32.26-29	27	3.1-12	20	3.1-4	30
34.11-16	25	3.6	20	3.3	31
34.11	25, 31	3.8	20	3.5	30
34.12	25	4.3	25	3.13	33
34.13	25	6.9	26	4.17-21	19
34.15	25	7	25, 26	5.1-31	36
		7.1-4	25	5.14	33
Leviticus		7.1-2	19	5.24-27	19
10.1-2	19	7.5	25	5.30	34
16	96	7.6	26	6.3	33

Judges (cont.)		8.8	34	Psalms	
6.33	33	9.20-21	30	7.17	18
7.12	33	9.21	30	38.12	19
8.21	36	11.16	16	46.5	42
8.22-23	36	12.21-24	36	83.5	34
9.24	18	12.26-31	22	83.7-8	33
9.42-49	19	14.21-24	22	83.9	34
11.4-11	36	16.30	31	94.1	34
11.29-40	19	18.40	19	95	101, 108
11.30-31	23	22	49, 50	137	35
11.34	36			137.8	35
12.15	33	2 Kings			
16.20	88, 89	3.5-27	23	Proverbs	
21.15-18	36	3.27	23	8.35-36	18
		9.15–10.31	23		
1 Samuel		10.16	23	Qoheleth	
11.5-15	36	10.18-28	19	8.4	43
11.12-13	36	15.16	16		
14.24	35	16.2-5	22	Isaiah	
15.1-3	33	18.3-7	22	2	10, 44
15.4-7	33	21.10-15	22	2.1-4	26, 43
15.5	33	22–23	32	2.2-4	41, 44, 45, 130
15.8-9	33	22.2	22		
15.13	33	22.16-17	22	2.4	41
18.6-7	36	23.20	32	4.2	42
18.25	35			4.3-4	42
22.17-18	34	1 Chronicles		4.3	43
24.12	34	4.41-43	34	4.4	42, 43
27.8-11	19	5.10	33	4.5	42
27.8	33	5.18-22	33	5.26-28	30
27.9	34	22.7-8	36	6.10	105
27.11	34			8.7-8	30
30.1-2	34	2 Chronicles		10.5-6	22
30.17	34	5.9	34	10.6	30
		25.11-12	16	10.12	22
2 Samuel				10.13	30
1.22	36	Ezra		10.16	22
5.1-3	36	9	96	10.28-32	31
7.1-16	36	9.1-2	26	34	35
7.9	36			34.2-3	48
8.2	19	Nehemiah		37.24	30
21	88	9	96	43.3	93
21.15-22	36			51.4-5	105
23.8-23	36	Esther		52–53	90
24.6-7	31	2.8	43	52.5	106
				52.10-15	105
1 Kings		Job		53.1-12	105
5.17	36	15.33	18	54.1-6	105
8.1-16	22			55.3-13	105

55.3-5	105	*Daniel*		*Habakkuk*	
58.1-12	105	9	96	1.2-3	18
59.6-7	19	11–12	90	2.17	18, 19
60.18	18, 19	12	128		
		12.3	55	*Zephaniah*	
Jeremiah				1.9	18
15.15	34	*Amos*		3.4	18
16.5-9	89	1.3	17		
22.3	18	1.6	17	**Apocrypha**	
31	45	1.9	17	*Tobit*	
31.31-32	105	1.11-12	33	4.17	88
50.34-39	35	1.11	17		
51.34-40	35	1.13	17	*Wisdom of Solomon*	
51.35	18	2.1	17	2–5	88
		6.7	89		
Lamentations				*Ben Sira*	
2.6	18	*Obadiah*		46.11-12	90
		1.10	18	48.11	90
Ezekiel		1.12-14	35	49.10	90
7.23	18				
16.17	24	*Micah*		*Prayer of Azariah*	
16.20-21	24	1.10-16	31	16-17	88
22.26	18	4	10		
36	45	4.1-5	26	*2 Maccabees*	
37	35	6.6-7	24	4.2	90
38.21-23	35			6–7	90
39	35	*Nahum*		6.29	90
39.9-16	35	3.18-19	22	15.12-16	90
39.17-28	35			17.21-22	90

NEW TESTAMENT

Matthew		*John*		8.3	96
5	10	1.14	116		
21.13	106	8	86	*1 Corinthians*	
21.23	106	10.33	86	5.7	96
21.27	106	11.49-50	93	7–8	122
27.25	9, 97	19.34	116	12–14	121
		20	98	15.3	96
Mark		20.20-29	116		
10	94	21	98	*Galatians*	
10.45	93			1.4	96
12	86	*Acts*		1.6-9	119
13.26–27	120	7.56–8.1	106		
15	98			*1 Thessalonians*	
		Romans		2.14	119
Luke		3.25	96	3.3-4	119
11.13	106	4.25	96	4.15-17	120
11.52	106	5.9-10	96		

2 Thessalonians		4.2	116	20.4-6	112
1	119, 125	4.3	117	21.8	123
1.5	121	5.6	116	21.27	123
1.6-9	119			22.15	123, 126
1.7-9	120	*2 John*		22.18	126
1.8	119	7	116		
2	118, 119			**Pseudepigrapha**	
2.1-2	119	*Revelation*		*4 Maccabees*	
2.5-6	119	1.16	123	6.29	93
2.8	120	2–3	124	17.21-22	93
2.10-12	119	2.9	122		
		2.14	124	*Apocalypse of Elijah*	
Titus		2.19-23	122	1	124
2.14	94	2.20	121, 124	4	124
		2.22-23	126	5	124
1 Peter		2.22	123		
1.18-19	94	3.9	122	**Mishnah**	
		7.3-4	122	*Yoma*	
1 John		9.3-6	123	6.6	96
2.15	116	9.4-6	122		
2.17	117	9.4	122	**Babylonian Talmud**	
2.18-22	117	11.5	123	*Rosh ha-Shanah*	
2.18-19	118	13.16	122	4b	7
2.18	117	14.4	123, 124		
2.19	116, 117	16.10-21	122	**Philo**	
2.20	116	16.21	123	*Contra Flaccum*	
2.21-22	116	17.4	123	6.36-39	97
2.26	116	17.6	125		
2.27	116	18	123, 125	**Josephus**	
3.7	116	19.16	123	*Antiquities of the Jews*	
3.8-10	116	19.17-21	122	14.2.1-2	91
3.9	116	19.17-18	123	14.2.22-28	91
4.1-6	117	19.21	123		

EARLY CHRISTIAN AND CLASSICAL TEXTS

Acts of John		7	96	Diodorus Siculus	
89-93	116	8.5	109	6.1.2	81
97-102	116				
		Callistratus		Diognetus	
Aristotle		*Judicial Examinations*		9.2	94
Rhetoric		6.15-16	108		
2.23.11 1398b	86			Epiphanius	
		Cassius Dio		*Panarion*	
Athenaeus		69.14.1-3	104	58.5	118
6.265c-266e	82				
		Didache		Euripides	
Barnabas		11	121	*Hippolytus*	
5	96			1423	81

Index of References

Eusebius		40.2-3	100	*The Passing of Peregrinus*	
Ecclesiastical History		40.4-5	107	11-13	102
5.16.12	124	41	107	33	82
5.18.2	124	43	100		
7.24.1-3	124	44	107	Pausanius	
		46	100, 107	9.17.1	89
Herodotus		47	102, 105		
2.145-46	81	48.4	102	Philostratus	
		49.1	102	*Heroicus*	
Homer		54	100, 107	9.141.6	81
Iliad		71–73	108		
16.791-92	92	71	109	Pindar	
18.28-31	92	72	100	*Nemean Odes*	
18.175-77	92	72.2-3	101	1.69-72	81
23.170	92	73	100		
23.218-21	92	73.1	101	*Olympian Odes*	
		76	100	7.77	81
Odyssey		80	112		
3.447-455	92	81	112	Pliny the Younger	
		86	107	*Epistles*	
Justinian		89	100, 108	10.96	111
Digesta		90	100, 107		
18.19.12	108	93	112	Plutarch	
48.19.1	108	94	107	*On the Malice*	
48.19.8	108	95	109	*of Herodotus*	
48.19.28	108	96	100	857d	81
		97	100		
Justin Martyr		108	113	*Pelopidas*	
Dialogue with Trypho		110	107	16	81
1	104	110.3	111		
10	108	110.4	110	Strabo	
10.3	100	111	107	9.2.11	81
11	105, 107	117	107, 112		
12	105	118.1	112	**Inscriptions**	
13	105, 107			*Enuma Elish*	
14–15	105	Lactantius		IV.1-10	43
16	104, 106	*Divine Institutes*			
18–19	106	4.18	109	*Mesha*	
18	106			11-12	28, 29
32	100	Lucian		14-17	28, 29
32.2	101	*Syrian Goddess*		14-16	27
38	108	6	92		
40	96				

Mesopotamian Legal Collections

Hittite Laws		*Laws of Eshunna*		*Laws of Hammurabi*	
17	67	13	58, 75-77	9	70
105-106	58	53	58, 59, 65, 66	14	58
				21-3	75

Laws of Hammurabi (cont.)		196-201	59, 67, 70	239	68
21	58, 75, 76	196-7	77	240	70
22-3	75	196	68	242	68
23	70	197	68	243	68
47.59–49.17	60, 61	198-9	73	244-9	59
47.59-73	61	198	68, 77	244	58, 70
47.75-78	61	199	68, 77	247	68
47.93–48.2	61	200-1	68	248	68
48.3-58	61	200	77	249	58
48.34-36	61	201	73, 77	250-2	59, 64-6
48.48-58	61	202-5	70	250	65, 66, 77
48.59–49.17	62	206-8	69, 70	251-2	68
57-8	58	206	59, 68, 70, 77	251	65, 66, 77
101	68			252	66, 73, 77
106-7	68	207	59, 66, 69, 70, 77	253-65	59
106	70			258-61	68
112-13	68	208	59, 70, 71, 77	264-6	59
116	59, 65, 66, 72, 73, 77	209-23	59	264-5	74
				264	68
117-19	59	209-14	59, 70	266-7	59
117	59, 72	209-10	67	266	70
120-1	68	210	65-69, 77	267	68
120	58, 59, 70	213-14	73	268-71	59
122-5	74	215-20	68	271	68
124-5	58, 59	215-17	70	273-4	68
124	68	217	68	276-8	68
125	58, 59, 74	218-20	70	281	70
126	68, 70	219	73	282	58
127-91	59	221-5	68		
138-40	68	221-3	70	Laws of Lipit-Ishtar	
148-9	59	228	68	d-e	67
175	59	229-30	59		
178	59	229	66	Middle Assyrian Laws	
182	59	230	65, 77	A 50	58, 67, 70
192-3	59	231	73	A 52	58, 70
195	59	234	68	A 53	67
196-205	59	238	68	A 55-6	59

INDEX OF AUTHORS

Ackerman, S. 89
Aitken, E. 79, 96
Anthony, D. 128
Aune, D.E. 79, 97, 123
Avalos, H. 1, 2, 4, 6-8, 10-12, 14

Bakhtin, M. 85
Barmash, P. 69
Beard, M. 125
Bellinger, C.K. 3
Berkman, J. 40
Bernat, D.A. 7
Betz, H.D. 87
Blenkinsopp, J. 89
Boatwright, M.T. 104
Bohak, G. 126
Bourdillon, M.F.C. 95
Bourne, F.C. 75
Boyarin, D. 4, 101, 110
Branham, J. 80
Bremmer, J.N. 88, 90
Brock, R.N. 94
Brown, R.E. 116
Buell, D. 107
Burkert, W. 82, 87, 90, 94, 95
Burrus, V. 110

Cardellini, I. 72
Cargal, T.B. 97
Carr, D.M. 18
Carrasco, D. 1, 2
Castelli, E.A. 103, 110, 114
Chilton, B. 92
Chirichigno, G.C. 72
Cohn, N. 115, 124
Coleman, K.M. 111
Coleman-Norton, P.R. 75
Collins, A.Y. 79, 86, 91, 95, 97, 98, 121, 123
Collins, J.J. 8-12, 32

Compton, T. 81, 84
Cooper, A. 89
Coser, L.A. 118
Cosgrove, C.H. 101, 102
Crossan, J.D. 96, 98

Dahl, N. 92
Daly, L. 84
Davies, E.W. 10
Davis, B.S. 96
Delaney, C. 5
Dever, W.B. 8, 9
Douglas, M. 5, 121
Dowd, S. 94, 95
Duff, P.B. 123
Duling, D.E. 88

Eberhart, C. 83
Ehrman, B.D. 109
Eilberg-Schwartz, H. 6
Eisenbaum, P. 96
Ellens, J.H. 2, 3, 8
Elsner, J. 107
Ember, C.R. 36
Ember, M. 36
Evans Pritchard, E.E. 5, 95

Feldman, L.H. 20, 28, 32, 36
Finkelstein, J.J. 57
Fiorenza, E.S. 94, 121
Foucault, M. 100
Frankfurter, D. 9, 10, 13, 14, 80, 101, 113, 116, 118, 121, 122, 124, 126
Frazer, J. 5
Fredriksen, P. 101
Fretheim, T. 38-40
Freud, S. 5
Frilingos, C.A. 121
Frykholm, A.J. 120

Gager, J.G. 118, 126
Galtung, J. 40, 41, 44, 46
Geller, S.A. 9, 11-14, 50
Girard, R. 1-6, 11, 14, 82, 100
Glancy, J. 111
Goldstein, B. 89
Green, J.B. 92
Greenberg, M. 22, 57

Hadas, M. 79
Hall, R.G. 127
Hallo, W.W. 35
Hamerton-Kelly, R.G. 3
Hansen, W. 84
Hartman, L. 119
Hauerwas, S. 40
Hayes, C.E. 27
Heine, R.E. 124
Hendel, R.S. 99
Hengel, M. 91, 92, 98
Henninger, J. 92, 95, 96
Heschel, A.J. 39, 44
Hoffmann, R.J. 2, 3, 6, 8, 11
Hoffman, Y. 26
Holzberg, N. 85
Hopkins, K. 110
Horner, T.J. 102
Hostetter, E.C. 39
Hunter, A.G. 32

Isaac, B. 104

Jackson, B. 63
Japhet, S. 34
Jay, N. 95
Jenkins, J.B. 120
Jensen, J. 42
Johnson, A.C. 75
Johnson-DeBaufre, M. 127
Juergensmeyer, M. 1, 3, 4, 6, 15, 127, 128

Kamionkowski, S.T. 7, 9, 10, 12
Kimball, C. 15
Klawans, J. 4, 27, 93, 95, 106, 110
Kluckholm, C. 17
Knust, J.W. 13, 80, 113, 122
Koester, H. 87, 96, 119
Kovacs, J. 124
Krakauer, J. 121

Krodel, G. 119
Kroeber, A.L. 17

Lahaye, T. 120
Landy, F. 44
Lang, B. 92
Larson, J. 81
Lefkowitz, M. 81
Levinson, B. 57, 63
Lewis, T. 89
Lieu, J. 101
Limburg, J. 41
Lind, M.C. 47
Lorenz, K. 1

Mach, M. 102, 103
Machinist, P. 30
Maclean, J. 79, 93
Malbon, E.S. 94, 95
Malul, M. 58
Marini, S. 13
Matthews, S. 106, 116
McGinn, B. 113, 125
McGuire, C. 3
McKenna, A.J. 3
McLean, B.H. 96
Milgrom, J. 27, 95
Moallem, M. 103
Mobley, G. 89
Morrow, W.S. 35

Nagy, G. 81, 83-85, 92, 95
Nelson-Pallmeyer, J. 2, 6, 8, 9, 11
Niditch, S. 24, 26, 36
North, J. 125

Olyan, S. 89
Orlinsky, H.M. 39
Otto, E. 63

Pache, C.O. 81, 82
Pagels, E. 113
Parker, R. 81-83, 95
Parkin, T.J. 104, 105
Patterson, A. 85
Paul, S.M. 57
Peerbolte, L.J.L. 117
Peterson, D. 1, 14
Pippin, T. 121, 123

Price, S. 107, 125
Prigent, P. 109
Pyper, H.S. 6

Raglan, F.R.S. 97
Rajak, T. 102, 110
Remus, H. 98, 99
Riccobono, S. 75
Riley, G. 84
Rives, J. 111, 122
Robbins, T. 128
Rofé, A. 25
Rohde, E. 90
Roth, M. 57, 59
Rothenbusch, R. 63
Rowland, C. 124
Ruether, R.R. 94

Samuel, M. 21, 36
Sarna, N. 57
Satran, D. 91
Schade, A. 28
Schenke, L. 98
Schille, G. 98
Schwartz, B.J. 42, 43
Schwartz, R.M. 2, 5-11, 14
Schwartz, S. 105
Schwemer, A.M. 91
Schwienhorst-Schönberger, L. 63
Seeley, D. 91
Segal, A.F. 116
Shaw, B. 110
Shuck, G.W. 120
Simmel, G. 117
Sivan, E. 115
Skarsaune, O. 109
Smith, B.K. 5
Smith, J.Z. 83, 87, 118
Smith, M. 79
Smith, M.S. 24, 89
Speiser, E. 67
Sprinkle, J.M. 57
Stackert, J. 69

Stern, M. 104
Stern, P.D. 28, 31
Still, T.D. 119
Stirling, M.C. 3
Stowers, S.K. 94
Strecker, G. 116
Strenski, I. 4
Stroumsa, G.G. 115, 128
Stylianopoulos, T. 102
Sweeney, M.A. 41, 42

Talbert, C.H. 79
Talmon, Y. 115, 121
Thompson, L.L. 125
Tigay, J.H. 26
Trevett, C. 124
Tutu, D. 3

Ussishkin, D. 9

Van Seters, J. 63
Vernant, J.-P. 83
Versnel, H.S. 95

Watson, A. 108
Weinfeld, M. 31
Westbrook, R. 68
Wexler, L. 103
Williams, J.G. 3
Williams, S.K. 90
Willis, J.T. 43
Wills, L.M. 11, 79, 82, 84, 89, 93, 97, 98
Wilson, R. 50
Wimbush, V.L. 101
Winkler, J. 84, 85
Wrangham, R. 1, 14
Wright, D.P. 9, 11, 58, 59, 63, 64, 67, 70, 95

Yee, G.A. 39

Zevit, Z. 5, 7, 9, 11-13, 17, 24, 29, 32

www.ingramcontent.com/pod-product-compliance
Lightning Source LLC
Chambersburg PA
CBHW071430160426
43195CB00013B/1861